Service At Its Best

Service At Its Best
Waiter-Waitress Training
A Guide to Becoming a Successful Server

Ed Sanders
Paul Paz
Ron Wilkinson

Prentice
Hall

Upper Saddle River, New Jersey 07458

Library of Congress Cataloging-in-Publication-Data

Service at its best : waiter-waitress training, becoming a successful server / Ed Sanders, Paul Paz, Ron Wilkinson.
     p. cm.
   Includes index.
   ISBN 0-13-092626-4
   1. Table service. 2. Waiters. 3. Waitresses. I. Paz, Paul. II. Wilkinson, Ron. III. Title.

TX925 .S47 2002
642'.6—dc21

2001036487

Editor-In-Chief: Steve Helba
Executive Editor: Vernon R. Anthony
Production Management: Linda Zuk, WordCrafters Editorial Services, Inc.
Production Liaison: Barbara Marttine Cappuccio
Director of Production and Manufacturing: Bruce Johnson
Managing Editor: Mary Carnis
Manufacturing Manager: Cathleen Petersen
Creative Director: Cheryl Asherman
Cover Design Coordinator: Miguel Ortiz
Cover Designer: Scott Garrison
Cover Image: Courtesy of Villeroy & Boch
Marketing Manager: Ryan DeGrote
Editorial Assistant: Ann Brunner
Composition: Pine Tree Composition Inc.
Printer/Binding: Banta Harrisonburg

Pearson Education Ltd., *London*
Pearson Education Australia Pty. Limited, *Sydney*
Pearson Education Singapore, Pte. Ltd.
Pearson Education North Asia Ltd. *HongKong*
Pearson Education Canada, Ltd., *Toronto*
Pearson Educación de Mexico, S.A. de C.V.
Pearson Education—Japan, Inc., *Tokyo*
Pearson Education Malaysia, Pte. Ltd.
Pearson Education, Upper Saddle River, New Jersey

10 9 8 7 6 5 4 3
ISBN 0-13-092626-4

Contents

Foreword

In today's competitive market, the need for restaurants to sell on tight margins while satisfying the customer is at an all-time high. Restaurant patrons have expectations that they want to have satisfied. At the top of their lists are quality, value, and service. In the final analysis, only those restaurants that continually seek to improve their service will survive and flourish. Exceptional service doesn't simply happen. It is the result of careful initial training and constant attention to ongoing training.

Ed Sanders, Paul Paz, and Ron Wilkinson have written a comprehensive and informative training and reference manual in *Service At Its Best*. This book has brought together all of the basic elements that can effectively inform and train the new waiter or waitress in all aspects of professional table service. It presents the material in an easy-to-read and understandable format. The book can further serve as a reference manual for the experienced server as new situations and circumstances arise.

This book has everything—from tips on professionally serving wines, cocktails, beers, and specialty coffee drinks to the latest in restaurant technology that will advance the level of table service.

Exceptional service starts with exceptional training.

Herman Cain
CEO, T.H.E., Inc. (The Hermanator Experience)
Former CEO and President of the National Restaurant Association

Perspective

As more and more people in America have come to recognize the critical contribution dining room service plays in a restaurant's business, there have been many unsuccessful attempts to set rules of service. The "melting pot" has melted together different service styles, names, rules, and influences of the old traditional European service culture to fulfill the New World's hunger for practical and innovative styles. This has resulted in a jungle of service practices published by a number of books. None sets down best practices as well as *Service At Its Best*.

Service At Its Best not only constitutes a concise and practical compilation of dining room techniques, but it also presents a clean standard for genuine hospitality and conveys a refreshing new message on the heightened significance of the dining room profession. It is easy to read; it makes sense; and it is the first publication I've seen in America that presents service methods and principles of work that demonstrate an outstanding balance between logic, reality, style, and business.

Good hospitality includes the genuine desire to serve, knowledge, integrity, and mastery of the basic mechanics. *Service At Its Best* has it all.

Bernard Martinage, C.H.E.
Founder/President, The Federation of Dining Room Professionals

Acknowledgments

The authors would like to acknowledge the following people for their inspiration, help, and support as the book was being developed:

Vernon Anthony, executive editor, Prentice Hall-Pearson Education for enthusiastically supporting the authors' vision for the book from the time of inception through its completion.

Brenda Carlos, publisher of the Hospitality News Group, who diligently reviewed the book as it was being developed, in addition to adding insightful comments that greatly improved the clarity and content of each chapter. Furthermore, she conducted and wrote up all of the interviews for the waiter–waitress profiles in Chapter 10. Her dedication to the book's professionalism is reflected in every chapter and appreciated in ever so many ways.

Earlene Naylor, who coordinated all of the photography and graphics contained in the book: maintained everything in a logical order, always had good suggestions that further enhanced the presentations, and kept pace in helping the project to be completed ahead of schedule. Lori Smith, who was always prompt in responding to any technical or computer problems; her expertise brings comfort for all of our projects—past, present, and future.

Linda Zuk, of WordCrafters Editorial Services, who supervised editorial production and interior design with superb attention to detail.

The professionals who reviewed the manuscript during its development and offered critical input that allowed the authors to bring additional focus to important topics, and further add to the book's detailed descriptions and accuracy. A heartfelt thanks to the following individuals: Eric Stromquist, Dean, Western Culinary Institute—Le Cordon Bleu Program; Tim Hill, Ph.D., FMP, Chairman, Business Department, Central Oregon Community College; Vivienne Wildes, Ph.D., School of Hotel, Restaurant and Recreation Management, The Pennsylvania State University; Chef Gene Fritz, Ed.M., CCE, Hotel and Restaurant Administration, Washington State University; Ray Colvin, Director, Le Cordon Bleu Restaurant Management Program; Jim Sullivan, CEO, Sullivision.com; John Antun, Ph.D., CEC, CCE, FMP, CHE, School of Hotel, Restaurant and Tourism Administration, University of South Carolina; and, Bernard Martinage, CHE, Founder, Federation of Dining Room Professionals.

Sharyl Parker, Executive Director of the Oregon Restaurant Education Foundation, for providing access to the Oregon Restaurant Association resource library while doing research for the book. Additionally, for her continued faith in a professional career waiter's ability to contribute to the restaurant industry.

Keith and Cathy Morrow, owners of The Deschutes River Trout House, and their family and staff for being excellent examples of hospitality professionals and for allowing their restaurant menus to be used as illustrations in the book. Their 18-year love affair with their restaurant has involved not only their children, but also their Central Oregon community.

Bryan Caldwell, Managing Partner, Beaches Restaurant and Bar, Beaverton, Oregon, for his gracious hospitality in allowing the authors the use of the dining room for a photo-shoot.

Tom Halligan, Rob German, and Ron Evans of MICROS Systems for their time and patience in explaining and demonstrating the complete functionality of the MICROS POS/Restaurant Management System. Richard D. Boyd, Co-CEO of Boyd Coffee Company, for his review and suggestions for the coffee and tea section of Chapter 6.

Mark Sanders, who encouraged his father to do another textbook, and was also quick to recognize the need to put a "human face" to the subject matter, which led to the development of the waiter–waitress profiles. Jay Sanders, who worked as a busboy and waiter during his senior year in college, and who shared personal experiences that brought focus to several topics. Katie Sanders, who always takes the opportunity to recognize, appreciate, and compliment "good service" whenever and wherever she finds it. Dad needed and appreciated the critical input. Linda Sanders for her suggestions, ideas, and constructive comments, who again brought great value to another of her husband's writing projects. Nick and Dorothy Drossos, lifetime restaurateurs, who introduced Ed Sanders to formal dining room service in 1971, and were still able to show him a few more tips in 2001.

Robert E. Farrell, whose philosophy and book *Give'Em the Pickle*, inspired Paul Paz never to lose touch with the only reason any of us have hospitality careers: to serve the customer. Besides being Paul's employer, his professional and personal friendship is profoundly appreciated.

Paul J., Jacqueline, and Dominic Paz for providing respect, love, and pride to their father, the waiter.

Darla Wilkinson for her insight and expertise on the subject of waiter–waitress training. Her suggestions and constructive comments contributed additional value to the book and the AIMHIRE® server profiles—from a most appreciative and loving husband.

Organization of Text

This book is written so that the chapters flow in a logical sequence, establishing a step-by-step procedure for understanding and learning appropriate server skills. The chapters are also self-contained, so that the reader can go directly to any chapter for specific information. Therefore, the book can be used as a training guide or a reference manual for specific service questions.

Chapter 1, "The Professional Waiter–Waitress," introduces the reader to restaurant industry statistics and income opportunities, and explains how tip credit is calculated. "The Saturday Market Theory of Waiting Tables" reflects how a server takes ownership in his/her job. The nature of tipping and tip income reporting responsibility to the Internal Revenue Service are explained. Occupational advantages and disadvantages are identified, along with the job qualifications and descriptions of advancement opportunities for servers.

Chapter 2, "Professional Appearance," discusses the many aspects of grooming standards, the importance of poise and posture, the types of uniforms and aprons that may be used, the value of safe shoes, and the importance of server health.

Chapter 3, "Table Settings, Napkin Presentations, and Table Service," identifies the basic table settings for breakfast, lunch, and dinner as the table is preset and as the meal is served, along with the appropriate wine and beverage settings. The use of placemats and the correct placement of salt and pepper shakers, sugar and creamers, and rolls and butter are explained. Twelve popular napkin presentations are illustrated with detailed steps for each presentation, along with the correct procedure for placing tablecloths. The specific types of table service are explained in detail, including the following: butler service, American service (individual plate service), English service, Russian service, French service, as well as counter service, banquet service, and room service. The use of salad bars and dessert tables and carts is highlighted.

Chapter 4, "Serving Food and Beverages," sets forth 25 tips for proper table service, the correct procedures for loading and carrying trays, and the techniques of carrying multiple plates. Service priorities and timing along with effectively handling difficult situations are identified and supported with positive responses. Table bussing is detailed with procedures for using a cart or tray, as well as the procedure for setting up with the use of a tray, along with identifying additional bus attendant responsibilities.

Chapter 5, "Service Preparedness," illustrates breakfast, lunch, and dinner menus, along with a wine list. The importance of menu knowledge by the server is emphasized along with the role of the server in helping the guest understand the menu and menu terms. The responsibilities of a server that support good service include completing side-work as well as following opening and closing procedures. The chapter also discusses when service teams are appropriate and how they function.

Chapter 6, "Wine and Beverage Service," begins with identifying the proper temperatures for serving wines along with the correct procedures for using an ice bucket. The presentation and service of wine is illustrated step by step, beginning with presenting a bottle of wine to a guest, properly opening it, and the appropriate method of pouring the wine. The reasons and the procedure for decanting wine are also discussed. The various shapes of wine glasses are shown, identifying their appropriate use for the type of wine being served. Wine varietals are introduced and explained so that the reader gains a basic understanding of wine. Spirits and cocktails are discussed along with popular spirit brands, cocktail choices, and related terms the server should know. Beers, lagers, and ales are defined, and the correct procedure for serving beer is explained. Responsible alcohol service is reviewed and emphasized. The correct procedure for serving bottled waters is discussed. Coffee drinks that include espresso, café lattes, cappuccino, mochas, and the application of coffee with a spirit beverage are explained along with the use of the French press for coffee service. Tea varieties and service are also presented.

Chapter 7, "Guest Communications," begins with the server personally connecting with the guest through an individual sense of enthusiasm. Varieties of possible guest types are discussed, along with tips for anticipating the guest's needs and how to look for nonverbal cues and prompts. Suggestive selling is detailed, with techniques for selling the guest up, suggesting related menu items, suggesting new menu items or the chef's specialties, suggesting items for special occasions, and suggesting take-home items. The guidelines for suggestive selling are presented and illustrated, along with methods of dining room showmanship. The correct procedure for taking the guest's order is discussed, as is the guest check and the importance of service timing. Correct reaction in a professional manner to emergency situations is also addressed.

Chapter 8, "The Technology of Service," identifies the basic point-of-sale (POS) terminology and presents technology applications. Table service management, guest paging system, product management software, hand-held touch-screen terminal, server paging system, two-way radio, electronic comment response, and various software applications are discussed, along with the benefits of technology. The uses of restaurant websites, e-mail, and fax applications are reviewed, as is employee training with technology.

Chapter 9, "The Host/Hostess," begins with effectively greeting guests and table selection. Professional courtesies, handling complaints, taking telephone reservations and "to go" orders, server supervision, and menu meetings are all detailed in the discussion of the responsibilities of this important position.

Chapter 10, "Waiter–Waitress Profiles," reflects the successful experiences of 10 servers as interviewed by Brenda Carlos, publisher of the Hospitality News Group. The servers were selected from fine-dining, family, and casual theme-type restaurants from across the United States. They range from a national waiter contest award winner, career professional, to a student working as a server part-time. The AIMHIRE® software program can be accessed via the Internet and will introduce the reader/user to personality assessment software developed specifically for the foodservice industry.

Appendixes A, B, C, and D have been designed to provide the reader/user with a quick reference source for common menu terms; wine terminology; spirit brands and related cocktails; and ales, lagers, and non-alcoholic beers.

The video production *Service At Its Best* (ISBN 0-13-094792-X) further enriches this book with real-life applications that will inform and inspire the viewer. Contact Prentice Hall at 800-526-0485 or www.prenhall.com.

An Effective Waiter–Waitress (Server)

■　　■　　■　　■　　■　　■　　■　　■　　■　　■　　　■　　■　　■

An effective server is a person who

- Has a pleasant manner and truly enjoys people. The server is able to sustain a friendly demeanor with poise and self-confidence while under pressure.

- Is organized and systematically follows up. The server is always on time for work, provides prompt service to guests, completes all tasks including opening, shift change, closing cleanup, and restocking service areas.

- Has a positive professional attitude that generates positive results. The server enjoys pleasing people and contributes to an atmosphere of trust and unity with co-workers and guests.

- Takes charge of his/her station, recognizes when and what kind of service guests need, and responds with a sense of urgency. The server enjoys working at a fast pace.

- Has a good cultural awareness of the lifestyle, ethnic and nationality mixes of co-workers and guests. The server enjoys and desires to work with many people of diverse backgrounds.

- Has the ability to be flexible, diplomatic, patient, understanding, and co-operative. The server cooperatively works with co-workers in the fast-paced work environment that supports a common goal of providing the highest quality of guest service.

- Is sensitive and is able to anticipate guest needs. The server has the ability to be a good and active listener, enabling guests to feel at ease. The server is able to quickly discern and understand guests' needs, and is concerned with accuracy and quality.

- Demonstrates loyalty and commitment to the restaurant operation and co-workers. The server has a strong sense of honesty when handling guest payment transactions, when sharing tips, and when sharing work responsibilities equally.

- Has the ability to adjust timing and service according to the expectations and needs of multiple guest situations. The server continually develops and refines his/her service skills based upon personal experience.

- Understands food and beverage menu descriptions and is able to comfortably guide guests through meal selections. The server constantly takes the initiative to keep informed about new food and beverage items.

- Demonstrates politeness, courtesy, and respect at all times, enabling co-workers and guests to feel comfortable. The server works to support an environment that is relaxed and free from discord.
- Has endurance and a high energy level and enjoys working at a quick, steady, and methodical pace. The server is enthusiastic and has the ability to step back and find a sense of humor in order to minimize the stress and tension of the job.

A Professional Association

■ ■ ■ ■ ■ ■ ■ ■ ■ ■ ■ ■ ■

The Federation of Dining Room Professionals™ (F.D.R.P.) is the first association dedicated to being the leading source of professional support and development for dining room staff, host-proprietors, and chef-owners. Founded in 1998, F.D.R.P. is the only organization that recognizes experience acquired in the field as credit toward its unique certification program. This program allows front-of-the-house personnel to become a *Certified Dining Room Professional, Certified Captain,* and *Certified Maître D',* securing a place as top front-of-the-house leaders in the hospitality industry.

F.D.R.P. has partnership agreements with a number of culinary schools around the United States, leading their graduates and continuing education students to become tomorrow's new generation of professional hosts, so desperately needed in the hospitality industry. Through its quarterly magazine, *Pro-Success,* members are kept abreast of an ever-changing industry and clientele. *Pro-Success* publishes a variety of articles dedicated to the improvement of dining room operations, from Maître D' interviews and studies of specific techniques and history, to a column analyzing actual guest letters, complaints, and compliments.

F.D.R.P. exists to honor and promote excellence in dining rooms. It exists to help consolidate standards of service at a worldwide level through its members in France, England, Italy, Estonia, Taiwan, Japan, and the United States, where the Federation was founded. For information about F.D.R.P. membership, services, and certification, contact the administrative office at F.D.R.P., P.O. Box 892, Mahwah, NJ 07430, or call toll free 877-264-3377. You may also visit the F.D.R.P. website at www.FDRP.com.

From the Authors

A professional waiter–waitress (server) has the opportunity to earn an unlimited income, work flexible hours, be involved in a life's work that can result in great personal satisfaction, and pursue career advancements within the hospitality industry.

Service At Its Best introduces the student to the many aspects of being a professional server. It can further serve as a training manual for the student and the restaurant operator seeking to implement and maintain a professional service standard. The experienced server will also find the book to be an excellent reference to consult for various techniques and service situations.

The key topics include the rules of good service, typical experiences for which a server needs to be prepared, how to deal with and solve problems, the value of good communication skills, and some of the best techniques used by professional servers. As a working waiter involved in practicing the correct principles and procedures of good service, co-author and professional waiter Paul Paz brought reality to every chapter.

Best of all, you will meet some of America's most successful servers as they were interviewed by Brenda Carlos, publisher for the Hospitality News Group. These waiter–waitress profiles appear in Chapter 10. The servers range from a national server award winner to a part-time waiter attending dental school, and from people relatively new to the profession to those who have made it their life's work. Plus, you can compare your personal characteristics to those of the typical successful server via Internet access as discussed in Chapter 10.

Welcome to *Service At Its Best: Waiter–Waitress Training*, a guide to becoming a successful server.

About the Authors

Ed Sanders

Paul Paz

Ron Wilkinson

Ed is the founder and editor in chief of the Hospitality News Group, which publishes regional foodservice industry newspapers and an international education guide. He is a Certified Food Executive and a Certified Purchasing Manager; his professional career has included being chief operating officer for a regional chain of restaurants, an associate professor of business, and procurement director of a large-volume foodservice operation. He has a master of science degree in international management from the American Graduate School of International Management, and a doctor of business administration degree in management and organization. He was the co-founder and director of industry relations for the Hotel, Restaurant and Resort Management Program at Southern Oregon University. He is also co-author of *Foodservice Profitability, A Control Approach, 2E* (Prentice Hall, 2001) and *Catering Solutions: For the Culinary Student, Foodservice Operator, and Caterer* (Prentice Hall, 2000).

Paul has been a career professional waiter for over twenty years. *Restaurants USA, Restaurants and Institutions, Nation's Restaurant News, The Washington Post, The Wall Street Journal,* and several other publications have featured him in his profession. He has also appeared on ABC's 20/20 news show. His column, "Tips for Tips," runs regularly in the Hospitality News Group of newspapers and he has written numerous articles for other publications. Furthermore, he is a hospitality consultant and has presented a variety of seminars throughout the Pacific Northwest. He developed a number of training programs for the Oregon Restaurant Education Foundation and is the only professional waiter ever to serve on the Board of Directors of the Oregon Restaurant Association. The Association voted him the 1997 Restaurant Employee of the Year. He also has served as president of the National Waiters Association.

Ron is the founder and CEO of Profit Power Systems, developers of Foodco-Cost Control Systems and AIMHIRE-Employee Selection Systems. He is also the founder and director of the International Food Service Foundation. His

Ed Sanders
Editor-in-Chief
Hospitality News Group

Paul Paz
Principal
WaitersWorld

Ron Wilkinson
President/CEO
Profit Power Systems

forty-year career has included owning and operating quick-serve, family, and formal dining restaurants, and he has been a training director and vice president of operations for several large restaurant chains. He has developed and written operational and service training manuals and has taught college foodservice and restaurant management courses. He has also served on academic advisory boards for restaurant and hospitality management programs. He has presented numerous workshops at food shows, hospitality association conferences, and restaurant chain management meetings. He is a recognized expert at maximizing profit for foodservice operations of all types.

1

The Professional Waiter-Waitress

Learning Objectives

After reading this chapter and completing the discussion questions and exercises, you should be able to

1. Understand the size and economic importance of the restaurant industry.

2. Analyze and project potential income opportunities derived from wages and tips.

3. Identify factors that can influence annual income.

4. Understand the entrepreneurial side of being a waiter/waitress.

5. Relate the standards and rules for table-service tipping.

6. Understand why a tip may be small or not given at all.

7. Understand that tips are taxable income and that accurate record keeping must be maintained.

8. Recognize occupational advantages and disadvantages.

9. Identify waiter/waitress job qualifications.

10. Recognize career advancement opportunities.

Being a professional waiter/waitress (server) can be profitable and fun and can offer opportunities for career advancement. For many, the most challenging aspect of this career is approaching it as a business opportunity while not being distracted by stereotypes and inaccurate negative assumptions.

The foodservice industry, in general, offers boundless opportunities for talented people.

The following list represents some impressive facts and figures taken from the 2000 National Restaurant Association Restaurant Industry Pocket Factbook.

U nited States Restaurant Industry Statistics

- $376 billion in annual sales
- 831,000 locations
- 11 million people employed in the industry (largest employer aside from government)
- 45.3 percent restaurant industry share of the total food dollar
- Nine out of ten salaried employees at table-service restaurants started as hourly employees
- One-third of all adults in the United States have worked in the restaurant industry at some time during their lives
- Almost 50 billion meals are eaten in restaurants, schools, health-care facilities, clubs, and casinos each year

Restaurant Industry 2010 Projections:

- Annual sales of $577 billion
- Number of locations over 1 million
- 53 percent of the food dollar will be spent at restaurants

Additional information can be obtained from the National Restaurant Association at www.restaurant.org or from The Education Foundation at www.edfound.org.

The restaurant industry continues to sustain record growth with increasing employment opportunities in all segments of the industry.

I ncome Opportunities

Professional waiters/waitresses (servers) are often stereotyped as having low incomes and poor prospects of ever achieving a successful career. However, server income averages and industry advancement opportunities do not support these assumptions. Waiting tables should be viewed as an entrepreneurial business opportunity.

A server's income is usually derived from two sources: wages and tips. Keeping talented employees has become increasingly difficult and has driven some employers to become more creative with incentives including signing bonuses, health insurance with shorter waiting periods, paid vacations, and

A total of $500 per day in customer sales based upon serving 50 people with a $10 per person average guest check is used for the following analysis.

$500 per day sales × 5 days a week × 50 weeks = $125,000 annual sales

Annual sales		Tip %		Annual Tip Income
$125,000	×	10%	=	$12,500
$125,000	×	15%	=	$18,750
$125,000	×	20%	=	$25,000

A weekly work schedule may include any one or a combination of the following hours per workweek.

Weekly Hours		Fed. Min. Wage				Annual Wage
10 hours a week	×	$5.15	×	50 weeks	=	$ 2,575
25 hours a week	×	$5.15	×	50 weeks	=	$ 6,437
30 hours a week	×	$5.15	×	50 weeks	=	$ 7,725
40 hours a week	×	$5.15	×	50 weeks	=	$10,300

A typical average income from 30 hours a week (1,500 hours annually):

$5.15 Min. Wage		Tip %		Tip Income	Annual	Monthly	Hourly
$ 7,725	+	10%	=	$ 12,500	$20,225	$1,685	$ 13.48
$ 7,725	+	15%	=	$ 18,750	$26,475	$2,206	$ 17.65
$ 7,725	+	20%	=	$ 25,000	$32,725	$2,727	$ 21.82

Note: Tip income is based upon $500 per day in sales

FIGURE 1-1
Potential Earnings as a Waiter/Waitress

401-K pension plans. For the most part, the wage standard for a server in the United States remains at minimum wage for the entire length of employment. It is not the industry standard for employers to offer merit increases based upon performance or length of employment.

So how does a career professional server get a raise? The answer is in one word: *tips*. The customers provide the raises. Furthermore, the level of the server's competence determines the size of the raise. But can one really make a living at this profession? See Figure 1-1, Potential Earnings as a Waiter/Waitress. The example given in the figure is based on the current federal minimum wage of $5.15. The example given in Figure 1-2 reflects the federal 50 percent tip credit reduction application.

The average dollar amount in guest check sales will vary according to the type of restaurant operation. A fast-paced coffee shop or deli may average 5 to 7 dollars per person, a casual or family restaurant may average 8 to 15 dollars per person, and a fine dining restaurant may average 25 to 50 dollars per person, not including wine or other alcoholic beverages. Guest check sales also vary at breakfast, lunch, and dinner, as the dollar amounts are smaller for breakfast, increase with lunch, and are greater for dinner.

Tip Credit

Many states have mandated the legal authority to apply what is known as a "tip credit." The formula is simple: The more one makes in tips the less the employer is required to pay in wages. These formulas vary from state to state but for the most part duplicate federal guidelines that dictate that the federal minimum wage cannot be reduced by more than 50 percent. It should also be noted that there are some states whose minimum wage is higher than the federal minimum wage. The example in Figure 1-2 demonstrates the effect of the tip credit application.

Additional factors can influence income:

1. Working more or fewer hours
2. Working at two or more eating/drinking establishments
3. Shifts worked: breakfast, lunch, or dinner
4. Weekday or weekend
5. Banquet or special functions
6. Equipment failures
7. Weather
8. Holidays
9. Seasonal fluctuations in customer counts
10. Product availability
11. Staffing shortages
12. Tip pooling. This (where legally allowed) occurs when all tips go into one pot and are divided equally among selected staff. Usually the

---

$500 per day sales × 5 days a week × 50 weeks = $125,000 sales

Annual sales		Tip %		Annual Cash Income
$125,000	×	10%	=	$12,500
$125,000	×	15%	=	$18,750
$125,000	×	20%	=	$25,000

Weekly Hours		Fed. Min. Wage			Annual Hourly Wage
10 hours a week	×	$2.57	×	50 weeks	= $1,285
25 hours a week	×	$2.57	×	50 weeks	= $3,212
30 hours a week	×	$2.57	×	50 weeks	= $3,855
40 hours a week	×	$2.57	×	50 weeks	= $5,140

Income from 30 hours a week (1,500 hours annually):

$2.57 Min. Wage		Tip %		Tip $$$	Annual	Monthly	Hourly
$3,855	+	10%	=	$12,500	$16,355	$1,362	$10.90
$3,855	+	15%	=	$18,750	$22,605	$1,884	$15.07
$3,855	+	20%	=	$25,000	$28.855	$2,405	$19.24

FIGURE 1-2
Applying the Federal 50% Tip Credit Reduction

employer determines who will share the tips and the percentage formula.

13. Tipping out other positions. Under this system, a percentage or specific amount goes to any one or a mix of the following positions: host, bartender, cocktail servers, or bus attendants. Again, the employer usually sets the house policy on distribution.

14. Menu prices.

Two critical variables within the server's control directly impact his or her earnings. They are

Personalized Service: Consistently creating and delivering a distinctively personalized service that increases tip percentages. This is accomplished by rendering the highest possible quality of service.

Marketing Skills: Suggestively selling items such as appetizers, beverages, and desserts to increase the dollar amount of guest checks.

The Saturday Market Theory of Waiting Tables

The following story, in his own words, is from the experience of a professionally trained waiter:

It's my morning opening shift for the restaurant and I have a new server trainee following me. We are going through the scheduled routine of opening and cleaning, including waxing tabletops and scraping gum off table bottoms. My trainee says, "For such a big company why don't they have a cleaning company do this? They're probably just trying to save a buck."

I looked at him and said, "Have you ever been to a Saturday Market?" You know, the craft fairs and flea markets where entrepreneurs gather to sell their crafts and services.

"Yep," he answers in a quizzical tone.

Well, here in this restaurant, I'm in the same boat as the entrepreneurs at a Saturday Market. You see *my* "sales booth" is *my* five-table section and *my* success is completely determined by what I am willing to do with it. Okay, yes I am an employee. But, when I encounter my customers, they only see me. I am the owner. I facilitate what they expect to happen. In my customer's eyes, I am responsible for everything they experience during their visit at my Saturday Market sales booth.

Now on a practical basis, that's a ridiculous concept. But, the reality of my professional and financial success is to understand and appreciate the entrepreneurial opportunity that has been given to me as a professional waiter. It's an opportunity to be rewarded based upon my personal performance.

The waiter continues his story.

Well, I got hired as a waiter by a restaurateur who allowed me to take a theoretical ownership in a restaurant that cost over $1,000,000. The restaurant operation had a food and beverage inventory exceeding $70,000 that I could offer to my customers. It also provided an accounting department to calculate my business costs such as taxes, health insurance, vacation pay, and even retirement. There was a manager that planned the daily operations, staffing levels, and provided guidance and personal support in helping me to better serve my customers. A professional support staff consisting of other servers, hosts, bartenders, cocktail servers, cooks, and dishwashers all worked as a team so I could focus on my customers' needs and requests. Then the restaurateur spent thousands of dollars for advertising to bring in customers for me. All of this for my own personal use!

You know what's crazy? The first day I showed up they paid me an hourly wage before I ever sold a thing. But you know what is really, I mean really nuts? I get all this opportunity handed to me for nothing. I didn't have to pay a dime for any of it. All I have to do is show up and invest an entrepreneurial effort using the resources given to me. I am responsible for my future. My challenge is how am I going to maximize all this opportunity given to me at no cost?

Who says I'm not an entrepreneur? All I have to do is think like a businessperson. I have my own business as a waiter.

A dignified profession, I must add!

T ipping

The current national tipping standard for table service is 15 percent of the meal's cost, excluding taxes. Tipping over 15 percent is quite acceptable and in certain establishments can average 20 to 30 percent. Figure 1-3, Tip Guide 15% and 20%, shows the tip amounts when the percentages are applied. Who made up this rule of thumb? It evolved as a "customary" standard via the hospitality industry and consumers. There are numerous stories of servers being "stiffed" (left with no tip) or of being given outrageous tips. News-making stories include those of the Chicago cocktail server who got a $10,000 tip from an English doctor, or the Boston bartender who shared her restaurant concept with a customer who turned out to be an investment banker. He liked her idea and as a result, made her a partner and put up over $1,000,000 to launch her dream restaurant. A server can never know in advance whether the person that he or she may be serving could in some way reward personalized service with an extraordinary benefit.

Tips are not mandatory. Some servers think that they are, and they are routinely outraged when a customer leaves a tip that is less than they think appropriate. Some establishments set automatic gratuities or a service charge of 15 to 20 percent for certain circumstances, such as special events, banquets, and groups of diners over a certain size. In these cases the customer is notified either on the menu, during the process of making reservations, or by the server.

G etting Stiffed

Many servers have experienced the "penalty" of a short tip or no tip as the result of a customer's dissatisfaction. There are occasions where indeed the server did not deliver the service expected and should be tipped (or not tipped) accordingly. Some conditions are beyond the server's control, such as being short staffed, being out of certain food items, a kitchen equipment failure, etc. As a result the tip is reduced or lost. For the most part, customers are forgiving of momentary glitches if they are informed of the circumstances and the house makes a sincere attempt to reconcile the inconvenience. What customers will not excuse is a bad attitude on the part of the server or a projected sense of "entitlement" when it comes to tipping. Sometimes the best tip is no tip at all. Figure 1-4 compares the best tippers and the worst tippers.

Check Amount	15%	20%	Check Amount	15%	20%
$ 1.00	$ .15	$ .20	$ 51.00	$ 7.65	$10.20
2.00	.30	.40	52.00	7.80	10.40
4.00	.60	.80	54.00	8.10	10.80
6.00	.90	1.20	56.00	8.40	11.20
8.00	1.20	1.60	58.00	8.70	11.60
10.00	1.50	2.00	60.00	9.00	12.00
12.00	1.80	2.40	62.00	9.30	12.40
14.00	2.10	2.80	64.00	9.60	12.80
16.00	2.40	3.20	66.00	9.90	13.20
18.00	2.70	3.60	68.00	10.20	13.60
20.00	3.00	4.00	70.00	10.50	14.00
22.00	3.30	4.40	72.00	10.80	14.40
24.00	3.60	4.80	74.00	11.10	14.80
26.00	3.90	5.20	76.00	11.40	15.20
28.00	4.20	5.60	78.00	11.70	15.60
30.00	4.50	6.00	80.00	12.00	16.00
32.00	4.80	6.40	82.00	12.30	16.40
34.00	5.10	6.80	84.00	12.60	16.80
36.00	5.40	7.20	86.00	12.90	17.20
38.00	5.70	7.60	88.00	13.20	17.60
40.00	6.00	8.00	90.00	13.50	18.00
42.00	6.30	8.40	92.00	13.80	18.40
44.00	6.60	8.80	94.00	14.10	18.80
46.00	6.90	9.20	96.00	14.40	19.20
48.00	7.20	9.60	98.00	14.70	19.60
50.00	7.50	10.00	100.00	15.00	20.00

FIGURE 1-3
Tip Guide 15% and 20%

Waiting tables is a craft. The level of income that one can earn is relative to professional customer service delivered. Servers certainly do not sustain their careers via minimum wage, although it is still an important part of their income. "Raises" are provided by the customers and not by the employers. If servers want to improve their income levels, they must enhance their craft and skills.

There are certain customers who do not believe in tipping. That is their choice; and it is one of the occupational hazards of the profession. Americans prefer having the option on tips and rebel at being told that they "owe" tips. A typical waiter/waitress can serve over 11,000 people each year; perhaps 1 percent are not satisfied with the service. That leaves 10,890 fabulous guests, who were a pleasure to serve and were willing to reward professional service. The tips of these fabulous guests allow the server to enjoy a good income.

The rule to remember when getting stiffed is: Get over it! Reset the table for the next party and work toward a 25 percent tip or more.

Best Tippers	*Worst Tippers*
Business people	Business people
Regulars	Regulars
Hospitality industry workers	Hospitality industry workers
Restaurant managers & owners	Restaurant managers & owners
Alcohol drinkers	Alcohol drinkers
Smokers	Smokers
New Yorkers	New Yorkers
Church people	Church people
Yuppies	Yuppies
Seniors	Seniors
Families	Families
Women	Women
Teenagers	Teenagers
X-Gens	X-Gens
Large parties	Large parties
Parties that want separate checks	Parties that want separate checks
Travelers	Travelers
Get the picture?	

FIGURE 1-4
Best Tippers/Worst Tippers

Tipping and the Internal Revenue Service (IRS)

Workers in general have tax responsibilities and are required to pay their legally owed taxes on income. The Internal Revenue Service estimates that $11 billion in tips are unreported by restaurant employees annually. Recent court rulings have reinforced the fact that employers are responsible for undeclared employee tips on payroll taxes. These were taxes that the employee should have paid if they had declared their tips properly.

The Internal Revenue Service is stepping up enforcement on undeclared tips with employers. This increased IRS activity is the result of court decisions ruling in favor of the IRS putting pressure on employers (not employees) to account for tip income. For example, in Chicago, in 1999, a restaurant was assessed over $85,000 in taxes for undeclared tips for 1993, 1994, and 1995. The employer was responsible and the employees were not held liable in this particular case. The employer was negligent in accounting for employee tip income during those years. Nevertheless, the employee is responsible for declaring tip income.

Potential penalties to tipped employees for underreporting tips are:

1. Prison sentence for failing to declare income

2. Additional tax

3. FICA (7% of unreported income)

4. Fifty percent penalty on FICA

5. Twenty percent penalty on the total tax liability for the year

6. Interest charges

7. A big fat headache!

Benefits of reporting tips:

1. Higher social security benefits

2. Higher unemployment benefits

3. Higher credit rating for loans

4. Higher amounts paid into participating 401-K plans

IRS allocated tip formulas are used to track the sales of restaurants against the percentage of declared tips by the employees. If the declared tip ratio falls below 12 percent of the gross sales, the employer may "allocate" tips on W-2's at the end of the year to those employees who under-declared throughout the year. The 12 percent figure is the minimum total tax due. If the IRS audits a server they will be looking for all tips and will calculate the tax liability along with any penalties accordingly.

Because of increased payroll tracking technology, it is very difficult to hide tips, especially charged tips. It is recommended that servers keep a record of sales, tips, and other employees who shared in their tips. If the IRS audits a server, and no records are available, the IRS can assess a calculated amount.

Ultimately the law is clear and simple. Tips are taxable income and, by law, must be reported to all applicable tax agencies.

Additional information on tip reporting requirements can be obtained from the Internal Revenue Service by calling 800 TAX-FORM or by visiting www.irs.com. The following tax reporting forms are also available from the IRS upon request:

IRS Form 4070A, *Employee's Daily Record of Tips*

IRS Form 4070, *Employee's Report of Tips to Employer*

IRS Form 8027, *Employer's Annual Information Return of Tip Income and Allocated Tips*

IRS Publication 531, *Reporting Income From Tips*

Occupational Advantages

The following advantages are attractive and motivating to many people:

1. *Time flexibility:* The server's time can be flexible to accommodate other things in life, such as family activities, continuing education, a second job, leisure time, other professional endeavors, etc. The nature of the business allows for flexibility in scheduling work hours and days off.

2. *Income flexibility:* The server can control his or her income by working more or less hours.

3. *Performance reviews:* The server gets immediate feedback on the success or failure of his or her work in the form of tips and/or customer compliments or complaints.

4. *High hourly wage:* The potential to earn a high hourly wage (wage plus tips) is substantially greater than in many other occupations and can be achieved faster.

5. *Job mobility:* When the server has mastered the basic skills of the craft, those skills are then easily transferable to any restaurant in the world, along with other occupations. Everybody wants good service in one form or another.

6. *Minimal clothing expense:* The investment in work clothing can be minimal, as most employers provide uniforms.

7. *Complimentary or discounted meals:* The server is typically provided either a complimentary or discounted meal during his or her work shift. The average discounted meal is 50 percent off the menu price.

8. *Minimal after-work stress:* When the server clocks out at the end of a shift, the job does not go home with him or her. The server is done for the day until the next shift.

9. *Physical fitness:* The nature of the work provides a high level of physical activity.

10. *Opportunity to meet interesting people:* The server has the opportunity to meet a wide spectrum of people every shift. Friendships and lasting customer relationships often develop.

11. *Interesting work:* The work is never boring, as different things occur during every shift.

12. *Entrepreneurial experience:* The server learns how to be an entrepreneur by being exposed to selling and the rewards of providing personalized service.

13. *Work unity:* There can be a unique sense of family and camaraderie among restaurant employees that is not often found in other occupations.

14. *Sales training:* The server has the opportunity to learn the art of sales and merchandising. This training to increase sales will result in increased income and greater customer satisfaction.

15. *Teamwork participation:* The server can learn to appreciate the value and importance of teamwork.

Occupational Disadvantages

The disadvantages can be discouraging for people who are not cut out for server work.

1. *Working weekends, nights, and holidays:* The nature of the restaurant industry often requires working weekends, nights, and holidays. These are typically the busiest times in most establishments.

2. *Work stress:* The work can be physically, mentally, and psychologically intense, and can be emotionally demanding. The burnout possibilities are high for those who do not take the time to relax physically and mentally after work.

3. *Minimal employee benefits:* The employee benefits are often minimal, although recent competition for labor has motivated the industry to offer better benefits than in the past. Examples include medical insurance, paid vacations, pension plans, access to free or discounted activities such as health clubs, and meal discounts as a customer.

4. *No employer-provided disability insurance:* Restaurant employers typically do not provide disability insurance or short-term income

replacement benefits. This is not to be confused with Workers Compensation or Social Security Disability.

5. *Minimum wage:* Minimum wage is the industry standard and merit wage increases are the exception.

6. *Reduced minimum wage:* In states where tip credit is applicable, the hourly wage payable by the employer is reduced to below the federal minimum standard.

7. *Lost income:* Events beyond the server's control, such as shutdowns because of weather or equipment failure, mean the server will not be working.

8. *Financial budgeting:* Those who have difficulty managing a cash income, may have budgeting problems.

Job Qualifications

To be successful as a server, an individual should review the following personal categories:

EDUCATION

There are very few training schools for professional servers. Formal education is important but not necessary. The aspiring server should possess the ability to learn quickly on the job.

INTELLIGENCE

A successful server should be alert and mentally sharp at all times. The job requires quick organized thinking under stress, with the ability to adjust timing and service according to the expectations and needs of multiple guest situations.

PRODUCT KNOWLEDGE

The server must understand the menu descriptions of the food and beverage items in order to guide the guests through meal selections. Given the wide selection of products available, and new ones continually being introduced, the individual must take the initiative to stay educated about the latest food and beverage items.

SERVICE KNOWLEDGE

A number of service methods, techniques, and standards require training (usually on the job) and experience to gain practice at understanding and executing basic tasks. The seasoned server will develop a personal style by drawing from what he or she learns of the basics. With a little imagination and creativity the server will become increasingly more effective and profitable.

TIMING AND ATTENTION TO DETAILS

Dining is like telling a good joke—good delivery is in the timing. Again, it takes training and practice to acquire the proper skills of timing during the dining experience, coupled with the attention to the details that can make the guests' experience complete in every way.

PERSONALITY

A server must have a pleasant manner and truly enjoy people. He or she must be able to sustain a friendly demeanor with poise and self-confidence while under pressure.

INITIATIVE

A server must take charge of his or her station and recognize when and what kind of service customers need and perform that service with a sense of urgency in every detail.

POSITIVE ATTITUDE

A positive or negative attitude affects performance. If one shows up for a shift in a bad mood, it is going to be a bad shift with bad customers and bad co-workers making bad tips. A positive "professional attitude" can generate positive, wonderful results.

TEAMWORK ABILITY

The server should be willing to work cooperatively with others in a fast-paced work environment that supports a common goal of providing the highest quality of guest service. Also supporting a mutual effort is completing all assigned work.

GOOD MANNERS

A server should have the understanding and ability to demonstrate the social skills of being polite, courteous, and respectful to coworkers and guests.

HONESTY

A server must have a strong sense of honesty when handling guest payment transactions, when sharing tips, and when equally sharing work responsibilities.

SENSE OF HUMOR

A good sense of humor is essential in order to survive the daily stresses of the job. When things seem to be getting a bit out of control, it is one's ability to step back and find humor in it all that helps to minimize the stress and tension.

DIVERSITY SKILLS

The lifestyle, ethnic, and nationality mix of co-workers and the public demands that the server have good cultural awareness.

RELIABILITY

The server must always be on time for work, provide prompt service to guests, complete all tasks including opening, shift change, closing cleanup, and restocking service areas.

```
                          Owner
                     General Manager
                   Department Managers
                    Assistant Managers


  Bar Manager        Dining Room Manager     Kitchen Manager/Chef
  Bar Staff               Maître D'             Kitchen Staff
                          Host Staff
                      Head Wait Staff
                         Wait Staff
                 Busser/Server Assistant Staff
```

FIGURE 1-5
Restaurant Organizational Chart

dvancement Opportunities

There is a basic hierarchy in a restaurant. This can vary depending upon the size of the organization and other services offered such as banquets, room service, outside catering, etc. The chart in Figure 1-5 reflects the organizational structure of a typical full service restaurant.

Besides the positions listed in Figure 1-5, there are a number of other lucrative career tracks that waiting skills can transfer to, such as those identified in Figure 1-6.

Overview

The restaurant industry is an integral and growing part of American life, as shown by the impressive facts and figures that describe the industry. As a result, the number of opportunities for the professional server continues to grow. The level of income that a professional server can earn will be increased or decreased by the number of hours he or she is willing to work, and by the type of restaurant operation (ranging from the coffee shop or deli, casual, family, or theme restaurant, to fine dining).

The nature of the work allows the server to develop and exercise entrepreneurial skills by offering a personalized service to customers. In addition, it advances one's marketing talents through the merchandising and upselling of food and beverage items.

The advantages of being a server are many and include the following: Time flexibility to accommodate one's lifestyle; flexible income; high potential hourly earnings; career and job mobility; complimentary or discounted meals while at work; physical exercise to keep fit; and the opportunity to meet interesting people. The disadvantages often discourage people from entering the occupation, and include the following: Working weekends, nights, and holidays; physical, mental, and psychological stress associated with the work; and the absence of good employee benefits.

The qualifications of a successful server include competencies in the following areas: Product knowledge with a sound understanding of food and

Private Catering

Lodging

Tourism

Transportation

Recreation

Resorts/Spas

Nutrition/Health-care

Food & Beverage Broker

Food & Beverage Distribution

Winery - Brewery - Spirits

Hospitality Equipment & Technology

Hospitality Internet Services

Hospitality Consulting

Customer Service Training

Hospitality Journalism

Retirement Living Facilities

Commercial Food Service

Institutional Food Service

Grocery/Deli Food Service

Quick Service Market

FIGURE 1-6
Restaurant Related Career Tracks

beverage items; service knowledge in being able to provide each customer with a personalized service; a good sense of timing in serving the ordered items; a pleasant personality with a likable manner and positive attitude, and the ability to support co-workers. A sense of humor coupled with the ability to handle the stress of the work, and an honest and reliable work ethic.

A wide selection of advancement opportunities exists within the restaurant industry, ranging from entry level positions to actual ownership. For individuals with the interest, talents, and enthusiasm, along with the willingness to make a long-term commitment to the industry, the income and professional development can be excellent.

DISCUSSION QUESTIONS AND EXERCISES

1. Discuss the economic importance of the restaurant industry by identifying some statistics that were compiled by the National Restaurant Association.

2. Name the two sources of income for the professional server.

3. How does a career server earn an increased income?

4. Explain what is meant by a 50 percent tip credit.

5. If the average daily total guest-check sales for each server in a fine dining restaurant were $800 and a server worked 5 days, 40 hours per week at minimum wage and earned a 20 percent tip average, what would be his or her annual income? Refer to Figure 1-1, Potential Earnings as a Waiter/Waitress.

6. Identify 10 factors that can affect a server's income.

7. What are the two critical variables that the server controls that directly impact his or her earnings?

8. Explain the entrepreneurial side of being a server.

9. List three reasons why a tip may be reduced or lost.

10. Discuss several of the potential penalties for under-reporting tip income.

11. List 10 occupational advantages of being a server.

12. List 5 occupational disadvantages of being a server.

13. Describe at least 10 areas in which an individual should have competence in order to be a successful server.

14. Discuss potential career advancement opportunities for a server.

15. Identify several occupations to which server skills and training could be transferable and effectively used.

16. Discuss an example of personalized service that you have experienced or observed.

17. How much could a professional server earn by working in a fine dining restaurant where the average guest check is $50 per person? Assume the following: He or she works 5 days, 40 hours per week at minimum wage and serves an average of 60 people per shift. He or she also earns an average 20 percent in tip income.

18. Interview a server and ask what he or she likes and dislikes about the occupation. Write down the responses and report to class.

19. How would you determine the amount of tip to leave a server?

20. Has your opinion of the server occupation changed after having read this chapter? If so, describe the change.

Professional Appearance

Learning Objectives

After reading this chapter and completing the discussion questions and exercises, you should be able to

1. Understand the importance of good personal grooming standards.

2. Evaluate your own personal appearance.

3. Recognize that a well-groomed appearance is absolutely essential to project the image of good service, quality food, and a pleasant atmosphere.

4. Identify the personal grooming standards that are basic for waiters/waitresses.

5. Understand the value and importance of good poise and posture, and the positive impression that it creates.

6. Know the importance of always wearing a clean fresh uniform each day.

7. Know what to look for when purchasing a quality pair of shoes for work.

8. Understand the importance of good server health.

The following message to the professional waiter/waitress (server) discusses the importance of good personal grooming standards.

Your personal appearance will reveal to your customers much about your personality and attitude, because while you are in contact with your customers, they will be judging you, and what they see is reflected in your personality, your attitude, and your appearance. Remember, as a server, you are on stage at all times.

Sanitation is essential to all foodservice operations and every employee who prepares and/or serves food must meet the highest standards of neatness, cleanliness, personal hygiene, and good grooming. In order to prevent the contamination of food and food-contact surfaces, and the resulting potential transmission of foodborne illness, it is essential that servers observe strict standards of cleanliness and proper hygiene. This is important during their shifts and before starting work or returning to work after breaks. A good appearance is necessary to project the image of good service, quality food being safely served, and a pleasant atmosphere. Your personal grooming takes into account more than just your uniform and your smile. It includes your hair, hands, teeth, posture, figure, and clothes.

Good grooming has many benefits and you, the server, benefit from all of them. The way to ensure good grooming is to go to a mirror and observe yourself very closely. Take a good look at yourself. Do you like what you see? Stand naturally. Look yourself over. Does your posture consist of a head held high with your chin parallel to the floor? Are your shoulders held up, back, and relaxed and your rib cage held high with the elbows slightly bent, and the hips tucked under? Are your knees relaxed?

How did you feel as you looked at yourself in the mirror? Did you feel good? Did it give you confidence in yourself? Did you appear to have poise and self-confidence? Make a note of your appearance and posture faults and work on correcting them.

Your appearance is your way of telling your customers how you value yourself. By being very critical of your appearance and taking the initiative to improve it, you are telling your customers, "I believe in myself." Personal grooming is as much a part of your personality as your feelings and actions. If you don't like what you see, improve yourself and your appearance by determining to work at it by spending the necessary time.

The principles for good appearance are the same for men and women. Taking proper care of oneself is essential, and devoting time to your appearance will add to your confidence and peace of mind.

Grooming Standards

Customers expect to see well-groomed servers just as much as they expect to see a clean restaurant. The well-groomed server conveys a professional image that supports an overall dining experience. A well-groomed appearance is absolutely essential to project the image of good service, quality food, and a pleasant atmosphere.

The individual server has a significant role in the restaurant. The server is the only contact most customers have with the business aside from the food itself and perhaps the cashier. Therefore, the restaurant operator is challenged in setting forth and maintaining server standards that will help to ensure that customers return.

Certain restaurant concepts in today's eclectic market offer a form of entertainment. Some of these concepts have impacted dress standards by providing uniquely designed uniforms that may serve as costumes. Servers may be allowed to have bold hairstyles and colors, and to wear excessive jewelry. However, these concepts are the exception, unusual and limited to a defined customer base.

The following is a list of personal grooming standards that are basic for servers.

Bathing and Deodorants Good personal hygiene begins with daily bathing and the use of unscented deodorants or antiperspirants. Offensive body odors caused by poor personal hygiene can cause coworkers and customers to complain to the management. Offended customers may choose never to return.

Hair Care The server should always have clean and fresh-smelling hair that is controlled in order to prevent hair from contacting or falling into food or onto food contact surfaces. When hair is uncontrolled, it can be difficult to manage and distracting when serving food. Natural hair colors are pleasing and acceptable in contrast to bold unnatural colors that have the potential of projecting an image that may be displeasing to some customers. The professional server will have his or her hair styled professionally. The hair stylist will recommend a hairstyle that is becoming and easy to take care of. The hair should not be too long and preferably not go below the shirt collar. However, long hair should be restrained in a ponytail or hair net. Servers should avoid fixing or touching their hair while in view of customers, and should wash their hands after coming in direct contact with their hair.

Skin Care If a server is having problems with skin—acne, or dry or oily skin—the server should take appropriate measures to control the trouble. Servers should never scratch dry or itchy areas of the body in view of customers. If the skin is dry, wash with a mild soap or cleansing cream. Apply a moisturizer to restore valuable lost oils and be sure to take care of chapped lips by using a lip balm. Proper care of the skin requires cleanliness and protection. Measures to prevent overexposure to the sun should be taken, such as using sunscreen. Men should be clean-shaven.

Cosmetics The proper use of cosmetics can enhance one's appearance; overuse can detract from it. Too much of certain kinds of cosmetics, such as body glitter, can "run" and get into one's eyes or food when the body heats up during a brisk shift. If the appropriate selection and application of cosmetics becomes a concern, the server should consult a cosmetic specialist.

Fragrances The server who uses a fragrance should choose among products that are lightly scented. Strongly scented fragrances may be offensive to some co-workers and customers, and actually be sickening to those who suffer from severe allergies; fragrances may conflict with the aromas of the food being served.

Beards and Moustaches A well-shaped clean beard or moustache can be very attractive and can enhance a man's appearance, but it needs to be washed and trimmed daily.

Teeth and Breath Good oral hygiene is maintained by frequent tooth brushing and flossing. A smile is always complemented by clean teeth and fresh breath. Breath fresheners should be used as needed. The chewing of gum should be avoided in order to maintain a professional image. Smoking should be limited to shift breaks and never in view of customers. The time reserved for eating is during a lunch or dinner break; the server should never consume food in view of customers. If a server suffers during an allergy season, the coughing and sneezing must be controlled with the proper allergy medication. A server cannot successfully work with a coughing and sneezing problem in view of customers. A server suffering from a cold or the flu should not be allowed to serve food, as colds and flu are contagious and unpleasant for customers.

Hands and Fingernails The hands of a server should always be immaculately clean. The server's fingernails should be smoothly filed and kept short and regularly washed with a fingernail brush. Clear polish or buffing can enhance fingernail appearance, versus striking fashion colors. A hand moisturizer should be used for dry hands and fingernails. Servers must thoroughly wash their hands and the exposed portions of their arms with soap and warm water for at least 20 seconds before starting work, during work as often as necessary to keep them clean, and after smoking, eating, drinking, using the toilet, or after performing a non-food-service activity. During busy periods when a sink may not be available, an alternative may be the use of a health department approved hand sanitizer.

Foot Care The correct type of shoes will minimize foot fatigue. The server walks many miles during the course of each shift. Therefore, it is essential to have well-fitting and comfortable shoes in an acceptable style that is complementary to the server's uniform. Fashion shoes are not a good choice. Rubber heels and soles are best for reducing slips and skids on wet floors. Shoes should always be cleaned or polished and have clean laces. Foot powder or spray should be used during warm weather to prevent excess perspiration and odor. Clean socks for the waiter and clean hose for the waitress should be worn daily, free of runs, and in a color that complements the uniform. The server may also find comfort in wearing support hose designed to help relieve leg stress. Support stockings or hose are available in basic black, brown, and navy blue for men, and in a variety of shades for women.

Jewelry The jewelry worn by a server should be simple and should not interfere with the performance of job functions. A plain watch, smooth ring, or small earrings are acceptable and reflect a conservative image. When jewelry is large, ornate, or dangling, it becomes awkward and potentially hazardous. Such jewelry may be displeasing to some restaurant customers. Body piercing and tattoos may also be displeasing to customers. Therefore, body piercing should be restricted and tattoos covered with clothing.

Poise and Posture

Although servers may devote time and energy to daily beauty routines, they will not look their best unless strict attention is given to poise and posture. Poor posture can reduce a meticulous lady to a less-than-attractive figure and a good-looking man to a sloppy-appearing slouch.

The professional server is always on display and should stand and walk with poise and self-confidence. By moving more gracefully, confidently, and efficiently, the server will not only make a better impression, but will also conserve energy. The working day of a server is very tiring, and good posture can make long hours less tiring. Being able to walk quickly with an erect, well-balanced, controlled posture will create the impression of a confident, healthy individual. On the other hand, having a slouching, poor posture will create a bad impression with customers. The way that a server walks and carries him or herself is almost as important as the way he or she speaks and looks.

Uniforms and Aprons

Most restaurants require that the server wear a special uniform and/or apron. Some uniforms and aprons are plain, while others are stylish and will accent the theme, décor, and colors of the restaurant as shown in Figure 2-1. Some uniforms are as formal as a tuxedo or can be as casual as a pair of khaki pants, a polo shirt, and white sneakers. If the restaurant does not require a specific uniform or apron, the server should select a type of clothing that projects a professional image. It has been said that the clothes make the individual. With the server this is especially true. The clothing that a person chooses to wear may very well reflect his or her personality.

The server should have enough uniforms and aprons to allow for daily changes. If scheduled to work five days a week, then three uniforms and aprons would be appropriate, allowing the server to wear a clean uniform and apron each day. The server should never wear a uniform that is obviously soiled or stained, because food may be repeatedly contaminated by food debris or other soil from the uniform of the server. The uniforms and aprons should always be cleaned carefully. They should never be wrinkled, torn, or frayed. Having a clean fresh uniform and apron is, of course, essential to good sanitation. If the server lacks the ability to keep the uniform and apron looking professional, then he or she needs to find a good dry cleaner or launderer. Uniforms should fit properly and allow for comfortable movement. Also, the restaurant operator should establish a policy regarding the hem length of uniforms or shorts.

Uniforms help the customer identify who the employees are when they need assistance. They also add to the customer's perception of the cleanliness and organization of the server and the dining establishment overall.

FIGURE 2-1
Uniform and Apron Varieties and Styles *Courtesy of Scorpio Apparel, Inc.*

hoes

Shoes are a significant part of the server uniform and should be selected for style, appearance, safety, and most of all total comfort. Shoes that have ergonomically designed shock-absorbent cushioned insoles, slip-resistant outsoles, and full grain leather uppers are readily available and competitively priced, as shown in Figure 2-2. An investment in a pair of good quality shoes pays for itself in a very short period of time. Sore feet can make a miserable shift and eventually lead to other physical problems, as well as increasing the potential for slips and falls. Two pairs of shoes are recommended for those working long hours. One pair can dry out and air while the other pair is being worn.

Many restaurant operators have identified shoe stores in their communities that offer slip-resistant footwear for servers to purchase. Also, many have brochures, catalogs, and Internet sources available to allow servers to make their selections. The popularity of these types of shoes is rapidly growing as the number of slips and falls have been reduced in establishments where employees are wearing slip-resistant footwear. Another benefit of this product is reduced stress on the feet and legs.

Server Health

The health of servers is critical. No server, while infected with a disease in a communicable form that can be transmitted by foods or who is a carrier of organisms that cause such a disease, or while afflicted with a boil, an infected

Wing Tips   Boots   Cross Trainers

FIGURE 2-2
Slip-Resistant Footwear *Courtesy of Shoes for Crews*

wound, or an acute respiratory infection, should work in a foodservice establishment in any capacity in which there is a likelihood of contaminating food or food-contact surfaces with pathogenic organisms or of transmitting disease to other persons.

Disease transmitted through food frequently originates from an infected foodservice employee even though the employee shows little outward appearance of being ill. A wide range of communicable diseases and infections may be transmitted by infected foodservice employees to other employees, and to the consumer, through the contamination of food and through careless food-handling practices. It is the responsibility of both management and staff to see that no person who is affected with any disease that can be transmitted by food works in any area of a foodservice establishment where there is a possibility of disease transmission.

Overview

The server is in contact with customers at all times; therefore, his or her personal appearance is important. A good appearance is necessary to project the image of good service, quality food, and a pleasant atmosphere. The way to ensure good grooming is for the server to go to a mirror and observe him or herself very closely. Taking proper care of oneself is essential. The following list of personal grooming standards are basic for servers: Bathing and deodorants, hair care, skin care, cosmetics, fragrances, beards and moustaches, teeth and breath, hands and fingernails, foot care, and jewelry.

The server should always stand and walk with poise and self-confidence. Poor posture detracts from the server's appearance. The way that a server walks and carries him or herself is almost as important as the way he or she speaks and looks.

Most restaurants require servers to wear a uniform. If the restaurant does not require a uniform, the server should select professional looking clothing. The server should have enough uniforms to allow for daily changes. A clean fresh uniform is essential for good sanitation.

Shoes are a significant part of the server uniform and should be selected for style, appearance, safety, and most of all, total comfort. Slip-resistant footwear is increasingly popular, as the number of slips and falls have been reduced with these types of shoes. An investment in a pair of good quality shoes pays for itself in a very short period of time.

Servers must always be in good health. No server, while infected with a communicable disease, should be allowed to work in a foodservice establishment in any capacity. The potential to contaminate food and food contact surfaces, and to transmit the disease to other persons, is too great.

DISCUSSION QUESTIONS AND EXERCISES

1. What does a server's personal appearance reveal to customers?
2. How does a server ensure good grooming?
3. List and discuss 10 grooming standards that are basic for servers.
4. When might a bold hairstyle be acceptable for a server?
5. What should the server do when in doubt about the use of cosmetics?
6. Discuss the importance of good poise and posture.

7. What is an adequate number of uniforms for a server?

8. If a restaurant does not have a specific uniform, what type of clothing should the server select?

9. What should the server look for when purchasing a quality pair of work shoes?

10. If a server comes to work with a head cold, slight cough, and occasional sneeze, how should management respond?

11. Discuss a positive or negative grooming issue that affected your dining experience.

12. Name three restaurants within your community that are noted for a professional server staff and impressive server uniforms.

3

Table Settings, Napkin Presentations, and Table Service

■   ■   ■   ■   ■   ■   ■   ■   ■   ■   ■   ■   ■

L earning Objectives

After reading this chapter and completing the discussion questions and exercises, you should be able to

1. Understand, explain, and demonstrate a breakfast and lunch table setting before the meal and as the meal is served.

2. Understand, explain, and demonstrate a dinner table setting before the meal and as the meal is served.

3. Identify the most commonly used pieces of flatware and serving pieces.

4. Correctly handle flatware, glassware, dishes, and cups.

5. Understand, explain, and demonstrate the correct placement of wine, champagne, cocktail, and liqueur glasses.

6. Understand, explain, and demonstrate the correct placement of placemats.

7. Determine how many salt and pepper shakers to place at each table and when they should be removed.

8. Determine how many sugar and creamer sets to place on the table and when to place them, when coffee or tea is served.

9. Explain the different ways that rolls and butter can be served.

10. Understand and demonstrate various napkin folds.

11. Explain and compare the five different methods of serving food, commonly referred to as service styles.

12. Explain how counter service functions and be able to demonstrate different counter service table settings.

13. Explain correct procedures of banquet service, the importance of adequate spacing for table and chair arrangements, and table settings.

14. Understand and explain the service procedure for room service.

15. Explain the workings of salad bars, dessert tables, carts, and trolleys; demonstrate the correct way of using each.

Waiter/waitress (server) training begins with an understanding of correct table settings, and the correct way in which to handle flatware, glassware, dishes, and cups. The server must have the knowledge and ability to properly place table settings in a fast and efficient manner in order to keep pace with the demands of a busy restaurant. In time, the server will be able to immediately identify the most-used flatware and different serving pieces, such as a pasta spoon, lobster fork, or escargot tong. The server will also know how many salt and pepper shakers, sugar bowls, and creamers to bring to the table, as well as the restaurant's method of serving rolls and butter.

Napkin presentations are elegant and impressive, and a professional server will have the opportunity to perform a number of different napkin folds. Therefore, he or she should be acquainted with the most popular folds and develop the ability to do them. Most restaurants will have identified one fold that it uses consistently, but in response to customers requests, may choose different folds for banquets or catered events.

The professional server should also be acquainted with the five distinctively different methods of serving food, as many restaurants have developed a contemporary style of food service that shares various aspects from all five methods. The server may have the opportunity to work in counter service, banquet service, or room service and should be knowledgeable in these types of service.

Salad bars and dessert tables, carts, and trolleys have become a significant part of many restaurants. The successful server understands their functions and setups, and how they have become part of the restaurant's service.

P reset Breakfast and Lunch Table Setting

The preset breakfast and lunch table setting is shown in Figure 3-1. The table setting includes a fork, knife, teaspoon, bread-and-butter plate, water glass, and napkin. The fork, knife, and teaspoon are set approximately 1 inch from the edge of the table. The blade of the knife is always turned inward toward the plate. The water glass is placed about 1 inch to the right of the tip of the knife, and the bread-and-butter plate is placed about 1 inch above the tines of the fork. The napkin is centered between the fork and the knife. There should always be approximately 12 inches between the fork and the knife, depending upon the size of the plate that will be placed between them.

FIGURE 3-1
Breakfast and Lunch Table Setting

FIGURE 3-2
Breakfast and Lunch Table Setting as the Meal Is Served

When coffee or tea is served, the cup and saucer are placed to the right of the teaspoon approximately 1 inch from the edge of the table with the handle angled at 4 o'clock (some prefer the handle angled at 3 o'clock). If breakfast toast or a lunch salad is served, the plate is placed to the left of the fork and approximately 1 inch from the edge of the table. When the breakfast or lunch plate is ready to be served, and the guest has removed the napkin, the plate is placed and centered between the fork and knife, approximately 1 inch from the edge of the table. Refer to Figure 3-2, Breakfast and Lunch Table Setting as the Meal is Served. If side dishes are ordered, such as a side of pancakes with breakfast or onion rings with lunch, the dishes, along with any accompanying condiments, may acceptably be placed in a convenient location on the table when served.

P reset Dinner Table Setting

The preset dinner table setting is shown in Figure 3-3. The table setting from left to right includes a salad fork, fork, knife, butter knife (or butter spreader), two teaspoons, bread-and-butter plate, water glass, and napkin. When a

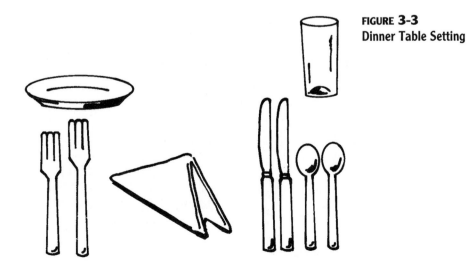

FIGURE 3-3
Dinner Table Setting

butter spreader is used, it could also be placed horizontally across the top half of the bread-and-butter plate with the blade turned inward toward the tines of the forks, or most often, parallel to the fork, the blade toward the left. The forks, knives, and teaspoons are set approximately 1 inch from the edge of the table. The blades of the knives are always turned inward towards the plate. The water glass is placed about 1 inch to the right of the tip of the butter knife, and the bread-and-butter plate is placed about 1 inch above the tines of the forks. The napkin is centered between the fork and the knife. There should always be approximately 12 inches between the fork and the knife, depending upon the size of the plate that will be placed between them. Formal dinner settings often include a decorative service plate, which will be removed and replaced with the actual plated entrée. At times, depending upon the menu, a salad plate or soup bowl may be set on top of the service plate, which is later removed with the salad plate or soup bowl.

When coffee or tea is served, the cup and saucer are placed to the right of the teaspoons approximately 1 inch from the edge of the table with the handle angled at 4 o'clock (some prefer the handle angled at 3 o'clock). When the salad is ready to serve, and the guest has removed the napkin, it is placed and centered between the fork and knife approximately 1 inch from the edge of the table. When the dinner plate is ready to be served, and the guest is not finished with the salad, with the guest's permission, the salad plate is placed to the left of the forks. The dinner plate is placed and centered between the fork and knife, approximately 1 inch from the edge of the table. Refer to Figure 3-4, Dinner Table Setting, as the Meal is Served.

When an appetizer such as smoked salmon with caper dressing or soup such as consommé spaghettini is served, it is placed and centered between the fork and knife, approximately 1 inch from the edge of the table. The appropriate flatware, such as a fish fork or soupspoon, is conveniently placed when the item is served, or the fish fork may be placed to the left of the salad fork and the soupspoon may be placed to the right of the teaspoon.

Bread baskets, butter plates, and side dishes, such as a side order of mushrooms, and condiments, such as Worcestershire sauce or Dijon mustard, may be placed in a convenient location on the table when served.

The dessert fork and spoon are in place for when the dessert is served, as shown in Figure 3-5, Dinner Table Setting With Wine Glasses, Dessert Fork,

FIGURE 3-4
Dinner Table Setting as the Meal Is Served

FIGURE 3-5
Dinner Table Setting With Wine Glasses, Dessert Fork, and Spoon

1   2   3   4   5   6   7   8

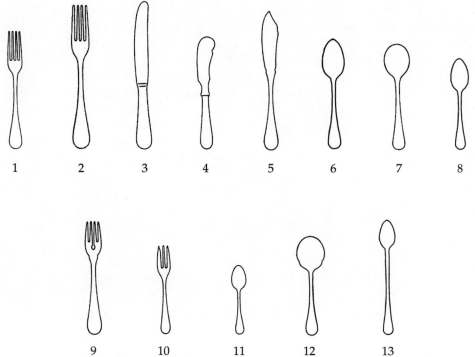

9   10   11   12   13

1. Salad Fork	6. Soupspoon	11. Dessert/Demitasse Spoon
2. Fork	7. Bouillon Spoon	12. Sauce Spoon
3. Knife	8. Teaspoon	13. Longdrink Spoon
4. Butter Spreader	9. Fish Fork	
5. Fish Knife	10. Dessert Fork	

FIGURE 3-6
Commonly Used Flatware

and Spoon. The small dessert spoon (or demitasse spoon) may be used for dessert or for an intermezzo course, which would be served during an up-scale dinner. The intermezzo is often served between salad and the entrée. The intermezzo typically consists of a small portion of citrus-flavored sorbet. The purpose of the sorbet is to cleanse the palate of strong flavors. The table setting also shows a napkin placed on a service plate. The number of courses in a given menu determines the number of forks, knives, and spoons that are selected for a preset table. Therefore, a seven-course meal may require five forks, four knives, a soupspoon, and three teaspoons. The rule to follow is that flatware is placed in order of usage from the outside inward. To be able to identify the most commonly used pieces of flatware refer to Figure 3-6, and for serving pieces refer to Figure 3-7. For safe and sanitary handling, the following procedures must be followed: Flatware should be held by the handles and never by the tines of a fork, the blade of a knife, or the mouth of a spoon. Flatware should be spotless when placed on the table. Once the guest uses a piece of flatware for its intended purpose, it should be removed from the table. For example, when a guest has finished a salad, the salad fork and

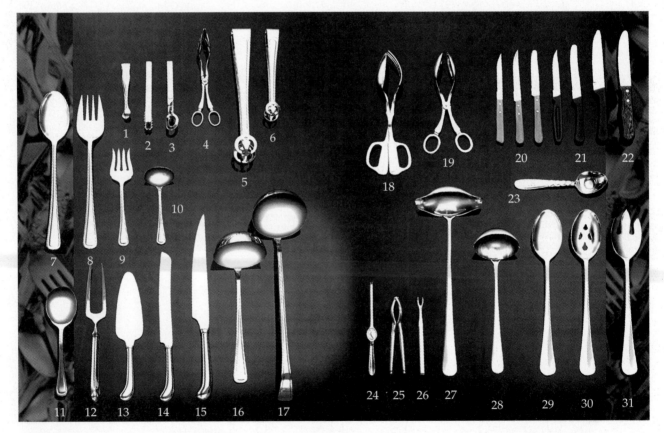

1. Sugar Tong	9. Serving Fork	17. Punch ladle	25. Lobster Crack
2. Ice Tong	10. Gravy Ladle	18. Salad Serving Scissors	26. Lobster Fork
3. Escargot Tong	11. Serving Spoon	19. Salad Serving Scissors	27. Punch Ladle
4. Pastry Tong	12. Carving Fork	20. Wood Handle Steak Knives	28. Tureen Ladle
5. Serving Tong	13. Cake Server	21. Plastic Handle Steak Knives	29. Buffet Serving Spoon
6. Tong	14. Cake Knife	22. Large Wood Handle Knife	30. Serving Spoon, Pierced
7. Banquet Spoon	15. Carving Knife	23. Pasta Spoon	31. Buffet Serving Fork
8. Banquet Fork	16. Soup Ladle	24. Lobster Pick	

FIGURE 3-7
Serving Pieces *Courtesy of Oneida Foodservice Flatware*

FIGURE 3-8
Preset Banquet Table Setting *Courtesy of Villeroy & Boch*

salad plate should be simultaneously removed. Glassware should be held by the stem or sides and never by the rim of the glass, and should always be spotless when placed on the table. Dishes should be held by placing the hand at the bottom of a dish with the thumb at the rim for balance, but never on the dish. Coffee cups should be spotless and held by the handle and never by the rim of the cup.

When a menu is predetermined, such as for a banquet or catered function, the tables are typically preset with the appropriate table settings to accommodate the menu and accompanying beverages, as shown in Figure 3-8, Preset Banquet Table Setting.

Wine and Beverage Setting

When wine is served, the water glass is moved above and slightly to the left of the knife. The wine glass is placed above and slightly to the right of the butter knife. Figure 3-5, Dinner Table Setting With Wine Glasses, Dessert Fork, and Spoon, shows a preset table, where two wines would be served during the meal. A wine would accompany one course of the meal and a second wine another course. There are fine dining occasions when different wines are served with corresponding courses of the meal. Thus a five-course meal could have five different wines. At the completion of each course, that glass would be removed. The wine glasses are set in order of use. Therefore, if a white wine was served first, the glass would be positioned to the right of the butter knife. White wine glasses are normally taller and narrower by design. If the second wine were a red wine, the glass would be positioned above the tip of the butter knife. Red wine glasses are a balloon-like shape, which helps the wine to "breathe" by exposing more of its surface area. The balloon-like

FIGURE 3-9
Glass Shapes *Courtesy of Cardinal International, Inc.*

shape allows the guest to swirl the wine in the glass as it reacts with air. If champagne were served, it would be positioned above and slightly to the right of the butter knife. If served with wine, the glass would be placed above the wine and slightly to the right of the water glass. Champagne glasses are a slim flute shape design, which keeps the champagne from losing its bubbles too quickly. Refer to Figure 3-9, Glass Shapes. When a before dinner cocktail or after dinner liqueur is ordered, it would be served centered between the fork and knife about 3 inches from the edge of the table.

lacemats

When placemats are used on rectangular tables, they should be centered between the fork and knife and approximately one half inch from the edge of the table, as shown in Figure 3-10. For round tables, rectangular placemats should be placed so that the corners of the placemat are one half inch from the edge of the table. Placemats of varying shapes and sizes, such as oblong, oval, or round, should be placed accordingly.

Salt and Pepper, Sugar and Creamer

Salt and pepper shakers should be preset according to the number of guests at each table, typically one set per four to six persons, depending upon the menu. As a general rule, they are removed after the main course and the same number of sugar bowls and creamers are placed just prior to coffee or tea being served. See Figure 3-11, Salt and Pepper Shakers, Sugar and Creamer in Use. It is important to recognize also that some restaurants may choose not to preset salt and pepper shakers, but to bring them to the table as needed.

FIGURE **3-10**
Placemats *Courtesy of Villeroy & Boch*

R olls and Butter

Rolls and butter may be served in several different ways, according to the policy of the restaurant. For example:

- A roll and slice of butter placed on a bread and butter plate for each guest.

FIGURE **3-11**
Salt and Pepper Shaker, Sugar and Creamer in Use
Courtesy of Villeroy & Boch

- Rolls in a basket and butter slices or balls in a dish for guests to serve themselves. The rolls may be served warm.
- Rolls and butter served to each guest by the server. This is typically done so that the rolls can be served hot.
- A small loaf of bread served on a cutting board with a bread knife, accompanied by a dish with butter slices.

N apkin Presentations

Napkins folded in a distinctive pattern can further add to the professional look of the table setting. Napkin folds can range from the simple flat fold to any one of the more elaborate folds shown in Figure 3-12. The napkin can be placed in the center of a service plate as shown in Figure 3-5. If a service plate is not used, the napkin can take its place. If tables are preset for a banquet or catered event, and salad is also to be preset, then the napkin would be placed above the salad plate.

T ablecloths

Tablecloths should always properly fit tables and drape approximately one inch above the chairs where guests will be seated. Before table settings are placed, the tablecloths must be clean and free of any spots or stains.

T able Service

There are five distinctive methods of serving food, often referred to as service styles: Butler Service, American Service, English Service, Russian Service, and French Service. The English, Russian, and French styles of service have changed over the centuries and evolved into different interpretations. Historical references correctly define these styles of service as they were originally set forth. Contemporary references are more focused on specific techniques that adapt the original definitions to what has transpired over the years.

Many restaurants have developed their own form of service that includes features from the different methods. This is often the result of a menu mix of international food items. The service style that a restaurant develops is one that will accommodate the menu, atmosphere, image of the restaurant, and nature of the clientele. What often develops are contemporary methods of serving food that are effective in meeting the individual restaurant's operational needs. These contemporary methods are a blend of one or more of the traditional methods, that fall into the following generally accepted definitions, combining some historical reference with a modern application.

BUTLER SERVICE

This type of service is provided during a cocktail party or during the cocktail portion of a banquet or catered event. Hors d'oeuvres and/or light refreshments are placed on hand-held trays and offered to guests by servers. This may also be referred to as "flying service" or "flying platters."

Clown's Hat

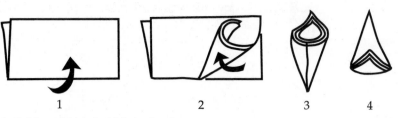

1. Fold napkin in half, bringing bottom to top.
2. Holding center of bottom with finger, take lower right corner and loosely roll around center.
3. Match corners until cone is formed.
4. Turn napkin upside down, then turn hem all around. Turn and stand on base.

Bird of Paradise

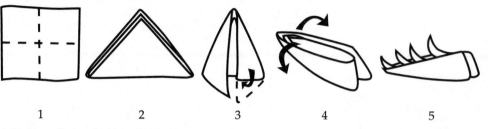

1. Fold napkin in half and in half again.
2. Then fold in half diagonally with points on the top and facing up.
3. Fold left and right sides down along center line, turning their extended points under.
4. Fold in half on long dimension with edges facing out.
5. Pull up points and arrange on a fabric surface.

Rose

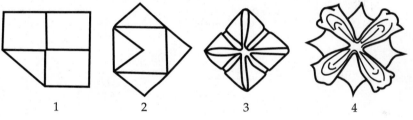

1. Fold all 4 corners of open napkin to center.
2. Fold new corners to center.
3. Turn napkin over and fold all 4 corners to center.
4. Holding center firmly, reach under each corner and pull up flaps to form petals. Reach between petals and pull flaps from underneath.

Candle

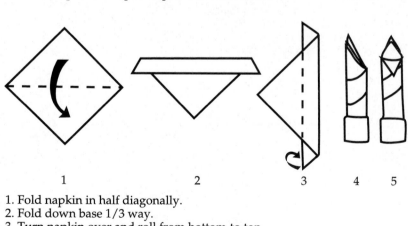

1. Fold napkin in half diagonally.
2. Fold down base 1/3 way.
3. Turn napkin over and roll from bottom to top.
4. Tuck corners inside cuff at base of fold and stand.
5. Turn one layer of point down and set on base.

FIGURE 3-12
Napkin Folds *Courtesy of Milliken & Company*

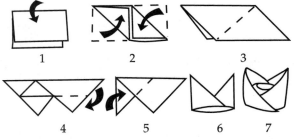

Bishop's Mitre

1. Fold napkin bringing top to bottom.
2. Fold corners to center line.
3. Turn napkin over and rotate 1/4 turn.
4. Fold bottom edge up to top edge and flip point out from under top fold.
5. Turn left end into pleats at left forming a point on left side.
6. Turn napkin over and turn right end into pleat forming a point on right side.
7. Open base and stand upright.

Oriental Fan

1. Lay napkin flat and fold along dotted lines.
2. Pick up from center where edges meet. This will give a "W" effect (if viewed from ends).
3. Pleat from bottom to top 5 times.
4. Grip from hemmed side at bottom.
5. Open accordion folds and pull down one side.
6. Repeat step 5 on other side.
7. Set napkin down and let fall into a fan shape.

Goblet Fan

1. Fold napkin in half.
2. Pleat from bottom to top.
3. Turn napkin back 1/3 of the way on right (folded) end and place into goblet.
4. Spread out pleats at top.

Rosebud

1. Fold napkin in half diagonally.
2. Fold corners to meet at top point.
3. Turn napkin over and fold bottom 2/3 way up.
4. Turn napkin around and bring corners together, tucking one into the other.
5. Turn napkin around and stand on base.

FIGURE 3-12 (continued)

Land Windermere's Fan

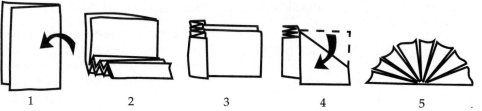

1. Fold napkin in half.
2. Starting at bottom, accordion pleat 2/3 way up.
3. Fold in half with pleating on the outside.
4. Fold upper right corner diagonally down to folded base of pleats and turn under edge.
5. Place on table and release pleats to form fan.

Cardinal's Hat

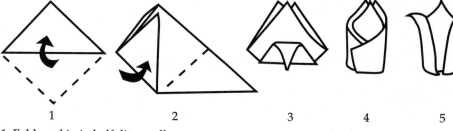

1. Fold napkin in half diagonally.
2. Fold corners to meet at top point.
3. Turn napkin over with points to the top, fold lower corner 2/3 way up.
4. Fold back onto itself.
5. Bring corners together tucking one into the other. Open base of fold and stand upright.

Pyramid

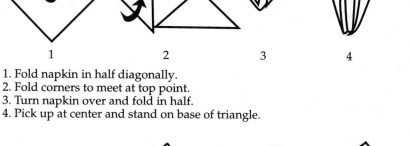

1. Fold napkin in half diagonally.
2. Fold corners to meet at top point.
3. Turn napkin over and fold in half.
4. Pick up at center and stand on base of triangle.

Crown

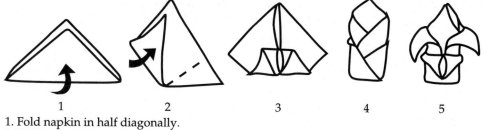

1. Fold napkin in half diagonally.
2. Fold corners to meet at top point.
3. Fold bottom point 2/3 way to top and fold back onto itself.
4. Turn napkin over bringing corners together, tucking one into the other.
5. Peel two top corners to make crown. Open base of fold and stand upright.

FIGURE 3-12 (continued)

AMERICAN SERVICE (INDIVIDUAL PLATE SERVICE)

This is the most popular type of service among today's restaurants. The service has been widely accepted because it is simple and quick, uses a minimum amount of serving equipment, and meets a wide variety of service needs. The food is plated in the kitchen and individually served to guests, either at the guest's right with the right hand (traditional) or at the guest's left for left-handed servers, if desired.

ENGLISH SERVICE

Formal English service is taken from the traditional service in English country homes where the head of the household acts as the carver and serves portions to family and guests with the assistance of servants. This type of service is often used in homes during holidays, such as Thanksgiving and Christmas. The head of the household (host) carves the turkey, ham, or roast and places an individual portion on each plate. The plate is then typically passed to another person (the hostess) who adds potatoes, vegetables, and other food items. Once the plate is complete, it is either served to a guest or given to the closest guests to be passed along to other guests. Soup is served in the same manner. That is, the host ladles soup from a tureen and either serves the guest or gives it to the closest guests to be passed along to other guests. The professional application in the catering and restaurant environment adapts the above technique to a more formal presentation. The server presents a platter to the guest by the guest's left side and serves the food onto the plate by using a serving fork and spoon with his or her right hand, the Pince (or Pliers) technique.

Bernard Martinage, Founder of the Federation of Dining Room Professionals, offers the following definitions for Russian Service *and* French Service.

RUSSIAN SERVICE

The food is brought out of the kitchen on attractive platters and serving dishes, then carved or finished in front of the guest on a side table. The service can be very formal and elegant as the food is displayed to guests before serving. This makes for an impressive presentation, such as when serving chateaubriand or for those sharing an identical meal. The guests experience a personalized service as the server places the food on each guest's plate. Prince Alexander Borisovich Kourakine imported this tableside service technique to France in the mid-1800s and it was so well received that it was incorporated into the French protocol of service, and has since been coupled with French service in countries where formal catering service was later imported. In an interesting twist, many professionals in the United States also associate a traditionally French technique with this service style. That is, the platters and serving dishes are placed on the tables for guests to serve themselves. The obvious advantage of this technique is that guests get to select only the items they enjoy.

FRENCH SERVICE

Historically, food arrived from the kitchen on any number of platters that were either placed at the center of the table for the guests to help themselves or passed around by servants. The servants would present the platters to the guests at their left sides, and the guests would remove food from the platters themselves. Two examples of this technique in practice today are the service

FIGURE 3-13
Gueridon or Flambé Cart *Courtesy of Lakeside™*

of bread, where the guest selects his or her own piece from the basket at the center of the table, and the act of selecting a tea bag out of a presented box. This technique of service is still associated with French service in Europe, as well as by traditionalists. In the United States and for a number of contemporary professionals, French service has come to signify a very sophisticated and spectacular level of service. As the French service incorporated the Russian tableside technique by the end of the 19th century, which is the practice of serving food from a serving cart, often referred to as a gueridon or flambé cart as shown in Figure 3-13, it has become synonymous with French service. A small heater, called a rechaud, is placed on top of the cart (except in the case of a flambé cart) and used to cook or warm food at the side of the table. The food comes from the kitchen either unprepared or semi-prepared, and final preparation is completed by the server for the guests to view. Since the food is being cooked for each guest, a considerable amount of time is required, along with specific culinary skills for the server preparing the food. The server typically needs an assistant to help in the preparation and serving of food. This type of service requires tables to be spaced farther apart to accommodate the carts. French service is reserved for very formal restaurants, as the cost to serve the food in this fashion is quite high. Some fine dining restaurants serve certain menu items from a cart, such as a Caesar salad or flamed desserts such as cherries jubilee.

Other Types of Service

Several other types of service can be offered in conjunction with the restaurant's table service. They are counter service, banquet service, and room service.

COUNTER SERVICE

This is a quick service and is generally found in coffee shops or old-fashioned soda fountains. The service is inexpensive and informal. The counter server will typically be assigned 12 to 18 seats depending upon the menu and how quickly the seats turn over. The table settings will vary from no setting at all until the customer arrives or orders, to a paper napkin with a fork, knife (blade turned toward fork), and teaspoon placed on top of the napkin and to the right of the counter seat as the customer would be seated. Or the table setting could include a placemat with the knife (blade turned inward), teaspoon to the right, a fork and napkin to the left. Water is placed above and slightly to the right of the tip of the knife and if coffee or tea is served, the cup and saucer or mug is placed to the right of the teaspoon with the handle angled at 4 o'clock. Condiments are usually within easy reach for the server, as are napkins, flatware, water glasses, ice, coffee cups or mugs, and tote boxes (bus tubs) for placing dirty dishes, flatware, glasses and coffee cups or mugs. The bus tubs are usually placed under the counters. The service pace is typically fast and the server is required to be conscious of keeping the condiments full and wiped clean, maintaining an adequate supply of napkins, flatware, water glasses, and coffee cups or mugs. The tote boxes (bus tubs) need to be removed quickly to the dishwashing area and replaced with clean tote boxes. This may be either the server's responsibility or an assigned bus person's. The guest check is given to the customer face down once the meal is served. Due to the nature of the service, customer tipping usually ranges from 10 to 15 percent and in some cases 20 percent or higher.

BANQUET SERVICE

This type of service can accommodate any size group ranging from a dozen to an unlimited number of guests. The capacity of the banquet room will dictate the maximum number of people that can be served. A banquet menu can be limited and served quickly, or it may consist of several courses, elaborately presented and served. It may be a traditional breakfast, lunch, or dinner menu. The nature of the event typically influences the menu, such as a wedding reception, birthday party, anniversary party, Christmas or New Year's Eve party, bar or bat mitzvah, business awards luncheon, retirement dinner, or any other special occasion. The menu is always predetermined. Occasionally a second choice may be offered to guests as part of the banquet menu, or to guests who may have some dietary restrictions. The tables should be set up well in advance of the banquet, allowing enough time to be thorough and complete. Tablecloths should be draped approximately 1 inch above each chair. The tables should be set with the appropriate plates, beverage glasses, coffee cups and saucers, and flatware to accommodate the menu being served. Each table setting should be approximately 24 inches wide and 15 inches deep. This will allow a comfortable space for guest seating and dining as well as adequate serving room. Tables and chairs should be arranged so that guests can be conveniently seated and served. Chairs, when in use, will normally extend 18 to 20 inches from the table edge and 18 inches in width. Allow 24 to 30 inches from back to back (when in occupied position) for comfortable service between tables. When a head table is being used, the other tables should be arranged so that the majority of the guests will be able to view the head table. The server is typically assigned 12 to 18 guests to serve, depending upon the menu and the method of service. For more extensive information on the mechanics of banquets, catering, and buffets, refer to *Catering Solutions: For The Culinary Student, Foodservice Operator, and Caterer,* by Ed Sanders, Chef Larry Lewis, and Nick Fluge (Upper Saddle River, NJ: Prentice Hall, 2000).

ROOM SERVICE

Many hotels and motels offer room service. The guests select from a room service menu and place their order over the telephone. The order is delivered to the room typically within 10 to 30 minutes from the time the order is placed. Delivery times can also be scheduled with advance ordering, such as for breakfast, which could be ordered the night before. The food is placed on a service tray or rolling cart and brought to the room from the kitchen by a server. Hot food plates are always covered to keep the food warm. The server has the added responsibility to double check the order for its appearance and completeness along with bringing the appropriate condiments. When the server arrives at the room, he or she knocks on the door and announces, "Room Service." The server, once having been admitted to the room, will typically set the table and serve the food. The cost of the meal is usually charged to the room, with the guest signing the guest check and either writing in a tip amount or giving a cash tip to the server. The tip will generally be 20 percent or higher. There are some operations that identify an automatic gratuity (service charge) on the room service menu. It is also common for the house to retain a portion of this charge, thereby sharing the gratuity (service charge) with the room service server.

S alad Bars

The server, once having taken the guests' food and beverage orders, invites them to visit the self-serve salad bar. On occasion, a guest may request the server to prepare and serve his or her salad with choice of salad dressing. Salad bars can be limited to lettuce and a few fresh vegetables to extensive offerings that include fresh fruits, sliced and grated cheeses, a variety of prepared salads, anchovies, pickled herring, seasoned croutons, bacon bits, assorted crackers, bread sticks, etc. The server keeps the water glasses full and serves the guests' beverages while the guests are eating their salads. When the meal is ready to be served, the server removes the salad plates and forks, if the guests are finished.

D essert Tables and Carts

Desserts can be attractively presented and displayed in several ways. Dessert tables are typically set up for guests to serve themselves. Desserts may be plated or dessert plates may be at the dessert table for guests to serve themselves. A dessert cart, as shown in Figure 3-14, with a display of desserts, is rolled to the side of the table by the server and offered for guests' selection. A pastry and dessert cart, as shown in Figure 3-15, has a larger capacity to display a greater variety of desserts that may include pastries, fresh fruits, and soft cheeses. A smaller variety of dessert offerings may be shown on a hand-held tray or covered cake dish.

O verview

Waiter/waitress (server) training begins with an understanding and demonstrated ability to prepare correct table settings for breakfast, lunch, and dinner, prior to and as a meal is served. Also, the correct sanitary handling of flatware, glassware, and cups must be understood and adhered to at all times. A server, with experience, will be able to quickly identify the most commonly used flatware and serving pieces, along with the correct number

FIGURE 3-14
Dessert Cart *Courtesy of Lakeside™*

of salt and pepper shakers and sugar and creamers to bring to a table. The different ways of serving rolls and butter should also be understood.

Napkin folding is an integral part of a server's functions; therefore, the server should be acquainted with the most commonly used napkin folds and have a demonstrated ability to perform the folds.

There are five distinctively different methods of serving food. These methods are often referred to as service styles, and are as follows: Butler Service, American Service, English Service, Russian Service, and French Service. It is important to recognize that many restaurants have developed their own service style that includes various features from the different methods. This is typically done in order to accommodate the menu, atmosphere, image of the

FIGURE 3-15
Pastry and Dessert Cart *Courtesy of Lakeside™*

restaurant, and the nature of the clientele. Therefore, many contemporary service styles have evolved in today's restaurant environment. Other types of service include counter service, banquet service, and room service.

DISCUSSION QUESTIONS AND EXERCISES

1. Demonstrate, with the use of tableware, the correct breakfast and lunch table setting before the meal and as the meal is served.

2. Demonstrate, with the use of tableware, the correct dinner table setting before the meal and as the meal is served.

3. Demonstrate the correct placement of a dessert fork and spoon for a pre-set dinner table setting.

4. Where possible, lay out on a table a variety of the most commonly used pieces of flatware along with various serving pieces and identify each one by actual use.

5. Demonstrate, with the use of tableware, the correct way to handle flatware, glassware, dishes, and cups.

6. Demonstrate the correct placement, with the use of wine, champagne, cocktail, and liqueur glasses, before, during, and after a meal is served.

7. Describe the shape of a champagne glass, white wine glass, and red wine glass.

8. Demonstrate the correct placement of the placemat with a lunch table setting.

9. How many salt and pepper shakers would be placed on a table set for eight people? Explain the general rule regarding the number of salt and pepper shakers to be set on a table and when they should be removed.

10. When would sugar and creamers be placed on a table? How many would normally be set?

11. Explain three different ways that rolls and butter could be served to guests.

12. Demonstrate six different napkin folds.

13. Define the five different methods of serving food and give an example of where each service would be used.

14. Explain how counter service functions.

15. Demonstrate different counter service table settings.

16. List several occasions that would require banquet service.

17. Discuss the importance of adequate spacing for table and chair arrangements during a banquet service. How many inches should be allowed between occupied chairs that are back to back in banquet seating?

18. What would be an average number of banquet guests assigned to a server?

19. Explain the service procedure for room service.

20. Explain the workings of salad bars, and dessert tables and carts.

4

Serving Food and Beverages

Learning Objectives

After reading this chapter and completing the discussion questions and exercises, you should be able to

1. Describe the 25 tips for proper table service.
2. Explain and demonstrate the procedures to follow when serving guests seated at a booth or next to a wall.
3. Explain and demonstrate the correct procedures for plate handling.
4. Describe and demonstrate the correct way to hold and serve a dish to a guest.
5. Explain and demonstrate the correct way to hold and serve beverage glasses, wine glasses with stems, cups, and mugs.
6. Describe the correct procedure to follow when serving wine.
7. Explain what additional items to bring to the table when serving specialty foods such as lobster.
8. Describe the correct way to prepare a finger bowl for use.
9. Explain the different ways that crumbs and food particles can be cleared from a table.
10. Understand, explain, and demonstrate how to correctly load and carry trays, such as the large oval, small rectangular, and round beverage tray.
11. Understand, explain, and demonstrate the three techniques for carrying multiple plates.
12. Recognize and define serving priorities and the importance of correct timing.
13. Explain how to handle difficult situations that a server may encounter.
14. Understand and explain the function of a bus boy/girl (bus attendant).
15. Know and explain how a bussing cart should be equipped.
16. Understand and explain the procedures to follow in order to properly bus a table with the use of a cart or with the use of a tray.

A restaurant's table service is developed to meet guests' expectations and designed to anticipate guests' needs. The particular demands or needs of the menu and dining room facility are also taken into consideration. Each restaurant will follow the method best suited for its particular condition. Therefore, the server must learn to follow the serving directions exactly so that service will be uniform throughout the restaurant. This chapter presents the basic service techniques that have been adopted at many restaurants throughout the country. However, each restaurant has its own set of standards and serving style.

During breakfast, fast, efficient service is essential; many guests are in a hurry. Service at breakfast may be limited to juice, toast, and coffee, or it may include a complete breakfast with an appetizer fruit cup followed by bacon, eggs, hash brown potatoes, and a side order of pancakes. It is important to remember never to have food in front of one guest while others have nothing to eat, unless it absolutely cannot be avoided. This usually occurs at the request of one of the guests who may have to leave the table before the other guests have finished their breakfast.

At lunch time it is also essential to serve guests immediately. Many times they have only 30 minutes in which to eat and get back to work. If an appetizer is ordered, such as a cup of soup or salad, place it in front of the guest as soon as possible. Rush the entrées and side dishes. If the guest orders nothing but a sandwich and beverage, serve them together. If there is extra time, serve the beverage first. However, it is equally important to recognize when guests may not be rushed and want to linger over coffee or dessert to discuss business or celebrate a birthday. Therefore, the server needs to exercise good judgment when asking whether a guest has any time restriction. The professional server is able to accommodate guests in a hurry as well as those who do not want to be rushed.

Dinner is generally more leisurely and allows the server to give guests extra special attention. However, at times guests may be attending the theater later in the evening or have another engagement, and they may want to eat quickly. Therefore, the server should inquire as to the guest's time frame for dinner. Often, dinner begins with a cocktail or two. The courses may include an appetizer, salad, soup, entrée, and a side dish. Rolls and butter should be served with the salad or brought to the table immediately following the order. The dessert can be served from a menu order, a dessert tray, cart, or trolley. When dessert is served, beverage refills should always be offered. After dessert the guest may want an after-dinner drink. Remember that if hot food is served on heated dishes, the guest should be warned that the dishes are hot.

T wenty-Five Tips for Proper Table Service

Professional servers traditionally serve food and beverages according to the following general rules and techniques:

1. Serve all dishes with the right hand, approaching the table to the right of the guest.
2. Serve all beverages and soups with the right hand and to the right of the guest.
3. Serve everyone at the table the same course at the same time, but serve a woman or older guest first as a matter of etiquette. When

there is more than one woman or older guest present, serve the woman or older guest on the host's right first. Then continue serving around the table clockwise, serving the host last. Treat children the same as adults, but serve them first if there is a problem.

4. Check the table setting for each guest to make sure that he or she has the necessary flatware for each course being served before serving the food. Flatware is to be held by the handles, never by the tines of a fork, the blade of a knife, or the mouth of a spoon. Preferably it should be carried on a tray or plate. Be careful never to serve bent or spotted flatware. The flatware should be clean and spotless. If water spots repeatedly occur, there may be a final rinse problem with the dishwasher that can be corrected. The manager should be informed of the problem.

5. Remove dishes and flatware from the right when each course is finished, using the right hand; then serve the next course from the right using the right hand. Exceptions to this rule are as follows:
   a. When it will inconvenience the guest.
   b. If the guest is leaning to the left to talk with another guest
   c. When serving a guest seated at a booth or next to a wall.

6. Serving guests seated at a booth or next to a wall requires the server to stand at the end of the booth or table and serve the guests seated farthest away first. Therefore, the guests seated on the right would be served with the left hand and the guests seated on the left would be served with the right hand. This reduces the possibility of the server accidentally elbowing a guest. Refilling water glasses or coffee cups may require the server to pick up the glass or coffee cup to be able to pour safely.

7. Serve all dishes by placing the thumb up or to the side of the outer rim of the dish and never inside, as shown in Figure 4-1, Plate Handling Procedures. Be careful never to serve a chipped or cracked dish.

Bernard Martinage, Founder of the Federation of Dining Room Professionals offers the following professional guidelines.

The way you pick up and carry a single plate is impacted by a number of factors: the temperature of the plate, the style of food presentation on the plate, the degree of accessibility to serve the guest and, finally, your personal preference or style.

The way the kitchen presents the food on the plate affects not only the server, but also the guest. Good food presentation dictates that the "decoration" shall never extend to the edge of the plate (past the inside rim). For example, if a chef covers an entire plate with powdered sugar, including the outer rim, it is guaranteed that the guest will see the server's finger imprints in the sugar.

For the basic technique of plate handling, the following rules, in Figure 4-1, apply whether or not the plate temperature requires it to be carried with a "service-napkin."

8. Serve beverage glasses by holding the sides or base of the glass, wine glasses by the stem, and cups or mugs by the handle, or, if placed on a saucer, by holding the rim and bottom of the saucer. Be careful never to serve a chipped, cracked, spotted, or stained glass, cup, or mug.

The worst way to handle a plate is to grab it by placing the thumb directly on the rim. There are several reasons not to handle a plate in this manner. First, it does not make the plate easier to manage. Second, this technique will leave a thumbprint on the shiny side of the rim for the guest to see. Third, if the plate is hot enough to require a service-napkin to hold it, the flap of the napkin will end up deeper in the plate than your thumb, possibly touching the food.

The server's personal preference and comfort will dictate how he or she will choose between this technique and the one that follows. The flexibility of the thumb position enables the server to remove his or her fingers smoothly from beneath the plate, allowing the server to bring the plate to table level in a perfectly horizontal position. This technique is also very elegant and discreet, but is uncomfortable to use when the plate temperature requires a service-napkin.

This technique sets the server's hand in the perfect position to serve a perfectly horizontal plate. Even though the amount of skin in contact with the upper side of the rim is greater than with the previous technique, it is still considered a very discreet style of plate handling, since the server's thumb is not sticking up. Also, this technique works well if the server must use a service-napkin, as the flap of the napkin would be folded back on the top of his or her hand, thus concealing the hand.

FIGURE 4-1
Plate Handling Procedures *Courtesy of the Federation of Dining Room Professionals*

9. Do not fill beverages or pour coffee to the rim. Leave room for cream with coffee. Constantly watch and refill water and coffee, and check to see if the guest would like a second beverage. When serving coffee or tea at a banquet where guests are seated closely together, hold a clean, folded napkin with the left hand and shield the guest from the hot pot when pouring. Note: When refilling coffee or tea, always ask first before pouring, as the guest may prefer an exact blend of sweetener and or cream. Adding more coffee or hot water to the tea may ruin the blend. After the third refill, a fresh cup is a nice touch.

10. When wine is ordered and brought to the table, the label is first shown to the host. The bottle is then opened and served to the host first by pouring about one ounce for tasting. Once the host has approved the wine, it is poured for other guests, filling each glass half way, beginning with the guest seated to the right of the host, with the host being served last. When the wine has been selected prior to the meal, as in the case of a banquet, serve the wine just before the main course. If more than one wine is served, serve the appropriate wine just before its designated course. Refer to Chapter 6 for additional information about serving wines and wine temperatures.

11. Follow the policy of the restaurant when serving rolls, breads, or crackers. If serving rolls or bread in a basket, the basket should be lined with a napkin.

12. Always handle butter with a fork, ice tong, or spoon.

13. When serving relishes, pickles, olives, or cheese, serve with a fork or spoon.

14. Salads as a separate course are served directly and in front of the guest. If the guest desires to finish his or her salad with the entrée,

then the salad should be placed to the left of the fork before the entrée is served. A side order salad would automatically be placed to the left of the fork when served.

15. When serving fruit cocktail, seafood cocktails, or any appetizer, place them directly in front of the guest. If guests are sharing an appetizer, be sure to bring an additional fork or spoon and appetizer dish. Some guests may appreciate having the appetizer split in the kitchen and served separately.

16. When serving specialized foods, such as lobster, bring a lobster crack, fork, and pick, as shown in Figure 3-7, and an empty plate for the lobster shell. Place the lobster crack to the left of the fork and the lobster fork and pick to the right of the teaspoon. If a pick is not used, place the lobster crack to the right of the lobster fork. Place the empty plate for shells above and slightly to the left of the lobster plate. Place the dish of melted butter above and slightly to the right of the lobster plate.

17. Formal dining sometimes includes the use of finger bowls at the end of a meal, such as lobster, chicken, or smothered ribs. Place to the left a small bowl filled with warm water on an underliner (small plate) garnished with a lemon wedge. Extra napkins are also provided for guests to wipe and dry their hands. Hot towels or a packaged moist towelette may also be used.

18. When serving steaks or fish, place the steak knife or fish knife to the right of the knife (or butter knife), followed by the teaspoon.

19. Always ask the guest if he or she would like any condiments that might accompany the meal, such as ketchup, mustard, Dijon, Worcestershire, or steak sauce.

20. Know the restaurant's policy regarding extra servings, so if a guest requests an extra portion, such as an additional serving of bleu cheese salad dressing or an additional slice of toast for breakfast, you will know how to respond (including any additional charges).

21. Dirty dishes should be taken to a side stand, a tray on a tray stand, or directly to the dishwashing area, and never scraped or stacked in front of guests.

22. When an ashtray is in use and needs emptying, simply remove it and replace it with a clean ashtray. Remove the ashtray slowly so ashes will not blow out, or cover the ashtray with another ashtray held upside down over it (capping), being careful not to clang them together to avoid chipping and unnecessary noise. Then remove both of them and replace with a clean one.

23. Completely clear all dishes, glasses not in use (leaving the water glass), salt and pepper shakers (if not normally left on the table), and condiments before serving dessert.

24. Tables should be cleared of all crumbs before presenting the dessert menu or serving dessert. This is done by using a crumber (handheld scraper), a mechanical handheld vaccum, or a clean napkin. When using a napkin, it should be tightly folded or rolled, then remove crumbs or food particles by sweeping onto a plate, small tray, or into another napkin, not into the other hand.

25. Desserts may be ordered from a dessert menu or selected from a dessert tray, cart, or pastry and dessert cart, as shown in Figures 3-14

and 3-15. After the guest has indicated a choice of dessert, the server should appropriately serve the dessert from the kitchen, tray, or cart. Place the dessert in front of the guest along with the dessert fork or spoon to the right of the dessert.

Loading and Carrying a Tray

There are various types of trays in general use, such as the **large oval** for bigger loads, **small rectangular,** and **round beverage trays.** Large oval trays are used when there are tray stands or side stands available to the server so that he or she can put the tray down before serving the guests. Rectangular trays are used for smaller amounts of food or for glasses. The round beverage trays are used for serving wine and cocktails. Restaurants that expect servers to handle full dinners for large parties generally use trays and tray stands. As a rule of professional service, a tray should not be placed on guest tables.

The following procedures should be followed when loading and carrying an **oval tray:**

- Make sure the tray is clean, top and bottom.
- Unless the tray has a nonskid surface of cork or similar material, cover the inside of the tray with a damp service cloth to prevent dishes or glasses from sliding.
- In most serving situations, hot and cold items will be loaded on the tray. Position on the tray is not determined by order of loading, but by the need to:
  a. Balance the tray.
  b. Keep hot foods away from cold foods.
  c. Preserve the food's attractiveness for the guest.
- Load the center of the tray first, and then work toward the outer edge.
- Load larger, heavier pieces toward the center of the tray or at the edge of the tray nearest the shoulder when carrying.
- Load lighter, smaller pieces toward the edges of the tray.
- Do not stack or overlap hot dishes with lids on cold dishes, or cold dishes on hot dishes.
- Keep plates with sauces or liquids level with the tray to prevent spillage.
- Do not place appetizers, soups, or cups on underliners (small plates) or saucers on the tray, but stack all underliners and saucers separately.
- Place coffee and teapot spouts away from food and plates, but not hanging over the edge of the tray.
- When stacking dishes with covers, do not stack more than 4 high or attempt to carry more than 16. It is possible to carry 5 stacks of 4 each, if done carefully.
- Never overload a tray. This will cause breakage as well as a possible accident or personal injury and loss of the spilled food.
- Balance the tray before lifting.
- Keep open dishes away from the side that will be nearest the server's hair.
- Leave one hand free to carry a tray stand.

An **oval tray** is carried on the server's shoulder; and it must be lifted to shoulder height. Since a tray may be fully loaded with covered dishes, it can be extremely heavy; therefore, it must be lifted properly according to the following procedures:

- Make sure the tray is properly loaded.
- Position the tray so that one side of the oval extends 5 inches off the service table, side stand, or tray stand in which the tray rests.
- Drop into a squat position by bending completely from the knees to get under the tray.
- Firmly place one side of the shoulder underneath the edge of the tray and slide the shoulder side hand toward the bottom center of the tray as the tray is being slid off the table or stand, as the other hand grasps the outer rim to steady the tray. See Figure 4-2.
- Stand up, keeping the back as straight as possible, using the legs to do the lifting; then the tray can be properly carried, as shown in Figure 4-3.

  Note: The server should never attempt to lift more than he or she is comfortable handling, nor should the server ever try to lift the tray to the shoulder using only the arms. This can result in twisted back muscles.

- Once the tray has been brought to the table, place the tray on a side stand or tray stand by keeping a straight back and again using the legs to drop into the squat position so that the tray can be slid onto the stand. Remove dishes evenly from the tray to ensure the tray remains balanced on the stand, and serve the guests.

Small rectangular trays are widely used in high-volume, limited-menu restaurants. They are used in some cocktail lounges, especially when the need to use all available space for seating leaves no room for side stands or tray stands.

A rectangular tray cannot be loaded as heavily as an oval tray, but a full breakfast or lunch for two people can be accommodated if properly loaded. The following procedures should be followed when using a rectangular tray:

- Make sure the tray is properly loaded and balanced.

FIGURE 4-2
Preparing to Lift a Tray

FIGURE 4-3
Properly Carrying a Tray

- Slide the tray broad side forward onto the left forearm.
- Hold the upper left arm close to the body.
- Use the right arm to carry a tray stand.
- Once the tray has been brought to the table, properly place the tray on the tray stand and serve the guests.
- When serving guests with the tray in the carrying position, unload it first from one side and then from the other in order to maintain balance.

Round beverage trays are best carried with the palm of the hand underneath and in the center of the tray, as shown in Figure 4-4. This enables the server to maintain balance and compensate for weight shifts while serving beverages. The tray should also be held close to the body to prevent spills or accidents.

FIGURE 4-4
Properly Carrying a Round
Beverage Tray

FIGURE 4-5
Items Clustered Together

When serving, slowly lift the glasses or bottles from the tray. If the tray starts to tip, quickly return the glass or bottle that caused the shift in balance. Then carefully slide the hand underneath the tray to the area that needs support, and resume serving. A good technique to keep the load steady is to make sure all items are clustered together and touching, as shown in Figure 4-5. This stabilizes individual items (tall beer bottles and wine glasses) and minimizes the possibility of a single item losing balance and knocking over the rest to the load.

arrying Multiple Plates

Some restaurants require servers to carry several plates from the kitchen at one time. This is often called arm service. Every server should learn the techniques of carrying multiple plates as this adds to his or her capability as a professional.

Bernard Martinage, Founder of the Federation of Dining Room Professionals, offers the following professional guidelines.

After a server has mastered plate handling techniques, the next step is to understand the different techniques used to carry several plates through the dining room and to the guest's table. The server should always use the proper plate handling technique to pick up each plate and then use one of the following three techniques to place each plate in the opposite hand for carrying, as shown in Figure 4-6, Plate Carrying Techniques.

PLATE CARRYING TECHNIQUE NUMBER ONE

This technique is particularly effective for carrying dishes in which the food presentation is high on the plate or very sensitive to remaining perfectly horizontal. The benefit of this technique is that it is fairly easy to practice

FIGURE 4-6
Plate Carrying Techniques: Technique Number One *Courtesy of the Federation of Dining Room Professionals*

and very elegant to serve; the downside is that it is a bit more difficult to perform when wearing a jacket, since the sleeve reduces the feel for the plate on the arm. To perform this technique properly, a server also needs to have a good sense of balance, especially with the third plate installed. As the third plate rests on the forearm, the server must always control his or her general body position. Shoulder moves will change the angle of the elbow and, therefore, the position of the plate on the forearm. Another inconvenience of this technique is that the plates must be removed in the same sequence that they were loaded. So the order of service must be planned while loading. Finally, this technique is very efficient for serving but not well suited for clearing a table.

Practice is required to get comfortable with this very elegant technique. The focus of your practice should be on the position of your fingers under the first plate, since it must support the others. If the first plate is not perfectly placed in your hand, there will be no way for you to correct its position once you add the other two plates.

The second plate must be oriented so that you will be able to place the third plate on the second plate's rim. If there are items such as bread sticks, cookies, or other food sticking out of one side of the plate, that food item should be placed away from your arm. Also, the third plate will be almost entirely resting on the second plate, so be sure the second plate position feels comfortable and strong before progressing.

The third plate is the most sensitive one, as it needs to be "locked" with the forearm. When adding this plate, fold your wrist "inside" to bring the second plate close to the forearm.

PLATE CARRYING TECHNIQUE NUMBER TWO

This is the easiest technique for stacking plates. It provides great flexibility in the way a server can position the arm to the body, and this technique is considered a strong and stable way to carry multiple plates. Because nothing rests any further up than the wrist, it is a great technique to employ in a busy establishment with a lot of traffic as the server can move the entire load freely in front of him or herself (or even to the side) without impacting stability of the load. It is not as aesthetic as the previous technique, but it is much more secure. One of the advantages of this technique is that it allows the server to unload the plates in any order, since none of the plates

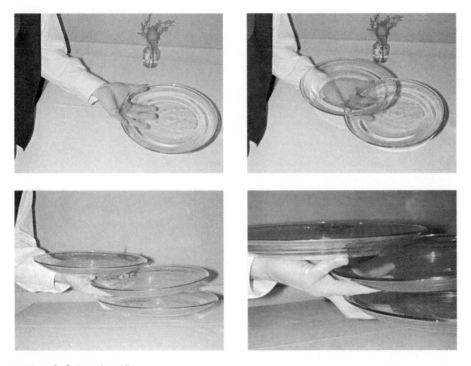

FIGURE 4-6 (continued)
Technique Number Two

rest on each other. This technique is practical for both serving and clearing of plates.

Here, the first plate to be placed in the hand is the middle one. This middle plate is called "the stabilizer" because it shapes the hand to support additional plates. Training for this technique can be painful, as it requires a big adjustment of your little finger and also puts stress on the thumb muscle. Once your body adjusts to this workout, you will no longer feel it.

The second plate to put in place is the one that rests in your palm. Because this plate rests almost on your full hand, it has great stability and strength, which constitute a perfect base for stacking.

The third plate is placed under the "stabilizer" and held by the major finger. The plate can rest there comfortably out of the way, right under the other plates. In order to carry more than three plates with this technique, the fourth plate rests on the second plate and on the server's forearm. However, this limits the freedom of movement this technique is designed to enhance.

For clearing using this technique, pick up the plate that contains the most food (or bones) left on it and use it as the stabilizer. Then place the fork sideways and lock the knife by sliding it perpendicularly and under the fork. Pick up the next plate and use the silverware to slide the food down to the first plate and then lock its silverware with the first ones on the stabilizer. Keep stacking, always making sure that your manipulation is performed out of the guest's view. By clearing in this manner, you can comfortably clear four guest's plates quickly and discreetly.

Using the forearm as a spare "parking lot" is acceptable when clearing two plates that contain food that will not stack well or when clearing salad or dessert plates (possibly of different sizes) at a large banquet. One person can stack well over 10 plates this way, if the plates are empty when they are

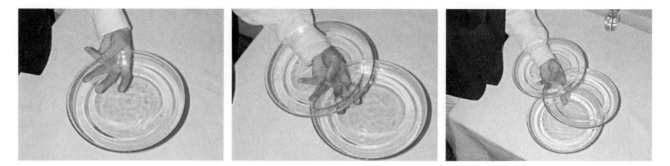

FIGURE 4-6 (continued)
Technique Number Three

picked up. This is not recommended for dining room service, but it is convenient for large catered events.

PLATE CARRYING TECHNIQUE NUMBER THREE

The third technique is very popular and is practiced industry-wide. It offers advantages over both prior techniques. Even though it does not provide the support strength of technique number two, it allows a server to unload the plates in any order. It does not offer the perfect horizontally layered plates of the technique number one, but it allows a server to comfortably carry plates with voluminous food presentation. Even though this technique can be used for clearing, a server needs adequate hand strength, since all the plates rest on the fingers.

Just like technique number one, the position of the first plate sets the comfort level for holding the following plates. There are different acceptable ways you can angle your wrist for this technique. You can maintain a straight wrist, bend your wrist toward the left to open your hand, or even fold the wrist inside. This flexibility allows you to move around between tables and around guests even in tight spaces more comfortably than with technique number one.

The second plate is the tricky one to set. It is easy to forget about the third plate when setting the second one. Positioning the three right fingers too close to the rim of the first plate will leave little support when adding the third plate. Remember that once the second plate is in place it is impossible to readjust the fingers without the help of the other hand, and this can be dangerous to do mid-dining room.

The third plate goes under both plates and is held by the "major" or "middle" finger. The plate is placed deep enough on the finger that even though it has only one finger's support, it is secure.

SUMMARY OF PLATE CARRYING TECHNIQUES

Any technique you learn will always feel awkward at first try, but it will become more natural with practice and will greatly improve the quality of your overall service. This impact is seen in saving extra trips to the kitchen, by saving a plate from going on the floor, or even in being able to hold a comfortable position while a guest is talking to you. These skills are as critical for a server as knife skills are for a cook. It is always important to keep it

FIGURE 4-7
Server Holding
24 Stemmed Glasses *Courtesy of the Federation of Dining Room Professionals*

as simple as possible, forget the idea that the more you can carry the better you are.

Carrying Glasses

It is possible to carry four glasses at one time, depending upon the size of the glasses and the size of the server's hand. Three glasses could be held in the left hand by fully spreading the fingers and using the thumb as balance. The fourth glass would be carried in the right hand. The stems of two or three glasses could be grasped with the left hand, with the right grasping the stems of the third or fourth glass. A number of restaurants' signature service includes the showmanship of carrying glassware, as shown in Figure 4-7. Advanced glass carrying skills would be learned from other experienced servers. However, when the potential for slippage exists the server should only use one hand to carry glasses.

Service Priorities and Timing

The server should always greet, welcome, and serve water to guests within seconds from the time they are seated (unless the policy of the restaurant is not to serve water to a guest unless requested). The server should be alert and attentive at all times and constantly aware of what is happening at his or her tables. This is accomplished by frequently looking at different tables and making eye contact with guests, even when engaged in taking an order or serving. Other tables may simultaneously need water or coffee refills, or may be ready to order dessert. Therefore, the server needs to cultivate service priorities and timing that convey a sense of urgency. This can be accomplished by developing the following techniques:

- Always make trips count. Never go empty-handed. The efficient server takes something that has to be delivered or removed from guest tables; for example, delivering an order from the kitchen to one table and removing dishes from another table to prepare for dessert. This saves time and energy and increases the speed of service by focusing upon efficiency and not wasting steps.

- Hot foods should be served the moment they are ready. The aroma, sizzle, and intensity of certain foods, such as soups, seasoned sauces, steamed vegetables, and steaks only last a short time and make up part of the guest's dining pleasure. Conversely, cold foods, such as seafood appetizers, fruit salads, or parfaits, must be served cold.

- After placing the guests' orders with the kitchen, promptly serve rolls and butter, appetizers, salads, soups, and/or drinks. Some restaurants have a policy of serving water as soon as guests are seated. Guests appreciate quick service and like to have enough time to finish one course before the next course arrives.

- Serve all the guests at the table the same course at the same time, without long lapses of time between courses. There is a delicate balance between not rushing guests and preventing them from fidgeting and getting impatient between courses. A constantly observant server will be able to accommodate guests.

- Pivot point service is a designated starting position with all orders served clockwise from that point. Servers should mentally number the positions at their tables with the designated starting pivot point and then go around the table clockwise as orders are taken. This allows the server to identify what each guest has ordered. The pivot point could be the party's host or, as with booths, the first person seated on the left and closest to the aisle. This can be critical if the point of sale (POS) system is designed to enter orders based on seating positions (as discussed in Chapter 8). Also, guest checks may provide table diagrams to assist in taking orders, as shown in Figure 4-8. When serving the food order, never ask guests what they have ordered. Be accurate and correct when taking the order and exact when delivering it.

- Keep water glasses refilled at all times. To some guests, nothing is more disturbing than to have an empty water glass. It is essential to check water glasses each time the server visits the guest, for any reason. For example, check water glasses when serving salads; when serving hot foods; when about halfway through with the meal; when suggesting dessert; and when serving dessert. Knowing which glass to fill first is important: a wine glass or coffee cup would be refilled before a water glass, for example.

- While it is important to follow the basic rules and techniques for proper service, successful servers focus on smooth, efficient serving procedures that are convenient for the guest, and that do not interrupt the guest's comfort. Also, remember that serving gracefully takes poise and know-how, and it brings pleasure and satisfaction to both the server and the guests.

- When taking orders, ask if the guests prefer individual checks or one check for the group. Never keep a guest waiting for the check. When presenting the check, place it in the center of the table face down, unless one of the guests has specifically asked for the check, or unless it was obvious when the orders were placed who would be paying. As soon as a credit card or money has been placed next to the guest check, the server should quickly process and return the credit card slip with the card and a pen or the change to the guest. The experienced server uses an

Table diagrams assist in taking orders
and serving correct meal to each guest.

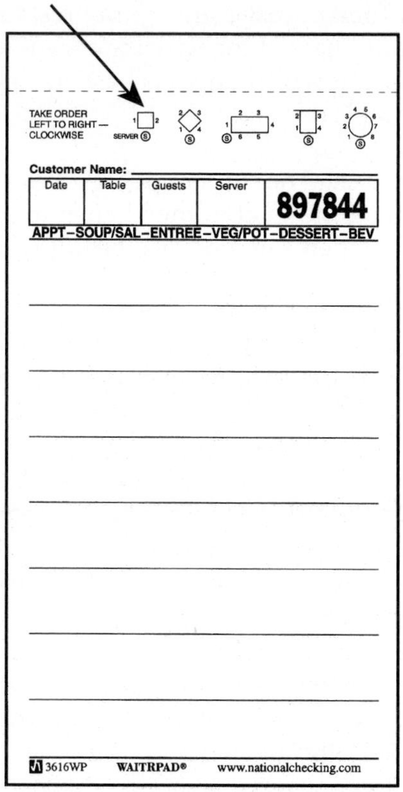

FIGURE 4-8
Guest Check, WaitRpads® *Courtesy of National Checking Company*

inexpensive ballpoint pen and removes the cap. This reduces the possibility that the absent-minded guest will place the pen in his or her pocket. The process for guest check payment should always be quick. If it is slow or delayed, guests may be displeased. Guest check processing and payment will be further discussed in Chapter 7.

■ Occasionally, guests take a leisurely approach to leaving after their meal. This may be acceptable when the restaurant is not busy, but when the table is needed for the next party, the guests may need a gentle hint that it is time to leave. The server may ask if the guests would like anything else, or start clearing the dessert dishes and glasses, thanking the guests and wishing them a pleasant evening.

Handling Difficult Situations

Difficult situations with guests arise occasionally in most restaurants. The server is typically the person who has to deal with and solve guest problems and complaints. Therefore, the server should remain calm, cool, and collected in working to correct a problem and satisfy the guest. The server needs to be confident of his or her abilities and remember that customer satisfaction comes before anything else. Difficult situations need to be resolved quickly. The following are examples of situations that occur most often, along with suggestions for effectively solving them.

Guest Receives Food Not Up to His or Her Expectations A good policy to maintain is that the "guest is always right." Food should be substituted or exchanged with an apology. The fact that the food is just right by the restaurant's standards is immaterial; the guests should have it the way they want it. This, of course, does not mean that the restaurant will change its basic recipe for each guest, a fact that most guests will appreciate.

Guest Complains that Food is Cold or Undercooked The server apologizes and immediately remedies the problem by returning the food to the kitchen to be warmed or fully cooked, and quickly returns when the food has been properly warmed or cooked.

Guest Says Food is Overcooked or Burned The server should follow the restaurant policy for how to handle this type of problem. A substitution may be offered or the food item can be replaced.

Guest States that the Portion Size is Too Small If the server recognizes that the portion is smaller than normal, the server should apologize and immediately take the guest's plate back to the kitchen for the correct portion amount. When the portion is the correct amount, the manager should be asked to visit the guest to resolve the problem.

Guest Says that the Order is Wrong When this occurs, it is not important who is at fault; what is important is to apologize and promptly correct the mistake. The error should be reported to the manager.

Guest Would Like a Baby Bottle Heated Although this may be inconvenient, do not give the guest the feeling, either by words or actions, that it is inconvenient or too much trouble to have the bottle heated. Be cheerful about doing it.

Guests Allow their Children to Wander the Floor Children should be asked to return to their table, or brought back to the table for adult supervision. Quite simply, the children would be at risk of getting knocked over, accidentally tripping a server, or annoying other guests.

Guest is Very Dissatisfied with Food and Does Not Want to Wait for a Replacement Apologize sincerely and suggest another entrée that is already prepared or is easily and quickly prepared. If the guest refuses, call the manager for help. The best decision may be not to charge the guest for the meal.

Guest Complains that Food is Undercooked, Although it is Half Eaten Apologize and offer to return it to the kitchen for additional cooking. If the guest refuses, some restaurants authorize the server to offer the displeased guest a complimentary dessert.

Guests Order Together and then Want to Pay Separately Do not become annoyed by this request, and by all means do not ask them to pay together and then figure it out themselves. Chapter 7 demonstrates a point of sale system that can quickly adjust to this type of situation.

Server Forgot to Turn in the Guest's Order to the Kitchen This might happen during a very busy shift. When it is discovered, the server should immediately place the order with the kitchen. Alert the kitchen and the manager to the problem. Then explain and apologize to the guest for the delay. Sometimes a free drink, appetizer, or beverage refill is necessary, if the server is authorized. This may appease the guest and salvage a tip.

Guest is Unhappy and Has a Bad Opinion of the Food and Service Always call for the manager when something like this happens. A third person often will be able to rectify the situation better than the server. Guests need to be satisfied before leaving the restaurant.

Guest is Intoxicated Inform the manager and bring coffee to the guest. If the guest becomes loud, obnoxious, or abusive, the manager may ask the guest to leave or may have to take other measures in having the guest escorted out of the restaurant. With the increase of liquor liability and laws passed specifically affecting alcohol service, the responsibility of monitoring alcohol service many times falls directly upon the server. The server should be completely informed about the legal statutes and house policies regarding intoxicated patrons.

Too Many Guests are Seated in a Server's Section When this occurs, and the server can't adequately handle the situation, the host or manager should be informed. Perhaps another server could be assigned to help, or the hostess or manager could step in to help. The mistake would be to try to serve more people than the individual server can effectively handle. The guest will not be pleased and the server's tips will suffer.

Guest Leaves Shopping Bag or Attaché Case in the Aisle The server needs to politely suggest that the guest move the bag or case out of the way of traffic to avoid possible trips or falls.

Server Spills Food or Drink on the Clothing of a Guest When a spill accident occurs, the server should react immediately by doing the following: Apologize and be certain that the guest was not hurt; assure the guest involved that the restaurant will clean the garment or replace it if necessary; replace the item that was spilled and alert the manager; and clean up the mess as quickly as possible.

Food is Slow Coming from the Kitchen Occasionally a kitchen may be temporarily backed up with orders. When this occurs, the server should explain the reason to guests—for example, a large party just arrived, or a tour bus just dropped off a large group. Most people are understanding and patient if they know why they have to wait and if they are not forgotten. The server needs to keep the rolls and butter replenished, water and beverage glasses full. If the delay is prolonged, some restaurants have a policy of providing guests with complimentary beverages, appetizers, or desserts.

Server is Informed that the Kitchen is Out of the Food Item Ordered When this happens the server should apologize to the guest for the inconvenience and suggest some comparable choices. It may be necessary to return the menu for the guest to review. Once the kitchen has run out of an item, the servers should be informed immediately. This will avoid or minimize the possibility of having to disappoint a guest once having placed the order versus being told ahead of time that the item is not available.

Foreign Object Found in the Food by the Guest This is among the worst possible situations. If a guest finds a piece of metal or glass, a bandaid, a bug, or anything else that would be dangerous and unappetizing, the server needs to immediately apologize and remove the plate, inform the kitchen and the manager, and return with fresh food for the guest. Most restaurants have a policy of not charging the guest for the meal along with offering the utmost apology for the unfortunate occurrence.

Guest Complains about the Food, Having Eaten Most of it Apologize and try to satisfy the guest in a reasonable manner. If that is not possible, the manager should be asked to resolve the situation. Some guests are never satisfied, and some are attempting to get a free meal. They still have to be treated with respect and dealt with fairly.

Guests Leave Without Paying Check with the cashier to be certain. Act quickly and inform the manager who in turn should follow them to their car, getting their license plate number. If they are not yet at their car, the manager should approach them and ask whether they paid, being polite but firm.

Customer Complaints—A Unique Opportunity for the Server

Stephanie A. Horton, CMP, a professional speaker/trainer/author in hospitality sales and service, and founder of Pacific Rim Protocol Server School in Seattle, Washington, offers the following advice to servers.

It is so easy to say, "turn lemons into lemonade" or "kill them with kindness." In this crazy business of hospitality, sometimes things go wrong. It is nobody's fault, there is just that moment when people, air, and food connect, then boom—something happens. Unfortunately, we cannot simply disappear (which seems like a pretty good idea sometimes)!

Your sense of humor is your finest attribute when an awkward situation looms. Remember, you can and you will get through it, because you are a hospitality professional. Then relax and enjoy the positive impression you have made! Now is the time to shine!

Listen to the parties involved, without interrupting. People need to "vent" when a situation occurs. Smile and focus entirely on the guest. Do not look around. Do not appear distracted. Empathize and acknowledge the complaint. Use words like, "I understand. You are absolutely right. Thank you for bringing this to my attention." Put yourself in their shoes. How would you react in the same situation?

Make sure your body language is "in sync" with what you are telling the guests—no crossed arms, sighing, shifting from foot to foot, or hands in pockets—all communicate negativism.

Do not argue. Whatever happens, resist the urge to defend yourself or the restaurant. The guest does not need to know how short on staff you are, or how the new oven just blew up. The guest is there for a relaxing, stress-free experience. All the guest cares about is what you are going to do about the problem!

Take action, fast! The guest needs to know that you can make something happen. Clarify with management in advance how much you are empowered to change. Can you bring a complimentary beverage or appetizer while the guests are waiting? If there is a breeze, perhaps a different table is in order, etc. Do something now! If you must get the manager—ask your team for help. Of course, jump in if one of your associates needs a hand. Once a problem has been solved, do not bring it up again or draw further attention to the situation. It is best forgotten!

Guests appreciate a server who takes action with a positive attitude. They are very understanding and forgiving, as long as their situation has become a priority. Take responsibility, and make something happen. You will be remembered for it!

Table Bussing

Being a bus boy or girl (bus attendant) is an excellent opportunity to learn the restaurant business thoroughly. Because of the wide variety of duties, the bus attendant can learn about waiting on tables, cooking, dishwashing, food preparation, and a variety of other areas—a little about every job in the restaurant. The bus attendant of today is often the waiter or waitress of tomorrow and the managers of the future.

Bussing is a very demanding job; it requires someone who can work quickly. The bus attendant must be able to perform under pressure when the restaurant is extremely busy and fast-paced. A bus attendant should be in excellent physical condition and should want to be of service to people. He or she should always be courteous and respectful to guests and other staff members.

Since the bus attendant is an assistant to just about every employee in the restaurant, he or she may take orders from the servers, host or hostess, cooks, and management, as well as the guests. During rush periods this may become frustrating. In the restaurant business it seems that everything happens at once, and this is a time when teamwork is essential. Through training and experience the bus attendant will be able to learn the order in which to perform tasks, always doing things that directly affect the guest first, working with speed and efficiency.

The personal appearance of the bus attendant is very important. Since the job puts the attendant in direct contact with guests, he or she must be neat, well groomed, and professional at all times. The same grooming standards that were discussed in Chapter 2 for servers apply to bus attendants.

Throughout the restaurant industry a common goal is to provide guests with quality food and good service, in a clean and sanitary environment. Therefore, the role of the bus attendant is critical in providing good service and in working to maintain a clean and sanitary restaurant. The best habit that a bus attendant can develop is to clean as he or she works. The key is not to wait until later to clean and straighten but to consistently do it as part of the work.

The manager explains general housekeeping duties and assigns specific responsibilities to bus attendants for each meal period during the day. Bus attendants may keep service stands equipped and tidy, replenishing supplies and ice, rolls, coffee, and other items as needed so that servers can serve guests quickly. The bus attendant works quietly, talking to others only when necessary and then in a low voice. This contributes to quiet and dignified service in maintaining good guest relations.

As soon as guests leave, the tables must be cleared. During the meal hours other guests are often waiting for tables; they are hungry and sometimes impatient; therefore, the bus attendant needs to act immediately in clearing and preparing tables. This can be accomplished by bussing with a cart or tray.

BUSSING WITH A CART

Using a cart to bus tables is the fastest, most efficient method of bussing. It is essential that the cart is clean, polished, and well stocked. It should have three or four shelves equipped with two clean tote boxes (bus tubs), with or without a flatware compartment, and two clean cloths, one dampened with a sanitizing solution and one dry. Some carts may also have a refuse bin attached. Refer to Figure 4-9 for an example of bussing carts.

The upper shelf of the cart may have a flatware bin (tub) filled with clean flatware. The top shelf may carry placemats and/or clean tablecloths and napkins.

Using a bussing cart allows the bus attendant to clear and clean a table and then set it up immediately. To properly bus a table, the following procedures should be followed:

FIGURE 4-9
Bussing Carts *Courtesy of Lakeside™*

- Pick up all flatware by the handles first, and place in a separate container.

- Put all paper and waste in a separate section.

- Put all "like" items together (example: glasses with glasses).

- Do not touch parts of dishes or flatware that may have come in contact with the guest's mouth. Avoid exposure to possible germs by picking up cups by the handles, glasses at the bottom or by stems, and flatware by the handles.

- Ashtrays should be emptied into a can or container, never in a dish or cup.

- Soiled napkins and placemats are rolled up and placed on the cart.

- Place condiments such as Dijon, Worcestershire, or steak sauce on the bottom shelf of the cart.

- Wipe off table, chairs or booth, table condiments (ketchup and mustard), etc. Remove crumbs or food particles by sweeping them onto a plate or into a napkin, not into the other hand. Do not allow crumbs or food particles to fall on the floor.

- Before leaving the table, check to see that the table has a clean ashtray (for smoking sections) and sparkling clean and filled salt and pepper shakers and sugar containers. Bus attendant should clean table, chairs or booth if needed. The floor around the table should be cleaned and vacuumed if needed. Check to see that the table has been set with flatware, placemats, and/or clean tablecloths, napkins, glasses, coffee cups, etc. in the proper places according to the restaurant's policy. Also, the bus attendant should make sure the chairs are straight and in order.

- Bus attendants should take bus carts to the dishwashing area and separate items in preparation for washing. The flatware goes in presoak tubs, glasses and cups go in racks, and dishes are scraped and placed together by size. Trash should be placed in the proper container.

- Work fast and efficiently.

Tables properly set up will enable the server to better serve the guests when they arrive. It is preferable to have the table set up before the guest sits down, but it is essential to have the table set up before the order is taken.

BUSSING WITH A TRAY

The tray is placed on a tray stand next to the table to be bussed. The dishes are stacked on the tray according to size—large plates together, small plates and saucers on top of large plates or on the side of the tray, glasses and cups around the edge of the tray as close to the plates as possible. Flatware should be placed together along the side of the tray. Stack the heaviest dishes on the side of the tray that will be carried on the shoulder. Lighter pieces can be placed around the edge. Soiled napkins and placemats are rolled and placed on the tray, unless it is the policy of the restaurant to place napkins and placemats on a separate tray. Care must be taken not to accidentally wrap any flatware in paper or it will end up in the trash instead of the dishwashing machine. Follow the procedures listed above to properly bus a table. Then lift the tray according to the loading and carrying steps previously discussed, remembering never to lift more than you are comfortable with handling.

SETTING UP WITH A TRAY

Setting up can be done with a tray. A rectangular tray is often used in the following manner. A linen napkin is unfolded on the tray to serve as a liner. Clean flatware (forks, knives, and spoons) is spread on the tray. Glasses and napkins are also included. This allows the server or bus attendant to quickly set up tables. All tables should be set up as soon as they are bussed.

ADDITIONAL BUS ATTENDANT RESPONSIBILITIES

The focus of the bus attendant is to do his or her best to keep the restaurant in top operating condition. Some additional responsibilities are as follows (Note: Porters may also be employed to perform some of these tasks.):

- During meal periods keep an eye on the floor. Crumbs and food particles should be swept up immediately with a small mechanical sweeper. Napkins, flatware, a piece of food, or any litter should be picked up as soon as it is seen.

- Spilled liquids should be cleaned up as soon as the spill occurs. If an area with a spill must briefly be left unattended, be sure that a chair or some other obstacle is placed over it so that no one will slip. Most spills can be soaked up quickly with a clean dry towel.

- All rugs and carpets should be vacuumed before and/or after meal periods, but never during a busy time. Vacuuming near guests should be avoided. The noise and activity can be irritating.

- Rest rooms need to be checked periodically for cleanliness and supplies. The rest rooms may need to be cleaned after every meal period, and soap, hand towels, and toilet paper replenished.

- Keep high chairs wiped clean with a safe sanitizing solution.

- The bus cart should be clean, orderly, and properly stocked with table set-up supplies, such as forks, knives, spoons, napkins, placemats, ashtrays, etc., ready to go into use.

- Server stand trash must be emptied periodically and replaced with a new trash bag liner. The station must be well-equipped with supplies, and replenished with ice, rolls, coffee, and other items as needed.

- Salt and pepper shakers, sugar bowls, and table condiments (ketchup and mustard) are checked and refilled as needed between meal periods.

- Some dining rooms have table candles that need to be lit before the dining room opens and checked throughout the evening.

- A salad bar or dessert table may need to be checked and refilled frequently.

- In addition to meal period responsibilities, the manager will assign and schedule daily and weekly housekeeping and cleaning duties. Most of these assignments should be scheduled so that the entire restaurant receives a thorough cleaning once a week. This means washing windows and cleaning all the small cracks and crevices where soil and food particles can accumulate.

In carrying out responsibilities within the restaurant, the bus attendant will often be dealing with guests. Bus attendants should be familiar with all menu items in case a guest asks a question. Courtesy is the key to good guest relations. If a guest requests some service from the bus attendant, such as a water refill, it is important that the bus attendant take care of it right away. If the request is for food or something that the attendant cannot deliver, the guest should be advised that the server will be informed without delay.

Overview

The general rules and techniques of proper table service are presented in 25 detailed procedures that apply to most restaurant operations. The correct methods of loading and carrying various trays are explained; every server should be competent in these methods. Some restaurants require their servers to be able to carry multiple plates, thus saving time and energy with fewer trips to the kitchen.

The server needs to cultivate service priorities and timing that convey a sense of urgency in meeting the needs of the guests. This is accomplished by developing techniques that include the following: Greet, welcome, and serve water to guests as soon as they are seated (unless the policy of the restaurant is to serve water only if requested by guests); always make trips count; hot foods are to be served the moment they are ready; after placing the guests' orders with the kitchen, promptly serve rolls and butter, appetizers, salads, soups, and/or drinks; serve all of the guests at the table the same course at the same time, avoiding long lapses of time between courses; when delivering the food order, never ask guests what they have ordered, develop a method to remember so that it will be correct; keep beverages refilled at all times; serving procedures should be smooth, efficient, and convenient for the guest; never keep a guest waiting for a check.

Never lose sight of the fact that the customer is the real "boss." If customers are not happy and satisfied today, they will not return tomorrow. Even worse, they can and will persuade friends to stay away too. One of the server's functions is to create and maintain the good will of the guests. When a guest complains about the food, the server needs to understand the complaint correctly and take care of it immediately. Several of the most common difficult situations that might occur in a restaurant are discussed in the chapter along with solutions and corrective actions.

The bus attendant has an important function in every restaurant. The most important duty is to please the guest. Nearly everything that a bus attendant does is aimed toward that goal either directly or indirectly. "Clean as you go" is one of the best habits that a bus attendant can develop, as this always contributes to a clean and efficient restaurant. The bus attendant is responsible for bussing and setting tables, replenishing supplies at the server's stand, and performing other responsibilities assigned by the restaurant manager.

DISCUSSION QUESTIONS AND EXERCISES

Note: An actual restaurant dining room setting or mock setup should be used in order to allow the student to demonstrate procedures, techniques, and functions that were presented in this chapter.

1. Explain and demonstrate the general rules and techniques of proper table service.

2. When there is more than one woman or older guest present at a table, whom would you serve first as a matter of professional courtesy?

3. How should children be treated when being served?

4. What should the server do if he or she continues to notice water spots on the flatware?

5. Explain the procedure to follow when serving guests at a booth or next to a wall.

6. Explain and demonstrate the procedures for correct plate handling.

7. Explain and demonstrate the correct way to hold and serve a dish.

8. Explain and demonstrate the correct way to hold and serve beverage glasses, wine glasses with stems, and cups and mugs with and without saucers.

9. What is the procedure to follow when serving coffee or tea at a banquet where guests are seated close together?

10. Explain the procedure to follow when wine is being served.

11. What additional items are brought to the table when specialty foods such as lobster are served?

12. How is a finger bowl prepared for use, and when should it be used?

13. What is a safe way to remove a filled ashtray?

14. Explain the ways that crumbs and small food particles can be removed from a table.

15. Explain or demonstrate the correct way to load and carry a large oval tray.

16. Explain or demonstrate the correct way to load and carry a small rectangular tray.

17. Explain or demonstrate the correct way to load and carry a round beverage tray.

18. Explain the correct procedure for carrying multiple plates. Demonstrate the three basic techniques.

19. Identify and discuss six techniques that a server could develop to help improve serving priorities and timing.

20. Discuss how the following difficult situations could be handled:

   - Guest receives food not up to expectations.
   - Guest complains that food is cold or undercooked.
   - Guest says food is overcooked or burned.
   - Guest states that the portion size is too small.
   - Guest says that order is wrong.
   - Guest would like a baby bottle heated.
   - Guests allow their children to wander the floor.
   - Guest is very dissatisfied with food and does not want to wait for a replacement.
   - Guest complains that food is undercooked and it is half eaten.
   - Guests order together and then want to pay separately.
   - Server forgot to turn in the guest's order to the kitchen.
   - Guest is unhappy and has a bad opinion of the food and service.
   - Guest is intoxicated.
   - Too many guests are seated in a server's section.
   - Guest leaves shopping bag or attaché case in the aisle.
   - Server spills food or drink on the clothing of a guest.
   - Food is slow coming from the kitchen.

- Server is informed that the kitchen is out of the food item ordered.
- Foreign object is found in the food by guest.
- Guest complains about the food, having eaten most of it.
- Guests leave without paying.

21. Define some of the functions of a bus attendant.

22. How should a bussing cart be equipped?

23. List the procedures for properly bussing a table.

24. Explain how a bus attendant would use a tray to bus a table.

25. How would a small rectangular tray be used in the process of setting up tables?

26. Identify seven bus attendant responsibilities.

5

Service Preparedness

Learning Objectives

After reading this chapter and completing the discussion questions and exercises, you should be able to

1. Explain the visual elements of a successful menu.
2. Relate what the server needs to know in order to help guests make the best selection.
3. Identify the differences between a breakfast, lunch, and dinner menu.
4. Describe an à la carte menu.
5. Explain what a table d' hôte menu includes.
6. Recognize the importance of server knowledge in wine selections.
7. Describe the purpose of "menu meetings."
8. Discuss the things that a server should learn about a menu in order to answer a guest's questions.
9. Explain how dining room stations are assigned.
10. Define zone coverage.
11. Define *mise en place* and know the responsibilities that accompany it.
12. Understand the importance of side-work.
13. Identify the items that are typically included on a service stand.
14. Understand the purpose of service teams and be able to explain how they function.
15. Define the basic steps and safety issues associated with closing procedures.

The server has many duties and responsibilities; once having mastered them he or she can provide the ultimate in service. Many times the server is the only individual who comes in contact with the guest, therefore the guest expects the server to be fully knowledgeable about menu items and the restaurant.

The server is responsible to ensure that everything needed to serve guests efficiently is done before the guests arrive. This includes assigned pre-service and ongoing duties. The server's efficiency will be measured by the care he or she takes in performing those duties before the guest arrives, during the meal service, and at the close of the server's shift.

This chapter introduces the new server to service preparation techniques that will help in providing the best in guest service; for the experienced server, it will reaffirm the importance of service preparedness.

The Menu

The menu is the focal point of a restaurant operation. It is the number one selling tool, and the first thing that a guest reads in determining what to order. Therefore, the menu should look attractive, use color appropriately, and reflect the quality and style of the restaurant. When a menu is professionally designed it can further support the restaurant's general appearance and ambiance, thus creating a positive first impression. If a menu is soiled, frayed, bent at the edges, or poorly printed and hard to read, it can create a negative first impression. Therefore, the menu should always be prepared, designed, and printed in the best possible manner to achieve its intended objective; it should always be crisp and clean when presented to the guest.

Although management can produce an effective menu, the individual who really determines the effectiveness of the menu for the guest is the server. It is up to the server to see that the guest understands what is on the menu. The server should be able to answer any questions the guest may have about menu items.

The server needs to be very familiar with the menu in order to guide and help the guest in making a selection. The server needs to know about every item on the menu; how they are prepared, with their ingredients, and when and if substitutions are allowed, such as a sliced tomato for an entrée vegetable. Furthermore, the server should know how to pronounce all of the words on the menu and be able to interpret them for the guest.

BREAKFAST MENU

Most restaurants have a separate breakfast menu, unless breakfast is listed and served 24 hours a day or all of the hours that the restaurant is open. Generally the menu consists of two sections. The first lists a combination of food items served at fixed prices, and the second lists items that may be ordered individually, as shown in Figure 5-1.

LUNCH MENU

The lunch menu is usually composed of appetizers, soups, salads, sandwiches, several complete entrées, desserts, and beverages. The menu selection typically includes several price levels, which are planned to cater to the wishes of different customer categories. Many restaurants feature special lunches, such as the business lunch, lunch special, chef's suggestions, manager's special, or *du jour*

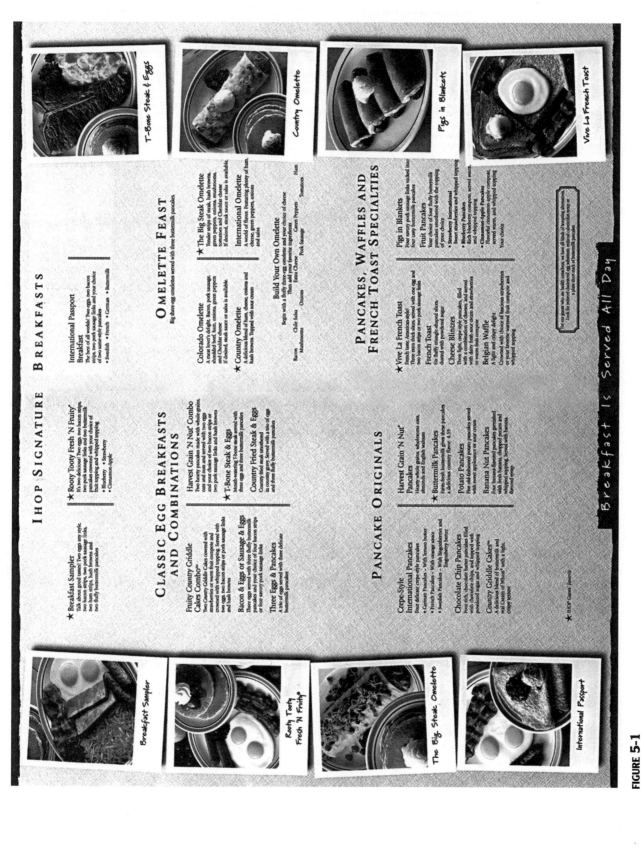

FIGURE 5-1
Breakfast Menu *Courtesy of International House of Pancakes*

Appetizers

Fresh Oysters on the Half Shell
Six oysters shucked to order. Ask your wait person for species.
Market Price/Availability

Fresh Northwest Oyster Shooters
$1.25/each

Fresh Manila Steamer Clams
Steamed in garlic, butter, and white wine.
Market Price/Availability

Razor Clams
Lightly breaded and grilled. Fresh in season.
Market Price/Availability

Fried Calamari
Calamari rings and tentacles flash fried and tossed in lemon butter sauce. $7.95

Cajun Popcorn
Bay shrimp in a cajun breading, fried golden brown. $6.95

Fresh Salmon Nuggets
Fresh salmon fried golden brown in dill tempura batter. $5.95

Escargot
Sauteed in garlic, white wine, and butter. Served with dipping croutons. $7.95

Bay Shrimp Cocktail
Bay shrimp served with cocktail sauce and a lemon wedge. $6.95

Dungeness Crab Cocktail
Dungeness crab served with cocktail sauce and a lemon wedge.
Market Price/Availability

Fresh Stuffed Mushrooms
Mushroom caps with bay shrimp, baked with sherry and cheese, topped with fresh scallions. $6.95

Fresh Sauteed Mushrooms
Whole button mushrooms sauteed in Madeira wine, garlic, and butter. $5.95

Baked Brie with Roasted Garlic
Served with dipping croutons. $5.95

Conch (konk)
Pounded thin like abalone, lightly breaded and grilled. $7.95

Onion Rings
Freshly sliced and fried golden brown in dill tempura batter. $4.50

Vegetable Quesadilla
Fresh sauteed vegetables and cheeses in a tomato basil tortilla. Served with sour cream and fresh salsa. $5.95

BEVERAGES

Bottle Wines	Coffee or Tea .85
Wines by the Glass	Soft Drinks, Iced Tea,
Beer on Tap	or Hot Chocolate 1.25
Bottled Beers, domestic & imported	Milk, Juice Lg $1.50 Sm $1.25
Cocktails	Stash Tea 1.75

Luncheon Entrees

Entrees served with Cole Slaw and your choice of French Fries, Potato Salad, Cottage Cheese, Cup of Soup, or Small Green Salad.

Fresh Salmon Filet
Your choice of char-broiled, grilled, poached, or baked. $7.50

Halibut
Your choice of char-broiled, grilled, poached, or baked. Fresh in season. $7.95

Fresh Northwest Cod or Red Snapper
Poached, baked or lightly breaded and grilled. $6.95

Fresh Northwest Sole
Lightly breaded and grilled or baked. Market availability. $6.95

Fresh Grilled Northwest Rainbow Trout $6.25

Razor Clams
Lightly breaded and grilled. Fresh in season.   Market Price/Availability

Fresh Northwest Oysters
Lightly breaded and pan fried. $6.95

Prawns, Scampi Style
Sauteed with white wine, lemon juice, garlic, capers and butter. $10.95

Fresh Manila Steamer Clams
Steamed in garlic, butter, and white wine.   Market Price/Availability

Conch (konk)
Pounded thin like abalone, lightly breaded and grilled. $8.95

Fresh 3-Egg Omelette
See wait person for today's selection and pricing.

Freshly-made Quiche
See wait person for today's selection. $6.25

Fettuccine Alfredo
Fettuccine alfredo-style or tossed with olive oil, garlic & parsley. $5.95

Liver, Grilled with Bacon & Onions $5.95

Fish & Chips

Northwest Cod - Dipped in dill tempura, then fried golden brown. $7.25

Halibut - Dipped in dill tempura, then fried golden brown. Fresh in season. $8.25

Fresh Salmon - Dipped in dill tempura, then fried golden brown. $7.95

Child's Northwest Cod & Chips $5.95

SIDE ORDERS

French Fries	$1.95	Cottage Cheese	$2..25
Potato Salad	$2.25	Small Green Salad	$2.25
Cole Slaw	$1.75	with Shrimp	+ $2.50
Loaf of Bread	$ .85	with Crab	+ $3.50

Split Luncheon Charge $2.50

FIGURE 5-2
Lunch Menu *Courtesy of the Deschutes River Trout House Restaurant*

(of the day) menu. These items can be printed on a daily menu, restaurant reader board, or announced to guests when they are handed the menu by the host or server. Figure 5-2 is an example of a typical lunch menu.

DINNER MENU

The dinner menu has an appetizer section and usually lists prices for complete dinners that include soup or salad and the entrée. There may be choices, such as mashed, baked, French fried potatoes or rice, along with a choice of

Favorite Sandwiches

Sandwiches served with your choice of French Fries, Potato Salad, Cottage Cheese, Cup of Soup, Small Salad, or Cole Slaw.

Trout House Cheese Steak
Thinly sliced New York steak grilled with peppers, mushrooms, onions, and cheeses. Served on a hand-made roll. $8.95

French Dip
Thinly sliced roast beef on a hand-made roll. Served with au jus. $6.95

Patty Melt
Ground chuck patty with grilled onions and Swiss cheese. Served on grilled rye bread. $6.75

Grilled Roast Beef
Roast beef, roasted peppers, and Swiss cheese. Served on grilled sourdough. $6.95

Sole Sandwich
Lightly breaded and grilled sole. Served on a sesame bun. $6.95

Barbecue Beef
Thinly sliced roast beef simmered in barbecue sauce. Served on a rosemary roll. $6.95

Turkey Reuben
Thinly sliced turkey breast with sauerkraut and Swiss cheese on grilled rye bread. $6.50

Club House
Ham, turkey, bacon, lettuce, tomato, and mayonnaise on toasted whole wheat or white bread. $7.25

Deli Sandwich
Choice of ham, turkey, roast beef, or tuna salad with lettuce, tomato, red onion, and mayonnaise on your choice of bread. $6.50

Half Deli Sandwich
Half Deli Sandwich with your choice of one side dish. $5.25

B-L-T
Your choice of bread. $5.50

Tuna Melt
Tuna salad, Swiss cheese, and tomato on grilled sourdough. $6.50

Grilled Ham & Cheese
Cheddar, Swiss, or jack on your choice of bread. $6.25

Grilled Cheese
Cheddar, Swiss, or jack on your choice of bread. $3.95

Peanut Butter & Marionberry Jelly
Your choice of bread. $3.95

Vegetarian
Cucumber, tomato, onion, mixed greens, carrots, mushrooms, black olives, Swiss cheese, pesto, and mayonnaise on your choice of bread. $6.25

Specialty Sandwiches & Hamburgers

Served with lettuce, tomato, and red onion. Your choice of French Fries, Potato Salad, Cottage Cheese, Cup of Soup, Small Salad, or Cole Slaw.

Pesto Chicken
Char-broiled with pesto, sauteed mushrooms, and Swiss cheese. Served on a rosemary roll. $8.25

Blackened Chicken
Served on a hand-made roll with citrus mayonnaise. $7.50

Sirloin Steak
Sirloin cooked to your taste, then sliced. Served on a hand-made roll with mayonnaise. $8.95

Boneless Pork Loin
Seasoned and char-broiled. Served on a hand-made roll with peppercorn mayonnaise. $7.95

Hamburgers
Served on a rosemary roll or sesame bun.

Plain - 1/3 pound ground chuck patty	$6.25
Bacon Burger	$7.25
Mushroom Burger	$6.95
Roasted Pepper Burger	$6.95
Garden Burger	$6.95
Add cheddar, Swiss, or jack cheese	+$ .50

Specialty Salads & Soup

Salads include tomato, cucumber, black olives, baby corn, beets, garbanzo beans, hard boiled egg, & lemon.

Our house dressing is Roasted Hazelnut-Honey Mustard. Other dressings: Ranch, 1000 Island, Bleu Cheese, and Italian.

Spinach Salad
Jack cheese and bacon served with Catalina mushroom dressing. $6.95

Chef Salad
Ham, turkey, cheddar and Swiss cheeses. $7.25

Garden Salad
Fresh and marinated vegetables with Swiss cheese over mixed greens. $7.25

Bay Shrimp Louie $8.25

Dungeness Crab Louie Market Price/Availability

Dungeness Crab & Bay Shrimp Louie Market Price/Availability

Bowl of Soup, Small Salad, & Loaf of Bread $5.95

Soup of the Day Cup - $1.95 Bowl - $2.95

Clam Chowder (Friday Only) Cup - $2.25 Bowl - $3.95

Desserts
We feature fresh homemade desserts.

FIGURE 5-2 (continued)

vegetable offerings. Also, the menu will have à la carte items that are individually priced, such as shrimp cocktail or fresh sautéed mushrooms. Very few restaurants have a menu that is either completely à la carte or complete dinners. Some fine dining restaurants offer a table d' hôte menu that includes a complete meal from appetizer to dessert for a given price. A restaurant may also offer early bird specials in the late afternoon, with menu entrées reduced in price or a few different entrées offered at a price lower than normal. A restaurant may also feature dinner specials that could include chef creations or the fresh fish catch of the day. The host or server normally announces these

Appetizers

Fresh Oysters on the Half Shell
Six oysters shucked to order. Ask your
wait person for species.
Market Price/Availability

Fresh Northwest
Oyster Shooters $1.25/each

Fresh Manilla Steamer Clams
Steamed in garlic, butter and white
wine. Market Price/Availability

Razor Clams
Lightly breaded and grilled, fresh in
season. $6.95

Fried Calamari
Calamari rings and tentacles flash fried
and tossed in a lemon butter sauce.
$7.95

Cajun Popcorn
Bay shrimp in a cajun breading, served
with cocktail sauce and
a lemon wedge. $6.95

Fresh Salmon Nuggets
Fresh salmon fried golden brown in
dill tempura. $5.95

Escargot
Sauteed in garlic, white wine and butter.
Served with dipping croutons. $7.95

Shrimp Cocktail
Bay shrimp served with cocktail sauce
and a lemon wedge. $6.95

Crab Cocktail
Dungeness crab served with cocktail
sauce and a lemon wedge.
Market Price/Availability

Fresh Stuffed Mushrooms
Mushroom caps with bay shrimp,
baked with sherry and cheese, topped
with fresh scallions. $6.95

Fresh Sauteed Mushrooms
Whole button mushrooms sauteed in
madeira wine, garlic and butter. $5.95

Fresh Cut Vegetable Crudite
With dipping sauce. $4.95

Baked Brie with Roasted Garlic
Served with dipping croutons. $5.95
    With pesto 6.95
    With bay shrimp 8.95
    With dungeness crab 10.95

Conch (konk)
Pounded thin like abalone, lightly
breaded and grilled. $7.95

Steak, Veal, Chicken & Pasta

6 oz. Filet Mignon
Choice cut 6 oz. steak char-broiled to your taste and served
with madeira mushrooms and bernaise sauce. $16.95
  • With sauteed prawns $21.95
  • With grilled razor clam $18.95
  • With pan fried oysters $18.95

10 oz. Choice New York Steak
Center cut steak char-broiled to your taste. $17.95

One Pound Porterhouse
Pressed with green and black peppercorns, char-broiled
to your taste, and topped with whiskey mustard sauce. $19.95

Veal Tenderloin
Lightly breaded then seared and topped with madeira
mushrooms, dungeness crab, and hollandaise sauce. $17.95

Rack of New Zealand Lamb
Char-broiled to your taste. $19.95

Boneless Pork Loin
Oven roasted with rosemary and juniper, sliced and
served with black currant sauce. $14.95

Chicken Breast
Boneless and skinless chicken breast
char-broiled, or ask your server for our
nightly chicken special. $12.95

Seafood Fettuccine
Bay shrimp, dungeness crab, sea scallops,
and fresh fish in white sauce. $15.95

Fettuccine Alfredo
Fettuccine alfredo-style or tossed with
olive oil, garlic & parsley. $10.95

Vegetable Fettuccine
Fresh seasonal sauteed vegetables served
in alfredo sauce or tossed with
olive oil, garlic & parsley. $12.95

Vegetarian Platter
Fresh steamed seasonal vegetables,
parmesan baked tomato, dill tempura
onion rings & artichoke hearts with
house potato or rice pilaf. $13.95

Desserts We feature fresh homemade desserts.

Selected Child's Portions $8.95 • Corkage Fee $7.00 • Split Dinner Charge $5.00
To serve you better, one check will be written for parties of 7 or more.

Child's Price   Corkage Fee   Split Dinner

FIGURE 5-3
Dinner Menu *Courtesy of the Deschutes River Trout House Restaurant*

items when the menus are handed to the guests, or the items may be listed on
a reader board. Figure 5-3 is an example of a dinner menu.

THE WINE LIST

Wine continues to grow in popularity and many restaurants have excellent
selections of wine. The wine list may also include a list of domestic and imported beers. The host or server will present the wine list to the guest along
with the menu. The server should be knowledgeable about the wines and be

All entrees served with
your choice of homemade
Soup or House Salad,
Chef's Vegetable, and
our fresh baked bread.

Choice of Rice or Potato
of the Day (except pasta
dishes).

Add-ons → Add shrimp for 2.50 or
crab for 3.50 to your
House Salad.

When we advertise
"fresh fish,"
it is fresh fish!

Signature Dinners

Dan's New York Steak, 10 oz.
Center cut choice New York steak stuffed with dungeness crab,
char-broiled, and topped with madeira mushrooms,
and bernaise sauce. $20.95

Mixed Grill
Venison, lamb rack, prawn saute, and razor clam with
whiskey mustard sauce. $22.95

Fresh Blackened Salmon
Fresh salmon filet with blackening spices pan seared, then baked
and served with a tequila-lime-sour cream sauce. $16.95

Fresh Stuffed Northwest Rainbow Trout
Rainbow trout stuffed with bay shrimp and dungeness crab, then baked. $16.95

Fisherman's Stew
Prawn, scallop, fresh fish, clams, mussels, dungeness crab,
and bay shrimp served in a rich tomato broth. $19.95

New Zealand Venison & Prawns
Medallions of venison and prawns sauteed
with whiskey mustard sauce. $20.95

Tournedos of Beef with Prawns & Artichoke
Two petite cuts of filet mignon char-broiled to your taste and
topped with artichoke bottoms, prawns, and bernaise sauce. $21.95

Fresh Seafood & Shellfish

Fresh Salmon Filet
Your choice of char-broiled, grilled, poached, or baked. $15.95

Fresh Baked Stuffed Salmon
Salmon filet stuffed with bay shrimp and topped with
a rosette of red wine butter. $17.95

Halibut
Your choice of char-broiled, grilled, poached, or baked.
Fresh "in season". $15.95

Fresh Grilled Northwest Rainbow Trout $12.95

Fresh Northwest Cod or Red Snapper
Poached, baked or lightly breaded and grilled. $13.95

Fresh Northwest Sole
Lightly breaded and grilled or baked. Market availability. $14.95

Prawns, Scampi Style
Sauteed with white wine, lemon juice, garlic,
capers and butter. $17.95

Fresh East Coast Sea Scallops
Baked in a mornay sauce. $15.95

Prawn and/or Scallop Saute
Sauteed with garlic, white wine and finished with
a creamy lemon-butter sauce. $16.95

Fresh Northwest Oysters
Lightly breaded and pan fried. $12.95

Fresh Manilla Steamer Clams
Steamed in garlic, butter, and white wine.
                          Market Price/Availability

Razor Clams
Lightly breaded and grilled.
Fresh "in season". $15.95

Seafood Combination Plate
Fresh pan fried oysters, grilled razor
clam, and prawn saute. $16.95

Conch (konk)
Pounded thin like abalone, lightly
breaded and grilled. $14.95

Lobster Tail
Baked with white wine and butter.
                          Market Price/Availability

Fried Calamari
Calamari rings and tentacles flash fried and
tossed in a lemon butter sauce. $14.95

Shrimp Louie
Chef's selection $13.95

Crab Louie
Chef's selection   Market Price/Availability

*All fresh seafoods are susceptible to
market availability and price.*

FIGURE 5-3 (continued)

able to suggest appropriate wines (or beers) to accompany the guest's meal, as discussed in Chapter 6, Wine and Beverage Service. Figure 5-4 is an example of a wine list.

DESSERT MENU

The dessert menu is typically presented in a way that is very enticing to guests. The description of each dessert item can tell a tale of great delight, and may include photos of the items as they look when served. The menu may be separate or part of a lunch and dinner menu as shown in Figure 5-5.

White Wines

Chardonnay

These are dry wines ranging from crisp, apple-like freshness to more pronounced varietal character and complexity, often with added dimension from aging in small oak barrels; the best are comparable to great white Burgundies.

	1/2 Bottle	Full Bottle
Duck Pond *Willamette Valley, Oregon*		14.00
Covey Run *Washington*		16.00
Chateau St. Jean *Sonoma County, California*		20.00
Kendall Jackson "Vintners Reserve" *California*	11.00	22.00
Beringer *Napa Valley, California*		24.00
La Crema *Sonoma Coast, California*		24.00
Rodney Strong "Chalk Hill" *Sonoma County, California*		25.00
Merryvale "Starmont" *Napa Valley, California*		27.00

Red Wines

Merlot

Excellent red wine similar to Cabernet Sauvignon but with a softness and suppleness that makes it very drinkable at an early age.

	1/2 Bottle	Full Bottle
Rosemont Estates Cab/Merlot *Southern Australia*		18.00
Clos du Bois *Sonoma County, California*	14.00	26.00
Kendall Jackson "Vintner's Reserve" *California*		27.00
Lambert Bridge *Sonoma County, California*		30.00
Canoe Ridge *Columbia Valley, Washington*		30.00
Whitehall Lane *Napa Valley, California*		32.00
Stag's Leap Vineyards *Napa Valley, California*		44.00
Mystal *Napa Valley, California*		44.00

FIGURE 5-4
Wine List *Courtesy of the Deschutes River Trout House Restaurant*

The Guest and the Menu

Guests naturally feel that the server should be able to answer their questions about the menu, such as, "What are the ingredients in a certain menu item or entrée? What does it include? How is it cooked and plated and how long will it take to prepare?" A guest may even ask how to pronounce the name of a menu item or sauce. Therefore, the server is expected to have a comprehensive knowledge of the restaurant's menu, being able to answer questions and offer suggestions. Appendix A, Common Menu Terms, lists many of the most commonly used terms to describe menu items and cooking procedures.

When new menu items and/or terms are introduced, the server should be eager to learn about them. The restaurant owner or manager should also schedule time for "menu meetings," informing the servers about the new items, and the daily specials that may be offered. These meetings usually take place just before the meal period. That is, if lunch starts at 11:30 A.M., then a "menu meeting" could take place at 11:15 A.M.

If a guest wants only a light meal, the server should know the menu well enough to suggest an appropriate item. The same is true for guests who say they are very hungry and want a full-course dinner. Also, if the guest is in a hurry, the server should be able to suggest an item that will not take much time to prepare, which means that the server should know how much time it takes to prepare each item on the menu.

Tiramisu
The classic Italian dessert. A frothy layer of creamy custard set atop espresso-soaked ladyfingers.

Berry Crostada
A flaky pastry featuring a filling of cranberries, blueberries and blackberries. Served warm with vanilla ice cream drizzled with raspberry syrup.

Strawberry Limone
A zesty lemon-infused custard and strawberries between layers of moist yellow cake. Set amid a delicious swirl of raspberry sauce and topped with whipped cream.

Black Tie Mousse Cake
Moist chocolate cake, dark chocolate cheesecake and creamy custard mousse, all layered beneath white and dark chocolate icing.

Chocolate Lasagna
Layers of chocolate cake and sweet butter cream. Sprinkled with semi-sweet chocolate.

Cappuccino Viva Italiano
Steamed coffee and cream, flavored with DiSaronno Amaretto, Frangelico or Sambuca.

White Chocolate Raspberry Cheesecake
Raspberry-swirled white chocolate cheesecake topped with slivers of white chocolate and a flourish of whipped cream.

© 2001 Olive Garden. Printed in USA. 031201 - 041601 YT14

FIGURE 5-5
Dessert Menu *Courtesy of Olive Garden Restaurants*

When a restaurant caters to senior citizens or families with small children, a separate menu or a separate section on the menu will typically be printed to honor these special guests. A senior menu traditionally includes smaller portions as well as diet-sensitive items and entrées. The children's menu typically includes a limited number of kid-proven favorites. A server should know when to offer these menus, and when in doubt, should inquire if the senior or young person would like to see the senior or children's menu. Also, a restaurant may have selected child's portions from the regular menu at a special price, as shown in Figure 5-3. If a child orders an expensive item from the regular menu, the server should get a parent's approval by asking if this is all right. Parents usually appreciate this. If it is not all right, the server should be prepared to quickly suggest another item or two from which the child can choose.

Some menus may include a short history of the restaurant, the chef's background and origin of some of the house specialties, historic sites and information about the community that may be of interest to tourists, and perhaps a list of nearby recreational areas or activities. The server should be able to answer any questions that a guest may have about such things. Some local and regional tourist associations offer complimentary maps for restaurants to give guests. This allows a server to offer additional service and help.

If a server cannot adequately answer a guest's questions about the menu, it weakens the guest's confidence in the server and reduces the opportunity for the server to suggestively sell other menu items, such as wines, appetizers, salads, and desserts. The server may be reduced in the guest's mind to just an order taker. Therefore, the opportunity to increase guest sales and tips is lost. Some questions that a server may need to be prepared to answer are as follows:

"Does the meat loaf contain pork?"

"What does the balsamic basil dressing taste like?"

"What is in the spicy sweet potatoes?"

"Can I substitute onion rings for French fries?"

"What is a New York Steak?"

"What is in the béarnaise sauce?"

"What are capers?"

"How do you pronounce 'gazpacho'?"

"Is couscous like croquettes?"

"Flan sounds good, what is it?"

"Is the Münster cheese smooth and sweet?"

"How long will it take for the rack of lamb to cook?"

In addition to knowing the menu's content, the server should be sure that menus are clean and in perfect order. If a menu is soiled or torn, it should be replaced immediately. If a restaurant has table tents (small pictures of menu or dessert items with brief descriptions and prices, placed upright in a stand on the table), they need to be clean and placed on the tables to look neat and professional.

The Server and the Menu

The guest assumes the server knows everything about the menu. Therefore, the server should take the initiative to master the menu in order to be prepared to answer questions and give explanations. Here are some tactical considerations to consider when learning a menu. Refer to the dinner menu in Figure 5-3.

1. Learn the menu by categories. That is, know where the signature (house specialty) items, appetizers, salads, sandwiches, entrées, features, à la carte items, beverages, and desserts are located on the menu. As you respond to a menu item question, point to the specific item on the menu. As you read, the guest will "read along," following your finger as it moves across the menu description. Reading the menu description eliminates the potential of describing the item incorrectly, and through repetition, the server gradually gains a confident and comprehensive knowledge of the menu.

2. Learn what items include soup and/or salad and the cost of the add-on items, such as adding shrimp or crab to the house salad that may be included with a dinner entrée. The add-on (additional) charge may for example, be $2.50 for the shrimp and $3.50 for the crab, for example, as shown in Figure 5-3, Dinner Menu.

3. Learn what (if any) beverages have complimentary refills, such as soft drinks or iced tea. Also, there may be a corkage fee when a guest brings in a special bottle of wine or champagne to have served with dinner, as shown in Figure 5-3.

4. Learn cooking and preparation times. Since each item on the menu takes a different amount of time to cook, it is important to keep guests informed. An easy tip to remember is that items such as thick meats require lower heat and a longer time to cook than pasta items, for example. Also, the degree of doneness of meats can change the cooking times, such as a steak cooked rare in 10 minutes or well done in 20 minutes. A server can quickly learn the cooking and preparation times through experience with the kitchen.

5. Learn that sandwiches and hamburgers often automatically include some or all of the following ingredients: lettuce, tomato, onion, mayonnaise, pickles, and mustard. Many people do not like some of these ingredients and become irritated when they find them on their sandwiches. Therefore, identify when and if these ingredients are automatically included with sandwiches and hamburgers. If they are, mention it to the guest at the time the order is placed. The guest may choose not to have some of these ingredients or may prefer to have them served separately.

6. Learn the ingredients of sauces and be able to describe their flavors. If a guest seems unsure about a sauce, offer to have the kitchen put it in a cup to be served on the side.

7. Learn the restaurant standard for the varying degrees of doneness in meat. Then be able to describe the degrees of doneness by color, such as the following:

Rare – brown, seared crust with cool red center.
Medium Rare – brown, seared crust, warmed through with a red, warm center.
Medium – outside well done, dark brown with reddish pink hot center.
Medium Well – outside dark brown, inside done through with little juice left.
Well Done – outside black-brown and inside brown throughout with no pink.

8. Learn the portion sizes of menu items, for example, three large pancakes as big as the breakfast plate, shrimp cocktail served with five jumbo shrimp, broiled lamb chops with a serving of three 4-ounce lamb chops, or a hot fudge sundae with two large scoops of vanilla ice cream. A guest who expects a different portion size may be either disappointed or overwhelmed. Therefore, you should be prepared to describe the portion size when asked by the guest or when you anticipate the need to do so. For example, you should know that a full-size sub sandwich is 10 inches long. If a guest states that he or she is full from dinner but can't pass up that hot fudge sundae, it may be appropriate to describe its size, two large scoops of vanilla ice cream. You do not want the guest complaining, "Why didn't you tell me it was so big?"

9. Learn what appetizers and entrées can be split for guests. Also, inform the guest if there is an additional plate charge when providing this service. An example might be when two guests are splitting an

entrée, such as a 10-ounce halibut steak, and they prefer not to split the baked potato, but request an additional potato. An additional charge of $5.00 may be appropriate, as shown in Figure 5-3.

10. Learn the restaurant's policy and pricing for extra portions and substitutions. It is not uncommon for guests to request extra portions, such as double the cheese on a cheeseburger, or to ask for a substitute, such as cottage cheese for French fries. When this occurs, the extra charge for the double portion of cheese may be 50 cents. The restaurant may have limits as to what will be allowed when substituting, and may not allow onion rings to be substituted for French fries. Therefore, the restaurant should identify the most commonly asked questions regarding extra portions and substitutions and have a clear policy for servers to follow. When a guest makes an out-of-the-ordinary request, you should make every effort to accommodate the guest, but you should first ask the manager for a decision.

11. Learn where to access information for recipe ingredients and cooking methods. Guests with dietary restrictions will expect the server to be able to answer their questions. They may have concerns about oils, butter, fats, sugars, dairy, and low calorie ingredients, as well as foods that may be fried, grilled, or sautéed. Also, people on vegetarian diets will be very specific about not wanting any food item that contains animal or animal byproduct. Ask the owner or manager where this information is available. Some restaurants may have it implemented into a point of sale (POS) system as product management software, as discussed in Chapter 8, The Technology of Service. At the touch of a button, you would find a list of recipe ingredients, cooking methods, and nutritional information, in addition to other related information, which could be printed on the POS printer and given to the guest. There are various types of recipe management software that can also generate the same information. A restaurant that does not have the technological advantage will have to rely upon the cooks and chef to be able to answer recipe ingredient questions.

12. Learn the restaurant's cooking methods for various menu items, as guests will expect you to be able to describe those methods. The following is a list of common cooking methods:

Baked – food is cooked in an oven with dry heat.

Boiled – food is cooked in boiling water.

Braised – a combination of dry and moist heat; usually cooking meat in a small amount of liquid in a covered pan, allowing the meat to cook in the moisture created from its own juices.

Broiled – quick cooking by direct flame or heat. (Note: *Pan broiling* is cooking in a hot frying pan or on a griddle without the addition of fat.)

Fried – food is cooked in hot oil or fat. Food is *deep fat fried* when it is placed or immersed in oil or fat at a sufficiently high temperature to brown the surface and cook the interior of the food. *Pan frying* or *sautéing* is done with a small amount of hot oil or fat in a pan, to which the food item is added.

Grilled – food is cooked with oil or fat on a griddle, or cooked over hot coals (*charcoal grilled*).

Poached – food is covered in water or other liquid and simmered.

Roasted – food is cooked in an uncovered pan without moisture in an oven using only dry heat (similar to baking).

Sautéed – a food item is browned and cooked in a small amount of hot oil or fat in a pan.

Simmered – food is immersed in a liquid and slowly cooked over low heat.

Steamed – food is cooked in steam.

13. Learn the definitions of the menu terms that name or describe food items and cooking procedures. Also, the pronunciation of the terms should be correct and adds flair to the merchandising description. Refer to Appendix A, Common Menu Terms.

Responsibilities that Support Good Service

The host, Maître D', or manager divides the dining room into work areas known as stations. The stations may vary in actual number of tables but each usually has approximately the same number of seats. Most restaurants have a diagram of the dining room showing each station according to a number, such as #1, #2, #3, etc. A number is assigned to each table. A server is assigned to a station and is responsible for a list of opening duties at that station to prepare for serving guests. The server must also maintain that station during the shift (the meal period) and be certain to follow the list of closing duties at the end of the shift. These duties are commonly referred to as **side-work.**

Many restaurants rotate station assignments on a regular basis, even daily. The typical restaurant may have certain areas that are more desirable because of a view or location. Therefore, the station will generate more activity due to guests' requests. Some stations may include booths or counters, or private dining areas that can seat groups up to 12 or more at one table. There are also smoking and non-smoking sections. New, contemporary-designed restaurants have often achieved ideal seating throughout the restaurant. For those guests who request the same server, seating is usually not a concern. New servers are often assigned to smaller stations or a station with less activity as they gain experience and confidence in handling larger numbers of guests and moving at a faster pace. Some restaurants have permanent station assignments for servers with seniority or for all servers based on good performance reviews.

As the dining traffic winds down, the number of servers on the floor is reduced. Terms used for this are "phasing" or "cutting" the floor. Zone coverage comes into play, as the remaining servers pick up tables in addition to their assigned station. In some instances, the manager will close areas of the dining room to seating and seat only in areas where there is a server available.

The French term *mise en place* is occasionally used in fine dining restaurants and means "put into place." It refers to the preparation steps from the kitchen to the dining room in terms of being prepared, with everything in place before service begins. Specifically, each server is responsible for his or her assigned station and should check it thoroughly with a visual inspection before guests are seated, during the shift, and at the end of the shift. Looking from top to bottom includes a quick glance up at the ceiling—a cobweb or birthday balloon may need to be removed; ledges may need to be dusted or a foreign object removed; lightbulbs may need to be replaced. Shelves should be stocked with appropriate serving supplies; counter tops and tabletops should be immaculately clean with spotless table-settings; table bottoms should be completely free of any gum or sticky substance; chairs, booths, booster chairs, and high chairs should be wiped clean and free of any crumbs, food particles, or grease. The floor should be swept or vacuumed and always safe, with nothing that a guest could slip on or trip over.

Side-work includes housekeeping chores that will ensure that every aspect of the restaurant is clean and spotless at all times. It also includes a detailed organization of each station and work area so that the server is better organized and able to provide quick service. The importance of side-work duties cannot be overemphasized. Many times up to half of a server's time will be spent on these items, which help to ensure better service for guests. This preparation always pays off during rush periods. It can make the difference between efficient and inefficient service. Most restaurants have a checklist of side-work duties, as shown in Figure 5-6. The letter (A, B, C, etc.) identification in the example represents a specific server and/or station assignment. It is important to recognize that most restaurants will have side-work duties that are somewhat standard within the industry, along with duties that are unique to the individual restaurant.

Each restaurant varies in what supplies are kept and what is kept at each service stand. Figure 5-7 shows an example of a typical service stand. The server should check that the correct items in the correct amounts are there before the shift begins. If items are low or out they should quickly be

Opening Procedures Foodserver

	Mon	Tues	Wed	Thur	Fri	Sat	Sun
1. Put ice in all bins.							
2. Make iced tea. Make coffee.							
3. Check details of last night's close. Inform manager of any missed items.							
4. Cut lemons, fill containers for the main station, patio and bar. (Mon-Thurs 1 gal/Fri-Sun 2 gal)							
5. Put ice under condiment caddie and fill 3 with lemons, limes and cherries.							
6. Restock glassware from dish station.							
7. Stock a 1/6 pan with creamers and butter. Put a pan of ice underneath.							
8. Check that straws, cocktail napkins, tip trays and mints are stocked.							
9. Be ready to go at ??:??am.							

FIGURE 5-6
Opening Procedures and Side-work *Courtesy of Sharyn Gardner of www.dinersoft.com*

Foodserver Side-work

A	Silverware. Sugar caddies. Salt and pepper shakers. Table tents. Chairs, tablecloths, windows and ledges in station.
B	To-go station. Wipe down and organize all shelves in kitchen server station. Restock straws and cocktail napkins in both stations.
C	Restock coffee cups, underliners and coffee spoons. Restock straws. Restock and clean garnish caddy-return to station.
D	Restock all dry goods: coffee, iced tea bags, hot tea bags, sugar, Sweet 'N Low, filters, salt and pepper containers.
E	Clean/restock all P.O.S. stations. Disperse tip trays to all stations. Restock cocktail napkins.
F	Wipe down all walls in station. Wipe down all shelves in station.
G	Clean all shelves and red mats under glassware. Run red mats through dishwasher. Restock red cups and soda cups. Melt ice.
H	Clean all coffee pots (not thru dish machine!) Wipe down coffee machine/grinder and underneath. Restock coffee grinder.
I	Clean iced tea bins -- do not give to dishwasher! Wipe down entire machine and underneath. Soak spout overnight.
J	Wipe down tray jack stands and kitchen doors including door jams.
K	Clean all high chairs and booster seats. Return all to main dining rooms.
L	Scrub small trays with degreaser.
M	Scrub large trays with degreaser.
N	Final wipe-down of station. Make sure everything is turned off, melt ice bin, wipe down soda dispenser and soak spigots over night.
O	Misc. – See Manager

Running Side-work	Server	4	5	6	7	8	9	10	11	12
Restock ice.		ABJMO	ABJM	ABJM	ABM	ABM	ABM	ABM	ABM	ABM
Restock condiments-coffee, tea, lemons, and limes.		ACDEL	ACDE	ACDE	ACDE	ACDE	ACDE	ACDE	ACDE	ACDE
Restock glassware and cups.		AFGHI	AFGH	AFGH	AFGH	AFGH	AFGH	AFGH	AFGH	AFGH
Follow up on running side-work. Keep stations clean.		AKN	AN	AN	AN	AN	AN	AN	AN	AN
Restock ice.			AIKLO	AIKLO	AILO	AILO	AILO	AILO	AILO	AILO
Restock ice.				ACDFGHI	ACDFK	ACDK	ACDK	ACDK	ACDK	ACDK
Restock glassware and cups.					AGHIJ	AFG	AFG	AFG	AFG	AFG
Keep stations clean.						AHIJ	AHIJ	AHIJ	AHIJ	AHIJ
Restock ice.							ACDEFGHI	ACDEFGHI	ACDE	ACD
Restock glassware.								AGHI	AFG	AFG
Keep station clean.									AHI	AHI
Restock ice.										AE

FIGURE 5-6 (continued)

FIGURE 5-7
Service Stand *Courtesy of the Beaches Restaurant and Bar*

replenished. Proper planning helps to eliminate wasted time in having to fetch items during rush periods. The work area should be arranged to allow for the maximum efficient service with the minimum amount of wasted time, energy, and effort. Everything should be within easy reach. This will reduce or eliminate the amount of unnecessary bending, reaching, twisting, and stretching. Utensils and supplies should always be kept in the same place at all times. This allows the server to pick up items without deliberate thought or effort during rush periods, increasing efficiency and conserving time and energy. The service stand will typically include some or all of the following items:

Beverages: ice, water pitchers, glassware, straws, coffee, tea bags, tea pots, cups, saucers, cream, sugar, honey, soft drinks, lemons, and limes.

Flatware: salad/dessert forks, dinner forks, knives, steak knives, teaspoons, soup spoons, iced tea spoons, serving spoons, ladles, tongs, and seafood (cocktail) forks.

Condiments: ketchup, mustard, Dijon, Worcestershire sauce, A-1 sauce, Tabasco sauce, salt, pepper, sugar, and sugar substitute. Breakfast: jams, preserves, and syrups.

Bread, Butter, and Crackers: bread, rolls, crackers, bread and cracker baskets, bread plates, and butter pats.

Linens: tablecloths, placemats, napkins (linen or paper), beverage napkins, children's bibs, and bar towels.

Miscellaneous Items: pens, peppermills, ashtrays, corkscrew, bottle opener, matches, food-to-go containers, and guest check trays.

The functionality of side-work coincides with the nature of the shift. The tasks, while similar, can vary in details from shift to shift; for example, baskets for jams and preserves during the breakfast shift could be used for bread or rolls at lunch or dinner. Servers will be assigned specific tasks for each shift to make the transitions smooth and efficient. Each restaurant will have guidelines for side-work, with some more formal than others. Assignments might be delegated by station or by the sequence in which servers start or end their shifts. In the long run it takes organization and teamwork to get all the bases covered throughout the day's shifts.

Examples of complications created when side-work is not completed are as follows:

1. During the lunch rush on a hot day, the iced tea runs out because the opening side-work function of brewing a 4-gallon backup was not completed.

2. The guest wants A-1 steak sauce but it was not stocked in the service station the night before, so the server has to run 25 yards (50 yards roundtrip) to the storage room to get it and to bring out the correct number of backups.

3. The server is getting three waters for a table but the glass-rack was left empty in the service station. The server responsible for ongoing side-work during the shift is not paying attention to stock levels, not to mention whoever took the last glass and did not replace it with a full rack.

4. The guest tries to use the pepper mill but it is empty. The server from the preceding shift did not complete the side-work of refilling all the pepper mills.

Service Teams

Some high-volume, fast-paced restaurants have developed service teams designed to give broad coverage of the dining room for all severs. A team of two servers may be assigned a large station with one taking beverage orders and the other taking food orders. Sometimes one may take all the orders and the other execute the delivery so that there is always a server attentive to the table. In some instances restaurants have eliminated bussing staff and reassigned bussing tasks to the servers.

Another service team procedure is team running of food and beverages; the priority is to get the food and beverages to the tables as soon as they are prepared and ready to be served. All servers participate in quickly getting the items to the tables. Having the servers bus all tables as they return to the kitchen dishwashing area furthers this efficiency. When they return to the service area after delivering bussed plates to the dishwashing area, they pick up clean plates and glassware for restocking service stations. This is sometimes referred to as "full hands in and out."

When service teams are used, tips are usually equally divided.

Closing Procedures

These procedures are basically the same as the *mise en place* steps described under the subject of dining room preparation, but somewhat in reverse. Ultimately the goal is to restock everything used and to clean the restaurant. Food and beverage products should be placed in their appropriate storage locations. Close attention should be paid to food storage safety. Primary attention should be given to securing the facility regarding safety issues: fire, water sources, security, and especially safe food storage. Again, these tasks would be assigned as described previously.

O verview

The menu is the focal point of a restaurant operation. It should be well designed and project the image of the restaurant. The server needs to be totally familiar with each item on the menu, so that he or she can answer questions the guests may have regarding the ingredients, preparation, cooking time, and pronunciation of a menu item or a sauce.

Generally there is a different menu for every meal, such as breakfast, lunch, and dinner, along with a wine list. Menus are priced à la carte, with a separate price for each separate item and also as full dinners, which usually include a soup or salad and the entrée. A table d' hôte menu includes a complete meal from appetizer to dessert for a fixed price.

The server can quickly learn a menu by remaining alert, attentive, and focused upon the following: Learning the menu by categories, that is, signature (house specialty) items, appetizers, salads, sandwiches, entrées, features, à la carte items, beverages, and desserts; learning what items include soup and salad, and the cost of add-ons; learning what (if any) beverages have complimentary refills; learning cooking and preparation times; learning the ingredients that automatically come with sandwiches and hamburgers; learning the ingredients of sauces and being able to describe their flavors; learning the restaurant standard for the varying degrees of doneness in meat; learning the portion sizes of menu items; learning what appetizers and entrées could be split for guests; learning the restaurant's policy and pricing for extra portions and substitutions; learning where to access information for recipe ingredients and cooking methods; learning the restaurant's cooking methods; and learning the definitions of the menu terms that name or describe food items and cooking procedures.

The server has responsibilities that support good service. The server is responsible for a list of opening duties at his or her assigned station to prepare for serving guests. The server must also maintain that station during the shift and be certain to follow the list of closing duties at the end of the shift. These duties are commonly known as side-work. The side-work includes housekeeping chores to ensure that every aspect of the restaurant is clean and spotless at all times. Each restaurant differs in what is kept at each server station, but the server should be certain that the correct items in the correct amounts are there before the shift begins, and again at the end of the shift.

Service teams have been designed to give broad coverage of the dining room for all servers, and can function in several different ways.

DISCUSSION QUESTIONS AND EXERCISES

1. What are the visual elements of a successful menu?
2. What should the server know about the menu in order to help guests make the best selection?
3. Explain the differences between a breakfast, lunch, and dinner menu.
4. Describe the differences between an à la carte menu and table d' hôte menu.
5. Why would a server need to know anything about wines?

6. List five things that a guest could possibly ask the server about the menu.

7. What would be discussed at a menu meeting?

8. If a child orders an expensive item from the normal menu, how should the server react?

9. What happens when a server cannot adequately answer a guest's questions about the menu?

10. List 10 things that a server should learn about a menu in being prepared to answer a guest's questions.

11. When a host, Maître D', or manager divides a dining room into work areas, what are those areas known as?

12. Explain zone coverage.

13. What does the French term *mise en place* mean and what does it specifically refer to?

14. Explain the importance of side-work.

15. How should a service stand work area be arranged?

16. List five different categories of items that a service stand typically includes and give examples within each category.

17. Give two examples of what can happen when side-work is not done.

18. What is the purpose of service teams? Explain two ways in which they can function.

19. What is the goal of an effective closing procedure?

20. What are the safety issues associated with an effective closing procedure?

6

Wine and Beverage Service

by Nick Fluge, CCE
Senior Vice President of Operations,
Career Education Corporation and
Chief Operating Officer,
Le Cordon Bleu Schools North America

Nick Fluge is the Senior Vice President of Operations for Career Education Corporation, and Chief Operating Officer of Le Cordon Bleu Schools North America. He served as president of Western Culinary Institute for nine years. He is a Certified Culinary Educator (CCE), and his many years of experience have included being a sommelier, captain, and Maître D' in leading hotels, restaurants, and private clubs. Nick is a Master Knight of the Vine and has received the prestigious Commanders Award. His wine columns in The National Culinary Review *and his position as chairperson of numerous wine fiestas and culinary salons have earned him regional and national acclaim. He is also the co-author of* Catering Solutions: For the Culinary Student, Foodservice Operator, and Caterer *(Prentice Hall, 2000).*

Learning Objectives

After reading this chapter and completing the discussion questions and exercises, you should be able to

1. Understand the importance of wine temperatures and know the recommended serving temperatures of various wines.

2. Describe how and when to use an ice bucket.

3. Understand and explain the correct way to present, open, and serve a bottle of wine or champagne.

4. Explain the process of decanting wine.

5. Identify the correct wine and beverage glass.

6. Understand that the climate in which grapes are grown affects the taste and color of wine.

7. Recognize the popular varieties of red and white wines along with some of their characteristics.

8. Understand when fortified wines would be served and why they are often used in cooking.

9. Describe the process of making vodka and the names of several popular vodka drinks.

10. Relate the origin and production process of Bourbon, Scotch, Tennessee Whiskey, Blended whiskey, and Irish whiskey.

11. Explain the process of producing brandy.

12. Name several popular drinks made with gin.

13. Identify several drinks made with rum.

14. Describe the process of producing Tequila along with popular drinks made with Tequila.

15. Identify popular liqueurs (cordials), and explain their characteristics.

16. Understand and explain the difference between beers, lagers, and ales.

17. Judge the quality of beers.

18. Describe malt liquor.

19. Define saké and explain how it is made.

20. List the recommended temperatures for serving beers, lagers, ales, and dark beers.

21. Understand the legal responsibility when serving an alcoholic beverage.

22. Correctly serve bottled water.

23. Understand and explain the various types of coffee roasts.

24. Describe how a French Press is used to make coffee.

25. Understand how espresso is made and explain how a caffé latte, cappuccino, and mocha are prepared.

26. Recognize some of the many coffee and alcohol combinations.

27. Describe how tea is prepared and served.

Many customers and restaurateurs alike feel intimidated by the mystique of formal wine service. Distinctive techniques and flair of service are as abundant as talented wine servers. However, the true key to serving a bottle of wine to a guest is as simple as knowing the basics. Once these are mastered, a server can slowly develop the time-honored panache of the great sommeliers of the world.

History tells us that humans have been offering and accepting wine since the beginning of documented time. Cave and tomb drawings, spanning ages, depict man in the company of a jug of wine. These early peoples did not have the glassware from which to sip nor the bottles to house wine, but their traditions, superstitions, and earthenware amphorae (jars) and cups were the precursors to the service we offer today.

Wine may not be ordered many times, because a guest is afraid of making a mistake. Therefore, the professional server needs to know the restaurant's wine list and be able to explain the selections to guests. Furthermore, for the guest to thoroughly enjoy the wine, it must be served properly. Also, the server needs to acquire the basic knowledge of the various liquor and beer types and brands, and the proper way of serving them.

Coffee and espresso drinks continue to grow in popularity; the professional server should know their flavor characteristics and compositions as well as techniques for serving.

Proper Temperatures for Serving Wines

Serving wines begins with knowledge of serving temperatures, which are as important to a wine steward as they are to a chef. A bottle of over-chilled Riesling will not exhibit its usual fruity and floral qualities. A cabernet served too warm may taste heavy and lack finesse. The vapors that are released from wine vary depending on their relative volatility. Red wine has higher molecular weight than white and is therefore less volatile. The aromatics of a red wine require a warmer room temperature to vaporize the wonderful aromas that are desired. Because lighter white wines and rosés are more volatile, they release their perfume at a much lower temperature. This requires chilling whites and serving reds near room temperature.

Generally speaking, white wines and sparkling wines should be served at between 45° and 50°F. Dessert wines should be served slightly cooler at 40° to 45°F. Cooler temperatures definitely contribute a perception of symmetry to sweeter white wines. Red wines are best enjoyed at a cool room temperature of between 60° and 68°F. Again, there are exceptions, as some very light reds, like Beaujolais, can be served at 50° to 55°F.

Some restaurants are guilty of keeping their white wines in multipurpose coolers set at 40°F. If this is the case, the wine should be removed a few minutes prior to service to ensure a correct temperature. Likewise, red wines can often be found housed in warm kitchens. Here, a quick chill in an ice bucket can revive a claret before it is served.

Ice Bucket Usage

Ice buckets are appropriate on many occasions. They can be used in conjunction with a stand, as shown in Figure 6-1, or set on a dining table as long as they do not overwhelm the china or glassware. It is a good idea to use a

bucket with Champagne or sparkling wines. A special occasion deserves an exceptional presentation. White wines probably do not require a bucket unless expressly requested. They will warm only slightly over the course of a meal, and this may even enhance their flavor. Another consideration for when to use an ice bucket is the number of people sharing the bottle of wine. Three or more will quickly empty the bottle, and thus will usually not require an ice bucket. However, one or two will take longer to consume the wine, making the use of an ice bucket appropriate.

Ice buckets should be filled half-full with shaved or cubed ice. If a bottle needs to be chilled quickly, cover it with ice then pour salt on top of the ice and let it stand for about five minutes. Add some water to loosen the ice and speed the chilling. Servers who choose to add water to their buckets should periodically check to make sure that the label is not sliding off the bottle. The server should also be available for prompt service so that his or her guests do not have to pour and risk water tracks running over the tablecloth if a side towel is not used.

Presentation and Service

The person who selected the bottle of wine is also the one who will taste it first. The server should present the bottle on a clean white side towel, held at an angle with the label facing the guest, as shown in Figure 6-2. The server should say the producer name and vintage in a soft but clear voice. Once the bottle has been approved, generally with a nod, it can be opened according to the steps in Figure 6-3.

FIGURE **6-2**
Presenting a Bottle of Wine to a
Guest

The lead or plastic foil must first be cut below the bulge to ensure that the wine will not have any contact with the foil during pouring (make sure the knife blade is sharp); see Step 1. A T-Screw wine opener, as shown in Step 2, is excellent to use because of its versatility. It has a knife at one end for cutting, a thin corkscrew for easy insertion into a cork, and a bottle opener at the opposite end. Wipe the neck of the bottle to remove dust or microorganisms that may have developed under the foil, as shown in Step 3.

The cork should be removed by following the procedure shown in Figure 6-3. Hold the neck of the bottle in one hand, pointing the bottle away from the guest, and with the other hand insert the tip of the corkscrew into the center of the cork, as shown in Step 4 (Note: many prefer to rest the bottle on a side-stand or on the corner of the table). Twist the corkscrew into the cork for a firm grip, hold the corkscrew straight and twist into the cork without pushing down on the cork; place the edge of the bottle opener on the lip of the bottle, holding it in place with your finger, and with a firm grip slowly pull out the cork, as shown in Steps 5 and 6. Unscrew the cork from the corkscrew; wipe off fingerprints or cork dust from the neck of the bottle with the side towel or a clean linen napkin. Practice will permit a server to remove even the most difficult corks without a break. Place the cork and the foil (make a small basket with the foil to hold the cork) next to the glass either on its side or on a bread and butter plate so the guest can inspect both as shown in Step 7; then pour the wine for the guest to taste and approve, Step 8. Take care not to stain the tablecloth with the cork.

Occasionally a cork may break. When this occurs the server should do the following: Remove whatever cork is on the corkscrew; reinsert the corkscrew into the center of the cork remaining in the bottle and gently twist all the way through the cork, being careful not to push the cork further into the bottle; slowly remove the cork. Place both pieces of the cork side by side for the guest to inspect. If the cork accidentally falls into the bottle, do not panic—apologize, and offer to bring the guest another bottle of wine. If the guest prefers a new bottle of wine, inform the manager and return the bottle with the cork to the bar for decanting (discussed in the next section)—this wine could later be served as a house wine by the glass.

Step 1 Cut and remove foil

Step 2 T-Screw wine opener

Step 3 Wipe the neck

Step 4 Insert the corkscrew

Steps 5 and 6 Remove the cork

Steps 5 and 6 Continued

Step 7 Place the foil and cork on a bread-and-butter plate next to the glass

Step 8 Pour the wine

FIGURE 6-3
Serving Wine *Courtesy of the Federation of Dining Room Professionals*

The practice of smelling and fondling the cork is somewhat open for debate. A century ago, wine enthusiasts checked the cork to ensure authenticity (some winemakers counterfeited labels but failed to stamp their corks with the same distinct logo or name). It is true that we can detect some early indications of quality by smelling or inspecting the cork. However, we can also be misled. The true measure of a fine wine is in its aroma and first taste from the glass.

Once the cork has been removed, and the lip of the bottle wiped with a clean side towel, the server should pour about one ounce of wine for tasting purposes. The bottle should be held firmly while pouring. While the guest who ordered the wine tastes the wine, the server should be holding the bottle at the base with one hand and the neck with the other hand, with the label facing the guest. After the guest has given approval, the server should pour the wine for the other guests at the table, starting with the guest to the right of the taster (or women and/or older guests first), with the taster's glass filled last. The bottle should be twisted with a turn of the wrist as poured to prevent dribbling on the table. Glasses are generally filled one third to half full, which permits swirling to experience the full bouquet that the wine has to offer.

When opening a bottle of champagne or sparkling wine, loosely cover the top of the bottle with a side towel or linen napkin as a safety precaution, as shown in Figure 6-4. Then remove the foil and wire cap (usually with five complete twists plus one half-twist of the wire). If the bottle has been shaken, the cork might pop off and accidentally injure someone if the bottle is not covered. As a further precaution, the server should have a hand on top of the cork. When removing the cork, firmly hold the cork in one hand, with the bottle pointing away from the guest, and slowly twist the bottle as the cork is removed. The cork should be removed with quiet precision, retaining the pressure in the bottle that creates the bubbles. Always have one champagne

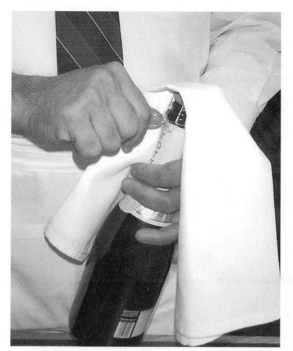

FIGURE 6-4
Serving Champagne or Sparkling
Wine

glass close at hand for quick pouring. Occasionally, when the cork is removed, the champagne may quickly overflow as the pressure is removed from the bottle. This is usually controlled after the first glass is poured.

ecanting Wine

Older wines sometimes have a layer of sediment at the bottom of the bottle, and therefore need to be decanted. The server should be careful not to shake the bottle, to avoid activating and distributing the sediment throughout the wine. Decanting a bottle of wine may present problems to a novice server, but it is not as difficult as it may seem. Most wine lists offer wine that is ready to serve straight out of the bottle. However, a great, old bottle of French Burgundy or Bordeaux that has thrown a good deal of sediment can be rendered clear by using the process of decanting. Decanting allows an older red wine to react with air, also known as "breathing." A very young red that is considered "closed in" will open up and appear less harsh and tannic once aerated.

Wine is decanted by slowly pouring from a bottle to a decanter without disturbing any sediment. A light source, such as a candle or flashlight, behind the shoulder of the bottle (entire foil should be removed) will be the clue when to stop as the sediment approaches the neck. The same process would be followed for a bottle having cork particles. Another method for removing cork particles is to pour the wine through cheesecloth.

When serving a bottle that needs to be decanted, present it to the guest at the table and open it in the normal manner, being careful not to agitate the sediment. Suggest that the wine needs to be decanted, and with the guest's approval, decant the wine. The wine will then be served from the decanter. The wine bottle should always go back on the table so the guests see what they are drinking.

ine Glasses

Wine glasses should always be clear and made of glass. Etched and colored glass are not suitable when one is attempting to appreciate the true color of wine. Colored stems may be acceptable if a Maître D' is attempting to create ambiance related to a regional or theme dinner.

Wine glasses should possess long stems for handling and have a wide enough bowl for swirling and smelling, as shown in Figure 6-5. Wine purists

FIGURE 6-5
Wine and Beverage Glasses *Courtesy of Cardinal International, Inc.*

prefer a smaller bowl for white wines and a larger one for red wines. The key is never to "crowd" the wine into a small glass that does not allow free movement of the wine.

Lengthy and multiple-course dinners often command several wine selections. The host will usually dictate which wine is to be poured first. However, a good rule of thumb is not to overwhelm the palate. White wines usually are better enjoyed prior to red wines, younger before older wines, and dry wines before sweet wines.

Basic knowledge goes a long way in any discipline. The often mysterious world of wine is no different. Servers should be trained in the fundamentals and let their personalities do the rest. The server who desires to go beyond the fundamentals should take a special course in wine and alcoholic beverages at a community college or culinary school.

Wine Varietals

When viewed from a distance, capturing wine knowledge can seem a daunting undertaking. This does not have to be the case, however. Although thousands of grape varietals exist, a command of perhaps 20 varietals will give the server a giant step towards recognizing wines from Bordeaux to Napa Valley and from Alsace to the Rhine Valley.

The *Vitis*, or grapevine, produces a number of different rootstocks. Each stock gives birth to many grape varietals. The European rootstock, *Vinifera*, is the family that produces the finest of the grape varietals. Riesling, Pinot Noir, Chardonnay, and Cabernet Sauvignon are only a few that grace the great wine lists of the world. *Vinifera* are grown in a number of areas throughout the world, but are best produced in Northern cool-climate zones.

At wineries in the United States, many vintners offer several different grape varietals in their tasting rooms. It is not unusual for a winemaker to bottle 10 different wines for the market.

While some of these wines are quite noteworthy, others seem less than memorable. The reason for this disparity probably lies in the fact that grape varietals prosper differently in varied climates. This concept is perhaps best understood when one drives through the great vineyard areas of Europe: Bordeaux, Burgundy, Mosel, and others. European winemakers are fiercely proud of one or two grape varietals they specialize in. After centuries of experience, they know which grape grows best in which climate. Why, then, will a tour of Napa Valley, California or other wine regions yield many wines to taste at each winery?

The answer is cash flow. In fact, many wineries are still paying for their vines. American vintners often find it necessary to make many different wines to accommodate the tastes of the public. The future of American winemaking will probably more closely resemble that of Europe, once the financial obligations are satisfied. The public, as well as the winemakers, are beginning to demand only those wines that have been made with the grapes that grow best in a given region.

In the United States we tend to name wines after the grape variety, while in Europe wines are often named after a town, a region, or a vineyard (winemaker).

In choosing wines for a restaurant's wine list, the owner/manager should take the same care that is taken with the produce or poultry selections. Begin by understanding which grapes grow best in which region and which wines will enhance the menu of the restaurant. Then, fill the needs with leaders from that area.

NOTABLE WINE VARIETALS

RED

Cabernet Franc (cab-er-nay frahnk): Used in Cabernet blending.

Cabernet Sauvignon (cab-er-nay so-vin-yon): Perhaps the grandest of the "reds." Big, bold, complex. Violet aromas, black currant flavors. Sometimes blended with Merlot (and other varietals) to "soften" the wine. Aged in oak. Very long-lasting.

Gamay (gam-ay): One of the lighter and fruitier red varietals. Best enjoyed young.

Grenache (gre-nash): Found in the Rhone Valley and Spain. Soft tannins and acids.

Merlot (mur-lo): Softer and rounder than Cabernet. Aged in oak. Gaining in popularity due to its ability to be consumed young.

Nebbiolo (neb-ee-oh-lo): Perhaps the greatest red grape of Italy. Deep, firm, and rich.

Pinot Noir (pee-no-nwar): Fine, full flavored, full body with an "earthy" nose. Velvety and long lasting.

Sangiovese (sang-joe-vay-zay): Rich garnet hue, deep when young, warm red-brick when mature. Slightly earthy and tannic. (Used in Chianti and other Italian wines).

Syrah (sir-ra): Full, heavy, long-lived wines of great color, scent, and body.

Zinfandel (zin-fun-del): Unique to California. Depending on winemaking techniques it can be made in bigger or lighter style. Berry overtones.

Note: The most popular red wine is Cabernet Sauvignon, followed by Merlot, Zinfandel, and Pinot Noir.

WHITE

Chardonnay (shar-dun-nay): Most classic variety. Pale to yellow color (aged in oak). Vanilla and oak flavors. Dry, rich, and fresh. Nutty and full bodied.

Chenin Blanc (shen-n-blahnk): Fruity with residual sugar (Honeyed richness). Found in Loire Valley and California.

Gewürztraminer (geh-verts-trah-mee-ner): From the German "gewurtz" or spice. Great food wine with increasing popularity. Strong and positive taste.

Muller Thurgau (mule-yer-tour-gow): At various times thought to be a cross grape of Riesling and Sylvaner. Now generally considered a Riesling hybrid. Mass produced in Germany. Light, inexpensive, and floral.

Muscat (muss-kat): Often made into sweet dessert wine. Pungent taste.

Pinot Blanc (pee-no blahnk): Light, good sipping wine, accessible to all. Fresh fruit.

Pinot Gris (pee-no-gree): (Gree, for gray color). Unrelated to Pinot Noir. Full bodied and great with salmon.

Riesling (rees-ling): Fruity, yet elegant wine distinguished in Germany, Alsace, and Pacific Northwest. Generally medium-dry. Crisp acidity.

Sauvignon Blanc (so-vin-yon blahnk): Produced in Bordeaux and California. Can produce big, dry wines. Occasionally found in dessert wines. Refreshing acidity. Aromatic.

Semillon (sem-ih-yon): Best utilized in Sauternes district of Bordeaux. Often blended with Sauvignon Blanc to make world-class dessert wines. Sweetness of freshly ripened fruit.

Sylvaner (seel-vaa-ner): Found in Germany, Italy, and Austria. Pleasant but unsophisticated.

Trebianno (tre-bee-ah-no): Light white wine from Italy. Often blended with other less than noble varieties.

Note: The most popular white wines are Chardonnay and Sauvignon Blanc.

Rosés or Blushes are made by fermenting red grapes, skins, seeds, and juice, but only for a short time. This produces a light pink or salmon color and can yield a fruity, light wine.

Sparkling Wine, called Champagne only when it originates from the Champagne region of France, is frothy or "impetuous" due to a second fermentation process. This second fermentation traps carbon dioxide bubbles in the bottle prior to corking. The following terms describe Champagne from the driest to the sweetest: Brute, Extra Dry, Sec, and Demi-Sec.

Fortified Wines were originally made in the seaports of Spain, Portugal, Madeira, and Sicily. Seafarers strengthened wines with distilled brandies so that they could travel for months aboard ships in both hot and cold cargo bays without spoilage. Fortified wines make great after-dinner drinks and also serve as basic sauce ingredients given their strong constitutions.

FORTIFIED WINE NOTABLES

- Sherry, Port, Madeira, Marsala

Knowing the characteristics of the wine varieties can help guide the server in offering suggestions to the guest who may request the server's opinion and/or recommendation for a wine selection. As a general rule, white wine is served with seafood and chicken and red wine with meat. Although there are no firm rules, ideally, the wine should complement the menu item, not dominate it. Consequently, dry wines are normally served directly with the entrée and sweeter wines with the dessert. Contemporary menus offer creative combinations of foods and sauces known as fusion foods, where a seafood item, for example, may be accented with a sauce that would traditionally go with a meat item. The same is seen with wines, such as a red wine being paired with a chicken entrée. Therefore, the server should be familiar with the preparation ingredients and accompanying sauces of menu items. Also, the time of the day can certainly dictate one's choice. A light, fruity, or even blush wine is an excellent choice for lunch. Ultimately, if the server can describe the wine's qualities, the guest will appreciate both the server's expertise and the wine selection.

Appendix B, Wine Terminology, identifies general descriptive wine terms, along with terms that describe wine by sight, smell, and taste.

Spirits and Cocktails

Spirits and cocktails have taken many interesting paths during the last several millennia. The history of alcohol is as old and intriguing as the study of humankind. Whether you are seeking the origins of bourbon or the ingredients of a Singapore Sling, you can be assured the results will be fascinating.

No primer on spirits would be complete without an overview of those beverages that find their way into all shape and sizes of glasses imaginable as they pass through the bars and restaurants of the world.

VODKA

Vodka, loosely translated, means "the water of life" or "little water." This top selling spirit was once almost exclusively consumed in Russia, Poland, and Scandinavia. Only after World War II did vodka become a favorite with Americans. Returning soldiers added lime and ginger beer to the clear liquid and the "Moscow Mule" was born.

We must also credit Smirnoff with "moving" Americans toward vodka. Established in Russia in 1818, it passed from the family's hands during the Russian Revolution. It was finally brought to America in the 1930s and remains one of the leading vodka makers in the world.

Wheat, rye, and sugar beets accompany the traditional potato as a base for vodka, with grain being the most popular. Advanced distillation and filtering techniques make for a clear and neutral finished product that accommodates many mixed drinks such as screwdrivers and Bloody Marys.

Aromatic vodkas (with small amounts of additives ranging from pepper to lemon) are also now making a large impact on the consuming public.

VODKA NOTABLES

- Moscow Mule, Screwdriver, Bloody Mary, Vodka Tonic, Vodka Martini, Straight, and Rocks.

SCOTCH, BOURBON, AND OTHER WHISKEYS

Whiskey comes from the Celtic word for "water of life." Both the Scots and the Irish claim invention of this widely used libation.

Grain is the base for whiskey making. The main differences between the leading producing countries of the United States, Canada, Scotland, and Ireland are in the type of grain used, the method of production, the method of aging, and the blending techniques.

Scotch is made in Scotland and its claim to fame is in the malted barley that gives a distinctive aftertaste. Single malts are produced from malted barley only. Blended scotch (the most popular) is made by combining single malts with unmalted grain whiskeys. The distinctive soft water (rich in minerals) is also the key to the unique quality of Scotch.

Scotch is aged in oak for at least 3 years. (Malt whiskeys require up to 12 to 15 years of aging). Grain whiskeys are best when aged for 6 to 8 years.

The name *bourbon* comes from a county in Kentucky (Bourbon) where the classic drink was first made. A freak incident caused a local maker to age his whiskey in charred oak. The resulting unique taste was outstanding. The practice continues today. Corn also is relied upon heavily and represents a minimum of 51 percent of the mash.

Tennessee Whiskey is essentially straight bourbon, made in Tennessee from a mash that contains at least 51 percent corn. It is mellower than other whiskeys because it is filtered through charcoal made from Tennessee maple.

Blended whiskeys are a blend of straight whiskey with other batches of whiskey and are probably best known as coming from Canada. The lighter styles come from Canadian Club, Crown Royal, and Seagram's V.O. (Note that America and Ireland use the "e" when spelling whiskey, while Scotland and Canada spell whisky without the "e".

Like Scotch, *Irish* whiskey is made from a mash based on barley (with added corn and rye). The difference is that in Ireland the malted barley is dried in coal-fired ovens—in Scotland the barley is dried over peat.

WHISKEY NOTABLES

- On the rocks or straight, in many cocktails and mixed drinks.

BRANDY

Brandy is simply wine that has been distilled. Grapes are fermented into wine. The resulting mixture is placed in a pot still to further refine the mixture. The name brandy comes from the Dutch Brandewign (or "burnt wine"—distilled).

The finest brandies come from the Cognac and Armagnac regions of France. They are generally sipped straight from a snifter. More common varieties are mixed with other mixers.

BRANDY NOTABLES

- Straight, coffee additive.

GIN

The Dutch gave the word "genever" to the drink that contained juniper aromatics and neutral-grain spirit. Hence the modern term, *gin*.

Gin was originally created as a tonic to cure various diseases. The diuretic properties of the oil of the juniper berry when added to a pure spirit base were looked upon as being a new, inexpensive medicine destined for the masses.

The early popularity and acceptance of gin led to many alcohol-induced problems in the 18th and 19th centuries. European authors from that time periodically cite the "madness caused by genever or gins."

London dry gin is generally the drink of choice, while Holland's gin has a stronger taste and full body, due to its lower distillation proof, malt aroma, and flavor.

If there is one drink to remember, it must be the martini. One ounce of gin, a sprinkle of vermouth, and ice should be shaken together and then strained into a Martini glass. A green olive caps the classic, unless you want a Gibson, in which case you should use a cocktail onion.

GIN NOTABLES

- Martini, Dry Martini, Gibson, Gin and Tonic, Tom Collins, Gin Rickey.

RUM

Rum is generally made from sugar cane or molasses. Because of this it is best produced in the tropical ports of Puerto Rico and Jamaica. Early Spanish settlers in the West Indies saw that the residual molasses from their sugar factories fermented easily. They experimented with distillation and rum was born.

For centuries, sailors used rum to keep spirits high and to cure scurvy. (While spirits always remained afloat, scurvy was not cured until sailors began relying on vitamin-C-rich limes and oranges).

Rums can be either light (or white) or dark. Light rums are made in column stills that distill away much of the flavor and color. Dark rums are made in pot stills to retain basic ingredients and aged in oak.

RUM NOTABLES

- Rum and Coke, Daiquiris, Rocks, Mixers (Tonic and 7-up), Rum Martini.

TEQUILA

"Pulque" is considered to be the first alcoholic beverage produced in North America. If this is true, tequila is a close descendant. The Aztecs drank the wine-like liquid called "pulque."

The blue agave plant is the source of fine tequila. Found near the town of Tequila in Mexico, the agave is steamed and then fermented until a coarse wine is produced. While many drink the pulque, most Americans prefer the distilled, more refined, Tequila.

Aged tequilas are called "anejo" and are more expensive. The oak aging also produces tequilas referred to as "gold" due to their rich color.

TEQUILA NOTABLES

- Margarita, straight with lemon and salt, with Sangria (a citrus juice).

LIQUEURS (CORDIALS)

Liqueurs, also called cordials, were originally produced as medicinal remedies for all ailments known to man. One can argue that the original distillers were not too far off their target. After all, various roots, herbs, seeds, and flowers do contain properties used today in various drugs.

When the practice of medicine took a separate path from spirits we were left with wonderful liqueurs (or cordials). These are generally sweet after-dinner drinks. Their essential oils make them a natural aid for digestion. These begin as neutral flavored spirits and are flavored by mixing or distilling in various fruits, herbs, seeds, spices, and flowers. They are then sweetened with sugar to finish.

Liqueurs must contain at least 2½ percent sugar (with many including as much as 35 percent). This makes liqueurs popular cooking and baking liquids as well.

LIQUEUR NOTABLES

- Benedictine, one of the oldest of liqueurs, developed in 1510. From many herbs and plants with a cognac brandy base.
- Chartreuse, still made by the monks in France. Yellow is low proof (80-86) Green is 110 proof. Both are spicy, aromatic, and based on brandy.

- Cointreau is an orange liqueur.
- Drambuie combines malt Scotch whiskey and heather honey.
- Grand Marnier is made from a cognac brandy base with orange peels for flavor.
- Irish Mist is a spicy Irish whiskey with a heather honey-flavoring agent.
- Kahlua is a coffee-flavored liqueur from Mexico.
- Southern Comfort is a blend of Bourbon whiskey, peach liqueur, and fresh peaches.
- Tia Maria, from Jamaica, is a coffee-flavored liqueur based on rum.

Appendix C, Spirit Brands and Related Cocktails, identifies some of the notable spirit brands along with popular cocktails.

Terms to Know

Aperitif: A drink before the meal to stimulate the appetite. Appetizer wine or spirit.

Bitters: Bitters are usually used to flavor mixed drinks.

Blended: Mixed in a blender until creamy. *Flash Blended:* A flash (quick) mix in a blender.

Brown Goods: A term often used to describe distilled spirits brown in color (whiskey and brandy).

Call Brand: When a guest requests a drink by brand name.

Coke: Any cola soft drink.

Diet: Usually diet cola.

Dirty: A beverage that includes green olive juice.

Dry: Usually refers to martinis, meaning a touch of vermouth. *Extra Dry:* no vermouth

Easy: Smaller portion.

Frappé: Iced. A liqueur served with finely crushed ice.

Garnishes: Products accompanying a cocktail used to enhance or alter the flavor. Also used to provide a decorative presentation. These could include olives, cherries, cocktail onions, pineapple, orange, grapefruit, celery, limes, lemons, and fruits in general.

High: A term indicating the beverage is to be served in a highball glass over ice.

Mary: Bloody Mary cocktail or spirits served with Bloody-Mary mix.

Neat: Not mixed. Liquor never touches ice. Brandy based spirits are served in a snifter glass and heated on request. Liqueurs are served in a cordial glass. Brown spirits are served in a rocks glass.

Proof: This is the alcohol content in a given spirit. Note that in America alcohol is doubled to equal proof. Therefore, 50% alcohol is 100 proof. This is how 151 proof rum consists of 75.5% alcohol.

Rocks: Served over cubed ice.

7-up: Seven-up, or lemon-lime soft drink.

Shot: Can range from 7/8 ounce to 1 ½ ounces depending upon the policy of the house.

Shaken: Shaken by hand, usually in a bar mixing tin.

Smokey: A beverage that includes a splash of scotch.

Soda: Club soda.

Tall: Tall glass.

Tonic: Tonic water.

Twist: A slice or sliver of lemon or lime rind.

Up: Usually refers to martinis and served in the classic martini glass. Spirits are chilled and strained.

Virgin: No alcohol.

Well Brands: Brands that the house has identified as a standard.

White Goods: A term often used to describe clear spirits (vodka, gin, rum, and tequila).

Beers, Lagers, and Ales

Ice cold beer! If you are thinking that beer is not always served "ice cold," you are right. That being said, can you imagine a better way to introduce a section on one of our favorite drinks, the beer?

Imagine for a moment the thousands (if not millions) of signs you have seen in your life that refer to "ice cold beer." From road signs, to supermarket displays, to television commercials, this never-ending barrage drives most of us to "reach for a cold one."

The impact of beer on humanity has been significant. Beer making has been dated to 5000 B.C. The religious priesthood and monasteries were central to its progression. However, neighborhood bakers also led the charge by combining barley and yeast to ferment and then finish beer.

Beer is the generic term for any malt beverage. However, what many people refer to as beer can generally be divided into two designations: *lager* and *ale*.

Beer is brewed and fermented using malted barleys, grains, and hops. The term "bottom fermentation" is used in reference to the yeast, which falls to the bottom of tanks during fermentation.

Bock beer is heavy, darker, and sweeter than regular beer.

Pilsner is generally used to refer to *light (lite)* style beers. The most famous of beers comes from the town of Pilsen in the former Czechoslovakia. Makers universally tend to use the pilsner name to reflect a style of light and bright beer.

Lagers represent most beers made in the United States. Like pilsner, lager is also light bodied, but somewhat effervescent. The storage (lager-age) or aging process creates a unique flavor. Once aged, lagers are carbonated.

Malt liquor is brewed like beer but generally has higher alcohol content.

Ale has a fuller body but more bitterness than beer, and is usually deep gold to amber in color. It is fermented at a higher temperature, and yeasts tend to rise; therefore, ales are "top-fermented."

Stout is very dark ale flavored and colored by the addition to the brew of roasted barley.

Porter is somewhat like Stout but lower in alcohol and with a bitter-sweet taste.

Non-alcoholic beer can be brewed by two different methods: traditional brewing and then removing the alcohol (an expensive process, but it maintains the taste of the beer), or brewing without alcohol, which often results in a grainy taste.

Saké is a specialized form of beer produced in Japan. It is made from rice and because of its high alcohol content many people refer to it as "rice wine."

Beer can be served with meals or by itself. The hops in beer stimulate appetites. Beer is used in various food preparations from soups to stews. It can be served with cheese and is used instead of yeast in some pancakes and fritters. The tangy quality of beer makes it popular with highly flavored or spicy dishes such as corned beef, Irish stew, sausage, cold cuts, pork dishes, fried dishes, or curry.

In judging the quality of beer one should look at bitterness levels (always present but never overstated), clarity (light or dark—but not cloudy), and the head (well formed and stable).

Let's return to our first phrase, "Ice Cold Beer." One of the main causes of "flat beer" is serving it too cold. The perfect temperature for most beers and lagers is 45° to 47°F. Ales are served a bit warmer at about 50° to 52°F. Dark beers should be served at a cool room temperature (but that of most European rooms, 58° to 68°F).

Glassware varies from pilsners, pub glasses, mugs, goblets, and specialty glasses (for those operations desiring an out-of-the-ordinary type of glass). Figures 6-6 and 6-7 show different types of beer glasses.

A clean glass is a must for the perfect head as well as the ultimate taste. Glasses should be free of oils, soaps, and fingerprints. A non-soapy detergent with a thorough rinse will ensure that the glass is clean and ready for the delivery of beer.

Many bartenders pour beer by tilting the glass at an angle to prevent an overwhelming head of foam. This style has its supporters. However, the traditional serving style is to let the glass remain standing on a flat surface. The beer is poured directly into the bottom of the glass. The foam should be about 1 ½ inches high, as shown in Figure 6-8. The key to this is to release carbon dioxide (U.S. beers in particular contain more carbon dioxide than their European counterparts). Beer drawn from tap should be promptly served to the guest.

Premium or imported beer is often served in the bottle to the guest. When the server is pouring beer at the table, the glass should be placed to the right of the guest. If the guest prefers to do the pouring he or she will inform the server. Most often the server pours the beer. The server should carefully pour the beer directly into the center of the glass, allowing about 1 ½ inches of foam to appear and come to the rim of the glass, followed by a quick twist of the bottle to prevent dripping. The bottle is then placed above and to the right of the glass.

In terms of storage, remember that beer is extremely perishable. Odors, bacteria, air, and even artificial or natural light can destroy a beer before it reaches our palates. Beer should be stored at around 40°F. Bottled beer should be stored in a dark, cool place. Beer in cans is not affected by light, but also needs to be stored in a cool place.

Appendix D, Ales, Lagers, and Non-Alcoholic Beer, identifies ale and lager types along with common brands of ale, lager, and non-alcoholic beer.

FIGURE 6-6
Beer Glasses *Courtesy of Cardinal International, Inc.*

Responsible Alcohol Service

The restaurant operator should be in full compliance with the laws that govern responsible alcohol serving within the state where he or she is doing business. Many states have a mandatory server education program for owners and employees of licensed businesses that serve alcohol. These states require

Football   Baseball   Golf   Basketball

Inside View   Inside View   Inside View   Inside View

Side View   Side View   Side View   Side View

FIGURE 6-7
Sports Pub Glasses *Courtesy of Cardinal International, Inc.*

alcohol servers to have a service permit. The permit is obtained by taking a class in responsible alcohol service.

The server is responsible for verifying that the person ordering the alcoholic beverage is of legal age. For proof of age, servers should accept only stand-alone identification, such as a valid driver license with photo.

Servers should always be conscious of taking good care of their guests and protecting them from the effects of alcohol misuse. In many states, a restaurant owner and/or the server can be held liable for actions of an intoxicated guest, so it becomes a liability issue. Along with being a legal obligation, responsible alcohol service constitutes good business, and is the "morally correct" thing to do. Therefore, the server should be aware of the number of drinks a guest has been served, and should know and recognize the signs of visible intoxication. The server should have a brief chat with the guest before serving, and at each visit to the table to determine if the guest is intoxicated or at risk of intoxication because of mood, fatigue, medications, or changes in behavior.

FIGURE **6-8**
Foam of about 1 ½ Inches When Beer is Poured
Courtesy of Cardinal International, Inc.

B ottled Waters

Bottled waters are typically opened, brought to the table, and poured by the server. The restaurant will determine the size and shape glass to be used for bottled-water service. The server places the glass with ice on the table to the right of the guest and pours the water to about three-fourths full. Occasionally, a guest may prefer not to have ice with the water. The bottle is then placed above and to the right of the glass. The guest may request or the server may offer (depending upon the policy of the restaurant), a lemon or lime twist. The glass may also be served on a paper coaster.

C offee

The origins of coffee date to before the Middle Ages. Legend has it that goats or sheep ate the small red berries that contained the coffee bean seeds. They became agitated and excited. The indigenous peoples (Ethiopians and Sudanese) decided to partake of the same plant. Their energy and alertness were also raised. The plant was passed on to monks who created various drinks including the current form of coffee.

Coffee quickly spread from Arabia to Syria to Constantinople. For centuries, coffee production was carefully guarded by the Arab world. The cartel was not broken until Dutch traders secured precious seeds to take to the west.

By the early 1600s coffee was enjoyed by the French. They soon introduced the style of serving coffee after dinner. Their method of preparation (the "French Press") is still used today and has seen a comeback in recent years, particularly in fine dining establishments. The superb quality of the coffee produced with a French Press and upscale presentation have added to its resurgence in popularity. Near boiling water is poured onto ground coffee—the coffee held together by disks that act as filters, as shown in Figure 6-9. A French Press can also create coffee for the drink that is unique. Prepared tableside, this visual display is tremendous, especially with the addition of a spirit cart. The press makes coffee for one or more guests (3-cup, 8-cup, or 12-cup French Press) and can be brought into any space without wires or plugs.

Over the centuries, cultivation spread from Africa to South America and then to the West Indies. Two types of coffee bushes supply most beans to the consumer. Arabica is considered the highest quality, while robusta contains more caffeine and yields a somewhat nutty taste.

Coffee beans are roasted to bring out various flavor characteristics. Beans roasted at lower temperatures are lighter and smoother than their darker roasted cousins. Higher temperatures during the roast produce dark, reddish-brown beans with "fiery" taste. Grinding is also a critical element in coffee making. While coffee can be ground weeks before it is brewed, the premium tastes and aromas are produced from beans that are ground directly prior to extraction, allowing time to stabilize.

Coffee service can be somewhat unique depending upon where it is served. In the United States, we now serve coffee in almost every possible way—black, with cream or milk, as espresso, as cappuccino, or with alcohol as an after dinner drink.

In Turkey, Greece, and in the Arab world, coffee is highly concentrated, strong, and often sweetened. Belgium, Germany, and Switzerland often serve coffee with chocolate. The British tend to serve coffee with scones or biscuits. Finally, in many regions of the world coffee is the base "entrée" for a wide range of alcoholic beverages.

FIGURE 6-9
French Press *Courtesy of Boyd Coffee Company*

Espresso is an Italian style of coffee. It involves a process in which a specialty blended and roasted coffee, finely ground, is brewed rapidly (20 to 25 seconds) under pressure, through a fine mesh screen filter. Espresso is traditionally served in a demitasse (small) cup.

Caffé lattes are approximately 10 percent espresso, 80 percent steamed milk, and 10 percent milk foam.

Cappuccinos are approximately 10 percent espresso, 45 percent steamed milk, and 45 percent foam. The resultant brown concoction is reminiscent of the color of robes of the Capuchin monks—hence the name.

Mochas are approximately 10 percent espresso, 8 percent chocolate syrup, and 82 percent steamed milk.

A wide variety of flavored drinks can be created by adding syrup flavorings to caffé lattes, cappuccinos, or mochas.

TYPES OF ROASTS

- Light roast: mild
- Medium roast: mellow, balanced
- Full roast: rich color with touch of roast flavor
- Continental roast: intense (for after-dinner drinks)
- Italian roast: black beans with strong flavor

FLAVORS

- Flavors can be added to coffee after roasting (flavored powders can be added to a brew). Chocolate, hazelnut, French vanilla, and raspberry have gained recent popularity.

DECAFFEINATED COFFEE

- A minimum of 97 percent of the caffeine is removed from coffee in this process. Unroasted beans are steamed to release caffeine from the bean. A decaffeinating agent (solvent or water) is then used to remove the caffeine. Many people feel that this process, while quite sophisticated, leaves coffee a shadow of its former self.

TIPS FOR CORRECT BREWING

- Always start with a clean coffee maker.
- Use only cold, fresh, pure water for brewing. Heavily chlorinated water should be filtered, or you should use bottled water.
- Temperature for brewing should be nearly boiling.
- Grind must be right for the type of brewing equipment.
- Follow a ratio of 14 to 20 ounces of water to 1 ounce of coffee, adjusting to taste.
- Always use superb quality coffee.
- Store coffee in a cool, dry place to preserve optimal freshness.

"A CUP OF COFFEE WITH A TWIST"

For centuries, people have enjoyed wine with their meals, but what about after dinner—the twilight hours of the day?

Some say the art of spiking coffee with alcohol began even before shepherds matched wine with food. Ghengis Khan was said to provide his invading soldiers with a hot drink made from pillaged wine and coffee before making forays into new lands.

Many who prefer wine as a complement to food still enjoy a properly mixed after-dinner drink utilizing coffee. It is often the perfect crowning touch to an evening.

Huber's of Portland, Oregon, has entertained thousands of patrons for decades with an offering of Spanish Coffee flambéed tableside. Their blend of Kahlua, coffee, 151 rum and triple sec are matched only by their showmanship and artistry. The Buena Vista Cafe in San Francisco, California, delights many with their version of Irish coffee. The tradition began in the 1940s when they mixed Irish whiskey with coffee and sugar, adding a dollop of whip cream. Tony's of Houston, Texas, makes their world-famous Café Diablo by flaming an orange peel into a silver chalice filled with coffee, brandy bitters and vermouth.

Some other favorites include: Café Royale (with bourbon or brandy) and Mexican Coffee (with tequila and sweetened with Kahlua). Café Pucci is an outstanding drink made with Trinidad rum and Amaretto; Kioki (or Keoke) Coffee tastes wonderful with brandy; and Royal Street Coffee is exceptional with Amaretto, Kahlua and nutmeg, served dry (no sugar).

Although wine is often the preferred choice with meals, coffee and spirits can add an exciting dimension to a memorable dining experience.

Tea

People around the world have enjoyed tea for over 5,000 years. Next to water, tea is the most commonly consumed beverage in the world, with an estimated one billion cups consumed daily worldwide. Numerous varieties of tea are found throughout the world. Some teas are named after their places of origin, such as Ceylon from Sri Lanka (formerly Ceylon) and Darjeeling from the Himalayas. Each tea has its own unique flavor, color, and aroma. Often different teas are blended to create a new flavor. Earl Grey, English breakfast, and orange spice are examples of teas that are blends of different varieties. Decaffeinated teas are available, and herbal teas are 100 percent caffeine free. The herbal teas are made from dried leaves and flowers that are steeped in boiling water.

Tea can be served with a cup of hot (near boiling) water and a tea bag placed next to the cup, with a teapot of hot water and the tea bag placed next to the teapot when served, or with a tea press that retains the leaves when pouring into tea cups. The teapot should be placed to the right of the cup with the handle turned at 4 o'clock. This allows the guest to open the package containing the fresh teabag and place it in the hot water to steep to the desired strength. The tea press should also be placed to the right of the cup. The tea press is used in fine dining restaurants that offer premium loose-leaf teas for guest selection. If the guest desires a lemon wedge and/or milk (or cream), it should be placed on a small plate lined with a doily. The plate is placed above and to the right of the cup.

Iced tea is served in a large glass with ice, a lemon wedge, and a long-drink spoon. The glass is typically placed on top of a small plate with a paper doily or coaster. Sugar and/or artificial sweetener are also brought to the table. When served, the iced tea is placed to the right of the guest. Iced teas flavored with syrup have become popular.

Overview

Wine service begins with the knowledge of serving temperatures and the correct use of an ice bucket during the service of wine. The importance of properly presenting a bottle of wine or Champagne to a guest along with being able to open and serve it is a measure of a server's professionalism.

Occasionally, wine will need to be decanted. The server should be able to recognize when this occurs and what the procedure is to decant a bottle of wine. Servers should be trained in the fundamentals of wine varieties and other alcoholic beverages such as vodka, scotch, bourbon, blended whiskeys, brandy, gin, rum, tequila, and liqueurs (cordials). Also, the server should know what to look for in recommending beer along with the best serving temperatures of beers, and to be able to explain the differences between beers, lagers, ales, bock beer, pilsner, malt liquor, stout, porter, and saké. Ultimately, if the server can describe the qualities of the various alcoholic beverages, the guests will appreciate the server's expertise and the selection.

Servers should always be conscious of taking good care of their guests and should protect them from the effects of misusing alcohol. Along with being a legal obligation, it constitutes good business, and is the "morally correct" thing to do. Many states have a mandatory server education program for owners and employees of licensed businesses that serve alcohol. These states require alcohol servers to have a service permit, which is obtained by taking a class in responsible alcohol service.

The server should know how to serve coffee, as well as espresso and espresso drinks, such as caffé lattes, cappuccinos, and mochas. In addition, he or she should understand the different types of teas and tea service.

DISCUSSION QUESTIONS AND EXERCISES

1. What is the recommended temperature for serving each of the following wines: white wine, red wine, and dessert wine?

2. Explain how to prepare an ice bucket for use and when salt should be added.

3. What is the correct way to present a bottle of wine to a guest?

4. Explain the procedure for removing a cork from a bottle of wine.

5. When a bottle of wine is opened, what should be done with the cork?

6. What is the true test of a bottle of wine?

7. Explain the procedure for pouring wine once the cork has been removed.

8. How full should wine glasses be filled?

9. Explain the procedure for opening a bottle of champagne.

10. Explain the process of decanting wine.

11. When red wine reacts with air, what is this called?

12. How does climate affect the grapes that produce wines?

13. When would fortified wines be served and how else could they be used?

14. List three examples of fortified wines.

15. Explain how vodka is made and name five popular vodka drinks.

16. Explain the origin and production process of both scotch and bourbon.

17. What distinguishes Tennessee Whiskey from other whiskeys?

18. Name two popular brands of Canadian blended whiskeys.

19. What is the difference between Irish whiskey and Scotch?

20. What is brandy?

21. What are two popular drinks made from gin?

22. What is rum generally made from?

23. Name three popular drinks that are made from rum.

24. Explain the process of producing Tequila and name two popular Tequila drinks.

25. What are liqueurs?

26. Identify seven different liqueurs and explain the characteristics of each one.

27. Define the following terms: aperitif, frappé, neat, and proof.

28. Describe Bock beer.

29. What are light style beers generally known as?

30. What is brewed like beer but has higher alcohol content?

31. Explain the difference between beer and ale.

32. Describe the difference between Stout and Porter ale.

33. What is saké and how is it made?

34. How is beer judged?

35. What is one of the main causes of flat beer?

36. What is the recommended temperature for beers, lagers, ales, and dark beers?

37. What is the server's legal responsibility when serving an alcoholic beverage?

38. Name and describe five types of coffee roasts.

39. How is a French Press used to make coffee?

40. Explain the process of making Espresso.

41. Name the ingredients and their approximate percentage in the following Espresso drinks: caffe lattes, cappuccinos, and mochas.

42. Discuss several coffee and alcohol combinations.

43. How are herbal teas made?

44. Explain two ways of serving hot tea.

45. How is iced tea served?

7

Guest Communication

Learning Objectives

After reading this chapter and completing the discussion questions and exercises, you should be able to

1. Describe how to make a personal connection with guests.
2. Demonstrate server introductory greetings to guests.
3. Understand how to develop server enthusiasm.
4. Measure the effects of server enthusiasm.
5. Identify and describe several different types of guests.
6. Anticipate the guest's needs.
7. Recognize nonverbal cues and prompts that can assist in anticipating the guest's needs.
8. Explain and demonstrate suggestive selling.
9. List the five different types of suggestive selling.
10. Describe the benefits of suggestive selling.
11. Explain the three basic guidelines for suggestive selling.
12. Give examples of when dining room showmanship suggestively sells.
13. Understand and explain the procedure to follow when taking a guest's order.
14. Identify several procedures that can help a server to conserve steps and improve service timing during rush periods.
15. Explain what the server should do in an emergency situation or when a guest becomes ill.

The servers are the individuals who put the "personality" in the restaurant. They are the salespeople and providers, selling food and beverages, and providing service. The server's job is to do the following:

1. Serve guests to their complete satisfaction.
2. Represent the restaurant and the management.
3. Perform within the restaurant's established standards of quality and service.
4. Earn the privilege of receiving maximum tips.

The job of a server requires the abilities of a psychologist, the technique of a super salesperson, the professional attitude of a nurse, plus the charming qualities of a "gracious society" host or hostess. Many people seem to believe that there is a mysterious "secret" to being a successful server. The fact is that there are no hidden secrets that cannot be learned. The personal attributes of self-discipline, hard work, and dedication; the satisfaction of serving people and the feeling of being qualified to perform with efficiency; and the instant money collected as tips are among the advantages that make the difficulties of the job not so difficult after all.

A Personal Connection

A server's task is more than taking an order. The server must be completely knowledgeable about the menu offerings and the wines, along with having a sense of the clientele and being able to help guests with menu selections. This begins with the server's ability to gain the guest's confidence initially, followed by an implied trust that generates a feeling that the server is prepared to provide the best dining experience possible. This personal connection can be initiated in several ways and, surprisingly, under the most common circumstances.

First and foremost is the server's attitude about service. At times the server's enthusiasm is more important than the service itself. Every restaurant has rules and procedures necessary for smooth, consistent operations. However, in the personal exchange between the server and guest it is important that the server show his or her personality in a manner that will have a positive effect upon guests. The result is a pleasantly smooth dining experience.

Acknowledging guests within the first few seconds after they are seated displays a sense of urgency on the server's part. This can be accomplished with a smile and a nod of the head, a small wave of the hand, or even eye contact, including raising the eyebrows while still serving another table.

Typically, the server greets guests by introducing him or herself. Often, a server wears a nametag that is clearly visible to guests. If the server learns the guest's name through a reservation or was introduced to the guest by the host or hostess, it is then appropriate to address the guest by name, for example, Mr., Miss, or Ms. Jones.

The server's introductory greeting must be genuine and original to each guest and table. Other guests seated at nearby tables will certainly hear the server's greeting for each arriving guest or group. The greeting should be different for each table; otherwise, the server may appear to be robotic, using the same script over and over. Here are three different greetings that can be used for arriving guests in an environment where the server has been "triple-sat" (three tables seated all at the same time).

1. "Good evening! My name is Paul, and I will be your server this evening."
2. "Welcome to the (name of the restaurant)! My name is Paul, will you be dining leisurely or are you on a tight time schedule?"
3. "Hello! My name is Paul. Is this your first visit to the (name of the restaurant)?"

Another invaluable technique is recognizing return guests. Remembering names, what the guests ordered at their last visit, their preferred beverage, the memorable event of their last dining experience with the server, are several factors that enhance the personal connection between server and guests.

When guests trust the server, they are inclined to respond favorably to appetizer, entrée, dessert, and beverage suggestions. This will affect sales and tips, and it provides the spark that encourages guests to return again and again.

S erver Enthusiasm

The server with enthusiasm demonstrates the following attributes:

- Smiles often.
- Always well groomed.
- Walks quickly and has good posture.
- Alert and attentive to guests.
- Friendly, tactful, and tolerant.
- Poised and composed.
- Speaks clearly and distinctly—voice carries conviction with proper inflections.
- Knows what he or she is doing and why.

Enthusiasm comes naturally to some people, but for most, it takes a concentrated effort to develop the traits that evolve into an enthusiastic personality. It begins with identifying where you are now and where you want to go. You have to visualize what you want to accomplish. This begins with asking, "How will enthusiastic behavior help me in becoming more professional as a server?"

Once you have answered that question, you can begin setting personal goals that will help you to develop the traits that promote enthusiasm. The goal achievement process is not just a one-shot deal. Rather, it is a continuous process. Success in reaching your goals is a "journey," not a destination. When one set of goals is accomplished, you pick another set and start to work on them. Your progress becomes limited only by your imagination and your desire for self-improvement. But do not feel that this is an entirely personal matter that concerns only you. On the contrary, share your goals with your fellow workers and especially with your supervisor. That way he or she knows what you are working on and may be able to help you or suggest ways you can define your goals or measure your achievements. A server can quickly recognize professional improvement when tips increase and repeat guests request the server's tables.

The act of smiling is the first step toward developing enthusiasm. What a difference it makes in your appearance! A smile communicates to the guest, "I am glad to see you." It is essential to start guests off right when they come to dine, so smile and greet them enthusiastically. Many servers may not be aware that they are smiling, because they usually do it as a natural reflex. If necessary, the server should become conscious of when he or she is smiling and work on increasing those smiles.

The server who develops vitality and a few internal creative forces will be able to generate an enthusiastic atmosphere for guests. When a server is sincerely enthusiastic, the server's face lights up, eyes shine, and the voice is vibrant. The server compels the guests' attention, and every word carries conviction. Enthusiasm is the key that unlocks the minds of your guests, causing them to like you, but it is also important to remember that it does not overshadow poor service and/or poor quality food. Remember, to be enthusiastic, you must act enthusiastic!

A server should always approach guests with the feeling that they are nice people who will be enjoyable to serve. This positive expectation can translate into a self-fulfilling prophecy. People tend to act as they are expected to act. Therefore, if you expect your guests to be nice people and you treat them that way, the odds are in your favor that they will be nice people. To be able to realize this full potential, a server needs to display an ability to generate sincere enthusiasm. If enthusiasm is not sincere, it may be seen as patronizing, which can generate negative feelings from guests. Genuine enthusiasm is contagious and a server who displays it in personal performance will achieve positive results. However, there are guests who are unpleasant no matter how positive and enthusiastic a server may be. Then it becomes a real opportunity for the server to turn a difficult guest into a happy, satisfied one.

D ifferent Types of Guests

The server needs to be prepared to serve all types of guests. Some are young, others are old; some are pleasant, and some are unpleasant. The server has to take them as they are and do the very best for each of them. They are the guests.

There are certain situations that require a great deal of patience and tact on the part of the server, especially when a guest is the problem. However, the guest is there and the server has to take care of that guest, and not allow him or her to disturb other guests. The following are some examples and approaches to handling different types of guests.

The Procrastinator This is a guest who just cannot make up his or her mind. This is where you have the opportunity to practice suggestive selling skills. The procrastinator would probably appreciate you helping in the decision making process. You can do this very skillfully by suggesting two or three menu items. If that does not work, allow the guest to have a little more time, mentioning that you will check back in a few minutes. Then check back every few minutes to see if the guest is ready to order.

The Skeptic This type of guest may be doubtful about the quality of food or the way it is prepared. The guest is often very fussy and wants it exactly a certain way. In this situation, your knowledge of menu item ingredients, cooking methods, preparation and serving methods, and cooking time of the items on the menu will help you to solve the problem. Furthermore, you need to be very positive with a guest like this, speaking with assuredness and in a professional manner.

The "Sender Backer" The guest who will send items back is a person who knows exactly what he or she wants. Therefore, it is important that you thoroughly understand the guest's complaint. Also, you must give this guest exactly what he or she wants. Demonstrate that you genuinely desire to please in every detail. The guest will appreciate it and you will have succeeded in turning around a difficult situation. Of course, if the guest proves to be a heckler or a person who is just trying to show off, or if it is impossible to meet his or her request, sincerely apologize, and report the situation to the manager. Most restaurants have a policy of allowing the guest to order something else. If something else is ordered, be very specific and ask the necessary questions to ensure that the guest's order is cooked and prepared exactly as desired.

The Handicapped Guest Be helpful with a physically challenged guest, and if possible, seat the guest away from the traffic flow. If the guest has a hand or arm injury that would make it difficult to eat, offer three menu suggestions. Suggest two easy-to-handle entrées and one that you could offer to cut up, if this seems appropriate. Be quickly willing to help the guest in any way needed. Also, the physically challenged guest may appreciate the server offering to take the guest check and payment to the cashier.

The Older Guest A little extra care goes into serving an older guest. Occasionally, help may be needed in seating the guest, in reading the menu, or in speaking a little louder. Some restaurants have a senior menu that offers smaller portions. Also, your knowledge of menu item ingredients, cooking methods, preparation and serving methods, cooking times, and nutritional information will be very helpful. The older guest will appreciate patience and not being rushed.

The Child Always ask the parents whether they want a booster seat or high chair for the child, being careful not to offend the child who may think that he or she is old enough not to need one. If the restaurant has bibs for children, special placemats, or games of any type, promptly bring them to the table. If appropriate, ask the parents if they would like you to bring some crackers for a small child or baby. This would help pacify the child until the meal is served. Furthermore, look to the parents for the lead in ordering for the child. If the restaurant has a special child's menu, make sure that it is available. If a child orders an expensive menu item, always check with a parent for final approval, and be prepared to suggest another item or two from which the child can choose. Be patient with children, alert for spills, and prepared to provide extra napkins if needed.

The Wise Guy This type of person seeks attention and as a result can be somewhat irritating. The person may pass a degrading remark, tell a crude joke, or ask the server for a date. The server should be polite, but firm in ignoring the comments. If the person continues, respond by stating that you will have to inform the manager. Give the person the same type of professional service you would give any other guest, remaining polite but firm.

The Talker The guest that wants to visit and impress you with his or her knowledge can be frustrating. This type of guest would like to dominate your time and receive all of your attention. Answer questions with short answers, have a pleasant smile, and keep busy.

The Silent Type This type of guest is a shy and soft-spoken individual, so listen with care. Smile and do everything you can to make this guest feel as comfortable as possible, as it will be appreciated.

The Dieter The guest who has diet restrictions will expect the server to be knowledgeable in answering questions and in making appropriate menu suggestions. The server should be competent in answering specific questions regarding menu item ingredients, cooking methods, portion sizes, preparation and serving methods, sugar or salt substitutes, etc. Also, most restaurants will try to accommodate a guest's special dietary request. But if it is impossible to fulfill the request, then the server should be quick to explain that fact and in turn suggest something else for the guest's consideration.

The Blind Guest A blind guest will typically be accompanied by a sighted person, but the server should not hesitate to offer services if needed, such as helping the person to be seated at a table or booth. Many restaurants have a menu available in Braille. When this is the case, it should be offered to the guest, or the guest may prefer the server to read several menu items along with the prices. The server should do everything in a normal way, the only difference being that when something is set on a table, the server should say the name of the item, such as, "Your salad, Sir/Ma'am." If the guest needs assistance in any way, the server should be available to promptly accommodate the guest. When the guest check is brought to the table, the server should offer to read the menu item and price, the sales tax amount (if applicable), and the check total. In addition, the server should inquire if the guest would like to have the check and payment taken to the cashier.

The Coffee Drinker The guest who only orders coffee and reads a newspaper or book or visits with a friend and sits at a table for an hour or more is using productive space without spending much money. This type of guest has to be carefully handled. The server should be tactful in not offending the guest, but needs to control the situation. The server may suggest a piece of pie or dessert item to accompany the coffee. If the guest declines, after the second refill, the guest could be charged for a second cup of coffee, depending upon the policy of the restaurant. If the dining room is busy and other guests are waiting to be seated, then the server, using good judgment, may need to inform the guest politely that the table is needed for lunch or dinner guests.

The Budgeter Many times the price of the menu item is a serious consideration for guests. An experienced server will quickly recognize when price is a factor, and will suggest medium and lower priced entrées. The important thing is that the guests do not feel ill at ease and that they enjoy dinner and feel that they got more than their money's worth.

The Bad Tipper When a guest who frequents a restaurant is recognized as someone who does not leave a tip or tips only a small amount, that guest should be served in the same professional manner as any other guest. Not every guest will leave the traditional 15 to 20 percent or higher tip. A guest may honestly not understand how to tip correctly. Also, there are some guests who do not tip for any reason, even when they receive excellent service. It is important for the server to remember that not receiving a tip should not affect his or her actions and service to other guests. The best way to react is to double the efforts in providing the best of service.

Anticipating the Guest's Needs

A professional server will always anticipate the needs of guests by keeping an alert eye on guests and by promptly attending to their needs before they occur. Anticipating guest needs is a combination of close observation and being able to interpret nonverbal communication from the guest. This is also referred to as "reading the guest," which involves determining the guest's priorities. For example, during lunch a guest may have time restraints that necessitate fast service. The nonverbal message from the guest might be frequently looking at his or her watch. By reading the nonverbal cue, the server may present the check right after delivering the entrée, at the same time suggesting dessert and coffee. Another example is when guests have business papers spread on the table and are engaged in conversation. The server should avoid interrupting the guests and wait for the proper moment (the same as if guests were engaged in social conversation) to become available to serve guests. Merely bringing glasses of water to the table and presenting menus could accomplish this.

The server must develop an expertise for "reading (observing and listening to) the guest" in order to build a comfortable personal connection. Servers with an anticipatory understanding of guest needs are perceived as providing exceptional service. "Reading guests" correctly allows the server to be proactive with responses that not only meet but also can exceed guest expectations. When service surpasses the guest's expectations, the guest may feel that the server has gone "beyond the call of duty," which is rewarded by a generous tip and the desire to return often. The reality is that often this perception is achieved via the simplest levels of "reading the guest" correctly. Some helpful suggestions are as follows:

- Always remove extra place settings as soon as the guests have been seated, to allow extra room on the table.
- If guests are seated in an area that may be drafty, or if the sun is shining in their eyes, the server should offer to seat the guests at another table or adjust the blinds.
- Salt, pepper, and sugar should be moved within easy reach of guests, particularly when guests are seated at counters.
- Never break into a guest's conversation, and time questions so that the guest will not have to try to answer with a mouth full of food.
- Check each food plate from the kitchen to ensure completeness and for the best plate presentation prior to serving.
- Be alert and notice when a napkin or piece of flatware has been dropped on the floor, pick it up, and immediately replace it with a clean item.
- Recognize when guests are not in any special hurry, such as after a movie, date, or ball game, allowing for additional suggestive selling opportunities.

Nonverbal Cues and Prompts

Nonverbal cues and prompts from the guest can assist the server in anticipating the guest's needs. They appear in common body language displays and facial expressions that are used every day in normal communications. There are also some behaviors unique to the dining experience, such as the following:

> *Menus:* Guests do things with menus that communicate when they are ready to order and their level of urgency. They will close the menus, and as the urgency increases they will stack them, or move them to the edge of the table, or even push the stack out over the edge of the table to get the server's attention.
>
> *Napkins:* Guests will unfold napkins and place them on their laps when ready to order. As the meal is completed they may lay the napkin back on the table or place the napkin on top of their empty plate. They may also push the plate to the side or center of the table when they are finished eating.
>
> *Looking Around:* When a guest is looking around it generally means something may be wrong or the guest may need something else.

Suggestive Selling

When a server uses suggestive selling, he or she is helping guests discover what is on the menu, and furthermore preparing the way for their desire to return again, along with increasing sales for the restaurant. Suggestive selling helps the server to engage in conversation with the guest instead of just taking an order. Guests generally appreciate it when a server takes a personal interest in helping them get better acquainted with the menu choices, and to further enjoy their meal by having items suggested that would complement their selection. This is a specific responsibility of the server and the more skillful the server becomes, the greater the opportunity to earn increased tips. The server's skill begins to develop with increased self-confidence, a firm belief that the guest will have a more enjoyable dining experience, and enthusiasm reflected in the server's voice and facial expressions.

To be successful at suggestive selling it is absolutely essential to know the menu, as presented in Chapter 5, Service Preparedness. The server should be prepared to answer any questions the guest may have about any menu item; for example, the quality and ingredients used, the method of cooking, the portion size, the way it is served, the flavor and taste, and the cooking time. Guest satisfaction should always be the first consideration.

There are several types of suggestive selling, and each is geared toward helping the guest enjoy the meal more, resulting in a better dining experience. The different types of suggestive selling are as follows:

SELLING THE GUEST "UP"

This type of suggestive selling entices the guest to spend more money and is a real service. Many times the guest is not aware that he or she can get more value and enjoy the meal more by spending a little more money—for example, by ordering the complete dinner instead of à la carte, by ordering an appetizer, Caesar salad, or a bottle of wine with dinner. Also, larger drink sizes are typically a better value than the regular drink size.

SUGGESTING "RELATED" MENU ITEMS

Related menu items refers to items that "naturally" seem to go with other items, such as soup or salad with sandwiches, cheese on a sandwich, French fries along with a hamburger, or a scoop of vanilla ice cream with apple pie.

SUGGESTING NEW MENU ITEMS OR THE "CHEF'S SPECIALTIES"

Most guests appreciate it when the server tells them about new menu items or "specialties" for which the restaurant may be known.

SUGGESTING ITEMS FOR SPECIAL OCCASIONS

On birthdays or anniversaries, and during holidays such as Mother's Day, Father's Day, Valentine's Day, St. Patrick's Day, or the Christmas and New Year's season, people are interested in creating a memorable occasion along with a fine meal. Most restaurants offer special menu items that can add to the festivities. Therefore, the server needs to suggest those menu items along with any other special items such as cakes for birthdays and anniversaries, if the restaurant offers them.

SUGGESTING "TAKE HOME" ITEMS

Many restaurants have items available for "take home," such as pies, cakes, cinnamon rolls, salad dressings, etc. The server should always take the opportunity to mention those items to guests. If the guest does not have a dessert with the meal, the server may suggest taking a dessert home.

Some guests welcome suggestions and others resent them. The experienced server will recognize the signs when suggestions are appreciated. It is also important for the server to recognize the importance and professionalism that supports suggestive selling versus high-pressure selling that annoys guests. Successful suggestive selling depends on the interest and enthusiasm of the server and a thorough knowledge of the menu, as well as knowledge of the different types of guests.

A server can quickly qualify guests by inquiring if they have eaten in the restaurant previously. If they are return guests they already have a feel for the menu items and staff, and may not require the full menu introduction given to first-time guests. But if it is their first visit, the server should be prepared to provide all the information necessary to make their dining experience complete.

Many menus have a "dinner section" and an "à la carte" section. On an à la carte menu, each item is individually selected by the guest, and is charged according to the selections. Therefore, the à la carte menu offers a greater opportunity to the server for suggestive selling. The dinner menu generally provides a greater value to the guest and therefore, it should be suggested first unless the guest specifically orders à la carte.

The menu itself is the best way to guide guests through a "tour" of the restaurant offerings. The server can guide the guest through the menu by pointing and highlighting categories. The dinner menu in Figure 7–1 is listed in the order of Appetizers, Steak, Veal, Chicken & Pasta, and Desserts on the left side of the menu. At the bottom of that side it details common guest

Appetizers

Fresh Oysters on the Half Shell
Six oysters shucked to order. Ask your wait person for species.
Market Price/Availability

Fresh Northwest Oyster Shooters $1.25/each

Fresh Manilla Steamer Clams
Steamed in garlic, butter and white wine. Market Price/Availability

Razor Clams
Lightly breaded and grilled, fresh in season. $6.95

Fried Calamari
Calamari rings and tentacles flash fried and tossed in a lemon butter sauce.
$7.95

Cajun Popcorn
Bay shrimp in a cajun breading, served with cocktail sauce and a lemon wedge. $6.95

Fresh Salmon Nuggets
Fresh salmon fried golden brown in dill tempura. $5.95

Escargot
Sauteed in garlic, white wine and butter. Served with dipping croutons. $7.95

Shrimp Cocktail
Bay shrimp served with cocktail sauce and a lemon wedge. $6.95

Crab Cocktail
Dungeness crab served with cocktail sauce and a lemon wedge.
Market Price/Availability

Fresh Stuffed Mushrooms
Mushroom caps with bay shrimp, baked with sherry and cheese, topped with fresh scallions. $6.95

Fresh Sauteed Mushrooms
Whole button mushrooms sauteed in madeira wine, garlic and butter. $5.95

Fresh Cut Vegetable Crudite
With dipping sauce. $4.95

Baked Brie with Roasted Garlic
Served with dipping croutons. $5.95
With pesto 6.95
With bay shrimp 8.95
With dungeness crab 10.95

Conch (konk)
Pounded thin like abalone, lightly breaded and grilled. $7.95

Steak, Veal, Chicken & Pasta

6 oz. Filet Mignon
Choice cut 6 oz. steak char-broiled to your taste and served with madeira mushrooms and bernaise sauce. $16.95
• With sauteed prawns $21.95
• With grilled razor clam $18.95
• With pan fried oysters $18.95

10 oz. Choice New York Steak
Center cut steak char-broiled to your taste. $17.95

One Pound Porterhouse
Pressed with green and black peppercorns, char-broiled to your taste, and topped with whiskey mustard sauce. $19.95

Veal Tenderloin
Lightly breaded then seared and topped with madeira mushrooms, dungeness crab, and hollandaise sauce. $17.95

Rack of New Zealand Lamb
Char-broiled to your taste. $19.95

Boneless Pork Loin
Oven roasted with rosemary and juniper, sliced and served with black currant sauce. $14.95

Chicken Breast
Boneless and skinless chicken breast char-broiled, or ask your server for our nightly chicken special. $12.95

Seafood Fettuccine
Bay shrimp, dungeness crab, sea scallops, and fresh fish in white sauce. $15.95

Fettuccine Alfredo
Fettuccine alfredo-style or tossed with olive oil, garlic & parsley. $10.95

Vegetable Fettuccine
Fresh seasonal sauteed vegetables served in alfredo sauce or tossed with olive oil, garlic & parsley. $12.95

Vegetarian Platter
Fresh steamed seasonal vegetables, parmesan baked tomato, dill tempura onion rings & artichoke hearts with house potato or rice pilaf. $13.95

Desserts   We feature fresh homemade desserts.

Selected Child's Portions $8.95 • Corkage Fee $7.00 • Split Dinner Charge $5.00
To serve you better, one check will be written for parties of 7 or more.

Child's Price   Corkage Fee   Split Dinner Charge

FIGURE 7–1
Dinner Menu *Courtesy of the Deschutes River Trout House Restaurant*

inquiries, Selected Child's Portions $8.95, Corkage Fee $7.00, and Split Dinner Charge $5.00.

The right side of the menu lists the Signature Dinners and Fresh Seafood & Shellfish. On the top it highlights, "See our reader board for tonight's special selections," which the server should know by memory. In the left margin next to the Signature Dinners, it details standard choices and accompaniments plus add-on suggestions including costs. Also, it emphasizes "fresh fish." All menu items have descriptions that promote, entice, and feature

See our reader board for tonight's special selections.

Choices →

*All entrees served with
your choice of homemade
Soup or House Salad,
Chef's Vegetable, and
our fresh baked bread.*

*Choice of Rice or Potato
of the Day (except pasta
dishes).*

Add-ons → *Add shrimp for 2.50 or
crab for 3.50 to your
House Salad.*

Fresh Fish → *When we advertise
"fresh fish,"
it is fresh fish!*

Signature Dinners

Dan's New York Steak, 10 oz.
Center cut choice New York steak stuffed with dungeness crab,
char-broiled, and topped with madeira mushrooms,
and bernaise sauce. — $20.95

Mixed Grill
Venison, lamb rack, prawn saute, and razor clam with
whiskey mustard sauce. — $22.95

Fresh Blackened Salmon
Fresh salmon filet with blackening spices pan seared, then baked
and served with a tequila-lime-sour cream sauce. — $16.95

Fresh Stuffed Northwest Rainbow Trout
Rainbow trout stuffed with bay shrimp and dungeness crab, then baked. — $16.95

Fisherman's Stew
Prawn, scallop, fresh fish, clams, mussels, dungeness crab,
and bay shrimp served in a rich tomato broth. — $19.95

New Zealand Venison & Prawns
Medallions of venison and prawns sauteed
with whiskey mustard sauce. — $20.95

Tournedos of Beef with Prawns & Artichoke
Two petite cuts of filet mignon char-broiled to your taste and
topped with artichoke bottoms, prawns, and bernaise sauce. — $21.95

Fresh Seafood & Shellfish

Fresh Salmon Filet
Your choice of char-broiled, grilled, poached, or baked. — $15.95

Fresh Baked Stuffed Salmon
Salmon filet stuffed with bay shrimp and topped with
a rosette of red wine butter. — $17.95

Halibut
Your choice of char-broiled, grilled, poached, or baked.
Fresh "in season". — $15.95

Fresh Grilled Northwest Rainbow Trout — $12.95

Fresh Northwest Cod or Red Snapper
Poached, baked or lightly breaded and grilled. — $13.95

Fresh Northwest Sole
Lightly breaded and grilled or baked. Market availability. — $14.95

Prawns, Scampi Style
Sauteed with white wine, lemon juice, garlic,
capers and butter. — $17.95

Fresh East Coast Sea Scallops
Baked in a mornay sauce. — $15.95

Prawn and/or Scallop Saute
Sauteed with garlic, white wine and finished with
a creamy lemon-butter sauce. — $16.95

Fresh Northwest Oysters
Lightly breaded and pan fried. — $12.95

Fresh Manilla Steamer Clams
Steamed in garlic, butter, and white wine.
Market Price/Availability

Razor Clams
Lightly breaded and grilled.
Fresh "in season". — $15.95

Seafood Combination Plate
Fresh pan fried oysters, grilled razor
clam, and prawn saute. — $16.95

Conch (konk)
Pounded thin like abalone, lightly
breaded and grilled. — $14.95

Lobster Tail
Baked with white wine and butter.
Market Price/Availability

Fried Calamari
Calamari rings and tentacles flash fried and
tossed in a lemon butter sauce. — $14.95

Shrimp Louie
Chef's selection — $13.95

Crab Louie
Chef's selection — Market Price/Availability

*All fresh seafoods are susceptible to
market availability and price.*

FIGURE 7–1 (continued)

attractive preparation and ingredients. The server should always include those descriptions to help develop a mental image when describing menu items. Words such as, fresh, tasty, mouth-watering, and scrumptious generate interest and build enthusiasm for the item.

The following example situation is given to demonstrate the importance of "reading" the guest prior to any suggestive selling.

After having quickly looked at the menu, the guest asks the server, "What do you recommend?" The server eagerly describes, in delicious detail,

"Our house favorite is fresh salmon filet with blackened spices pan seared, then baked and served with a tequila-lime-sour cream sauce." With furrowed brow and pursed lips the customer replies, "I hate fish!"

The server made a mistake by not asking about the guest's interests before launching into a recommendation. The server has been placed in an awkward position, and possibly annoyed the guest.

The server should have responded with the following inquiry: "Do you prefer beef, chicken, seafood, or pasta?"

When narrowing the guest's interests the server can then make the appropriate suggestions from the menu. By asking the right question(s), listening to the answers, and being alert to nonverbal cues, the server can guide the guest to the appropriate choices. This illustrates the importance of reading the guest first in order to effectively anticipate guest needs and expectations.

The effect of suggestive selling is to let the guest know what is available and to suggest items that "go with" the ordered menu item, because they fit into and create the guest's "needs." If the guest does not "need" the suggested item, he or she will reject the suggestion. The server's experience will help to develop an intuitive understanding of what the guest's needs are and then guide the guest into making decisions through suggestive selling. Also, the server should typically suggest two of the possible choices within each food and beverage category, so that the guest's choice will be made easier, as compared to five or six choices. Following are a number of examples showing how suggestive selling works.

BEVERAGES

The server should always suggest one alcoholic and one non-alcoholic beverage choice. Furthermore, the server should note whether the guest's eyes are scanning the beer or wine list, or looking at table tents. These are nonverbal cues to what may interest a guest. If it is beer, ask the guest if he or she prefers light or dark beer, imported or domestic. If it is wine, ask the guest if he or she prefers red or white wine, dry or sweet. These are excellent opportunities to suggest regional wines or local microbrews. When a guest asks, "What do you recommend?" the server should respond with questions like, "What do you drink at home?" "What is your favorite type of beer or wine?" The answers will indicate the guest's flavor and taste preferences. Many wine menus have suggested pairings of wine and food, as shown in Figure 7–2. The Pinot Gris in the wine menu describes the characteristics of the wine and includes a recommendation with seafood, notably salmon. This is especially helpful to the guest because reading the menu and hearing the server describe it provides further assurance that the Pinot Gris would be a good choice. Occasionally a restaurant may use a wine cart to further promote the sale of wine, as shown in Figure 7–3. The server pushes the cart next to the guests' table, with the labels on the bottles facing the table for the guests to inspect. Once a selection is made the wine is served immediately. Restaurants that are promoting certain house brands may even offer sample tasting to guests.

For spirits, again inquire what type the guest may like. Then suggest common name brands that are easily recognizable. For example, if the guest likes scotch, suggest Chivas Regal, JB, or Cutty Sark. These three scotch brands are internationally recognized and offer three levels of quality and price. If the guest says, "I'll just have water," ask if he or she prefers bottled or tap. If the guest wants coffee, suggest the choices that may be

Pinot Gris

Pinot Gris is a crisp, full-bodied, full-flavored wine; similar to Chardonnay but with a spicy edge; a perfect accompaniment to seafood, especially salmon.

	1/2 Bottle	Full Bottle
Hinman		17.00
Oregon		
King Estate		19.00
Oregon		
Eyrie		22.00
Willamette Valley, Oregon		
Lange "Reserve"		24.00
Willamette Valley, Oregon		
King Estate "Reserve"		26.00
Oregon		
Archery Summit "Vireton"		36.00
Willamette Valley, Oregon		

Sauvignon/Fume Blanc

A full-bodied white wine with a distinctive spicy and/or herbaceous aroma often reminiscent of fresh cut grass. A great dry wine to match with any seafood dish.

	1/2 Bottle	Full Bottle
Hogue		14.00
Columbia Valley, Washington		
Kenwood	9.00	18.00
Sonoma County, California		
Robert Pepi "Two Heart Canopy"		19.00
Napa Valley, Callifornia		
Robert Mondavi		22.00
Napa Valley, California		
Duckhorn		30.00
Napa Valley, California		

FIGURE 7–2
Wine Menu *Courtesy of the Deschutes River Trout House Restaurant*

available, such as espresso, latte, cappuccino, mocha, and decaffeinated, along with any specialty blends that the restaurant may have, as presented in Chapter 6.

APPETIZERS

Appetizers should be suggested in pairs. The dinner menu in Figure 7–1 has a variety of appetizers and the server could suggest two of them as follows, "We pride ourselves on our fresh oysters on the half shell, and among our most popular appetizers is the baked Brie with roasted garlic; if you prefer our chef will add Dungeness crab." It is important to include the word "add," which implies an increased cost (or simply state the increased cost), so the guest will not be surprised to see an extra charge on the guest check. While this can easily be done, the server must also be prepared to promptly provide additional information when asked, such as the size and species of oysters, or the portion size of the baked Brie and Dungeness crab. Also, when guests

FIGURE 7–3
Wine Cart *Courtesy of Lakeside™*

may want to split an appetizer, such as the oysters on the half shell, and want to add two more oysters, the server should know what the additional charge would be.

ENTRÉES

Suggesting entrée selections should begin with finding out the guest's preferences. The dinner menu in Figure 7–1 has a variety of meats, chicken, pasta, seafood, and shellfish selections, along with a vegetarian choice. Ask what the guest enjoys from those categories, and then offer two suggestions, being ready to follow up with additional information in response to questions regarding cooking methods, sauces, portion sizes, accompaniments, etc. For example, if the guest orders Dan's New York Steak from the Signature Dinners, the questions could be, "Who is Dan?" (the restaurant owner or chef); "What is charbroiled?" (quick cooking by open flame and/or direct heat); "What is Madeira?" (a rich brandy-based wine from Spain); "What kind of mushroom is used?" (Portobello); "What is in a bernaise sauce?" (eggs, butter, shallots, tarragon, and lemon).

DESSERTS

Desserts can be suggested with a menu, as discussed in Chapter 5, or by a presentation tray or cart, as discussed in Chapter 3. In either case the words used to offer the suggestions are important. Saying something like, "Our home baked ginger cake with fresh sliced peaches topped with fresh whipped cream is sensational, can I bring you one?" While presenting a dessert tray, the server could say, "The five layer chocolate cake is my favorite." Another approach if a dessert menu is used is to place the menu on the table for the guest to pick up and review. This can prepare and entice the guest, and the server can then follow up with some great suggestions.

AFTER DINNER DRINKS

These include coffee, espresso drinks, teas, alcoholic beverages, and house specialty drinks. Again the key is to suggest two items every time, such as "May I bring you an Irish or Spanish coffee?"

GUIDELINES FOR SUGGESTIVE SELLING

The basic guidelines for suggestive selling are as follows:

- When taking the guest's order, always suggest.
- When reading back the order for accuracy, always suggest.
- Before finalizing the guest check, suggest if appropriate.

Always suggest during the following situations:

- If an à la carte item is ordered, suggest "Would you like the dinner special?" Then explain that the dinner is a better value.
- If no beverage is ordered, suggest "And what would you like to drink?" Then suggest the large size, if appropriate for the guest.
- When an order has been placed à la carte, read back the order and suggest items that will "go with" the item ordered, suggest "Would you like soup or salad?" "May I recommend either French fries or onion rings?"
- When a salad is ordered, suggest an "add-on" by suggesting "Would you like it topped with shrimp or crab?" If there is a large size, suggest, "We have a special chef's bowl which is a complete meal."
- If the guest check appears to be complete, always ask, "Will there be anything else?" Never say "Is that all?"

The server should know what to suggest and understand the relationships between food items. Also, the server should be specific in naming food and beverage items, not categories. Say "Would you like a piece of our popular hot cherry or apple pie for dessert?" not "Do you care for dessert?" Say "Would you like a root beer or coke?" not "Do you want a beverage?" Dessert and beverage are not descriptive words. They do not taste like anything to the guest. When you suggest and describe specific items, a picture develops in the guest's mind, which may make it difficult for the guest to refuse. Furthermore, while the server is creating this mental picture, if he or she smiles and approvingly nods "yes," the guest quite often will be inclined to smile and nod "yes" back, agreeing that the server's suggestion is a good one.

SHOWMANSHIP SELLS SUGGESTIVELY

Certain food items can be served with flair, excitement, and showmanship by displaying a special technique or method of presentation. When these items are served, they have a visible presence in the dining room that attracts guests' attention, and creates interest and curiosity. The result is that other guests will be tempted to order the same items. Also, the server has the opportunity to point these items out, as they are being served and/or enjoyed by other guests, while suggestively selling. For example, the server could say, "Our sizzling T-bone steak is outstanding, and it has just been served on a hot platter to the guest seated at the nearby table."

FIGURE 7–4
Thermo-Plate Platters *Courtesy of Service Ideas, Inc.*

Foods that can be fun and exciting for guests are flamed dishes and sizzling platters. Examples of flaming dishes include flaming salads, shishkabobs, desserts, and the famous crepes suzettes. Certain techniques are used to light the different foods, to display them, and to skillfully put them out at serving time. Cognac, fruit liqueurs, and rum are generally used in flaming desserts. Flaming requires time and special equipment and is suitable only for certain dishes. Flaming does not actually cook the food but does add to the flavor. Restaurants that offer flamed dishes typically have one or two people trained to provide the service competently, such as the maître d' or dining room manager.

Sizzling platters, as shown in Figure 7–4, allow entrées to be attractively displayed and served. The pre-heated Thermo-Plate inserts keep foods hot from the stove to the table. Steaks and fish platters sizzle and emit a delectable aroma, as they are being brought through the dining room and served to guests. The French Press (discussed in Chapter 6), that is used in some fine dining restaurants, prepared tableside can fill the dining room with the irresistible aroma of fine coffee. Guests will look to see the tantalizing display.

Taking the Guest's Order

Knowing when to approach guests to take their order can be a challenge to the server, because guests vary in their likes and dislikes in terms of service. However, the best practice is to approach the table with a welcoming smile as soon as guests are seated. First impressions are important, so the server should be prompt, organized, and professional. Courtesy is essential in every detail, beginning with "please" and followed by "thank you" as part of the conversation while taking guests' orders. The server should ask the guests if they would like to dine leisurely or if they are in a hurry. Many people want to have a casual dining experience, have one or more cocktails, and enjoy the process. On the other hand, other guests may have a limited amount of time and expect to be served quickly.

When taking a guest's order, the following procedure should be followed:

- Stand straight, at the left of the table if possible, and close enough to hear the guest's voice.

- Listen carefully and lean forward slightly to hear if necessary.

- Some guests may need assistance in reading the menu.
- Be prepared to explain the menu and answer the guests' questions.
- Utilize suggestive selling techniques.
- Write the guests' orders using a guest check (as shown in Figure 7–5) or POS terminal (according to the restaurant's procedure).
- Read the order back to the guests in order to prevent any possible misunderstanding.
- Thank the guests for their order.
- Immediately place the order with the bar and/or with the kitchen if using handwritten guest checks.
- Begin the service at the table as soon as possible.
- While all of this is happening, be enthusiastic, smiling, courteous, and efficient.

When taking guests' orders a system needs to be followed and most restaurants have such a system. The purpose of the system is to help the server remember who is served what dish, so when the meal is served it is done in a fast, efficient manner. Chapter 4 discusses a pivot point service system with a designated starting position with all orders served clockwise from that point. Chapter 8 explains how server banking functions when a

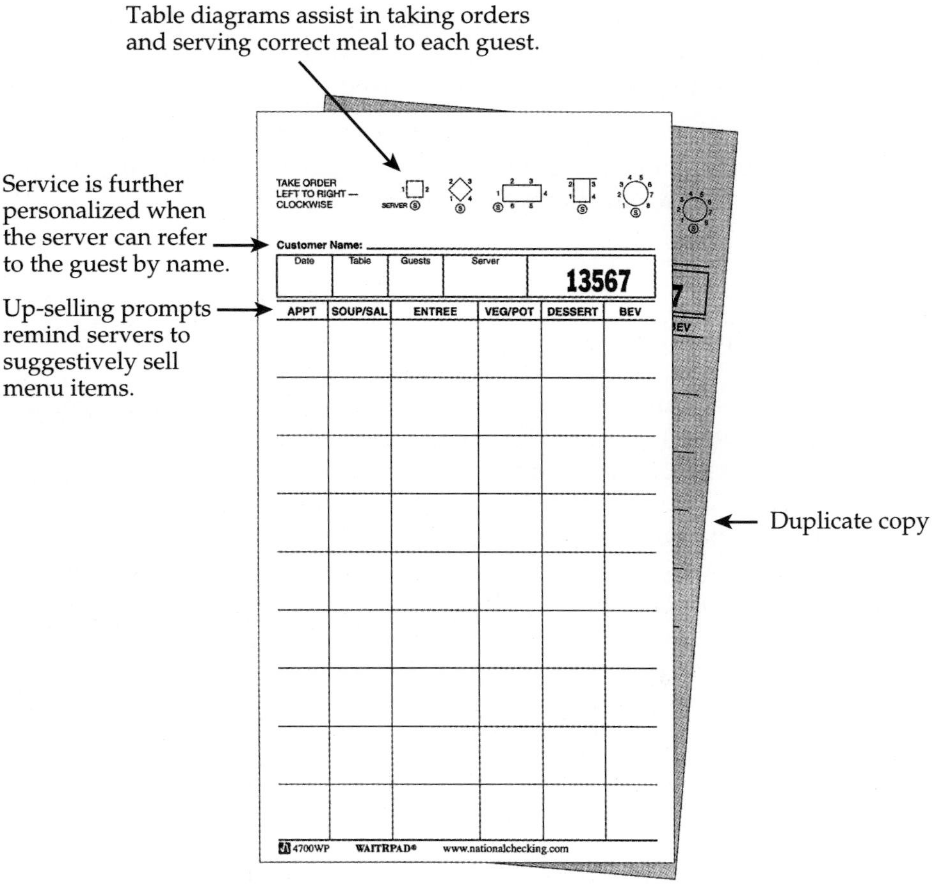

Table diagrams assist in taking orders and serving correct meal to each guest.

Service is further personalized when the server can refer to the guest by name.

Up-selling prompts remind servers to suggestively sell menu items.

Duplicate copy

FIGURE 7–5
Guest Check, WaitRpads® *Courtesy of National Checking Company*

restaurant requires its servers to handle payment transactions directly for the guest without going through a cashier.

Service Timing

During a normal shift an adequate amount of time can be allotted to serve each guest. However, during a Friday night dinner rush, the server's speed and efficiency are critical to giving proper attention to all the tables without seeming to "rush" the guests. During these rush times, the server may constantly have to change speed and direction. Therefore, reading each table and anticipating its needs is critical in controlling the service timing for all tables in the server's station. The server must observe them carefully and plan steps in advance of guest requests. This will save the server time and stress, and ensure good tips because the guests did not have to wait or ask for service.

The following procedures can help to consolidate steps:

- When two or three tables are seated at the same time, the server should take the orders from each table, one right after the other, using good judgment and considering how many people are seated. Then submit the orders to the kitchen and/or bar at the same time.

- If one person orders a second beverage, invite the other guests at the table to have a second beverage.

- When returning to the station, take several seconds to size up each table. What is each table going to need next? That is, beverage refills, prebussing, desserts, entrée orders, guest check, initial greeting, appetizer plates, etc. It is critical to always stay focused.

- When leaving the station follow the same procedure. Look to see what needs to be brought back out to the tables when returning to the station. Never leave or go to the dining room empty-handed.

Emergency Situations

If a guest becomes ill during the meal, or is choking, notify the manager immediately so that action can be taken. The server should try to remain with the guest as much as possible to attend to any needs, such as bringing a drink of water or a cold towel. If a guest has fallen, do not try to move the guest. Also, do not attempt to administer first-aid, except to ensure the guest's comfort. The manager or a designated person on the staff should be certified in first-aid training and qualified to provide immediate care. Ask the guest or those accompanying him or her if you should call 911 for emergency help. The restaurant should have standard guidelines for all employees to follow during any type of emergency situation.

Overview

A server's task is more than just taking an order; it begins with the server's ability to gain the guest's confidence that the server will provide the best in food and beverage service. A server who generates an enthusiastic atmosphere for guests, coupled with personal enthusiasm can produce a positive dining experience that will result in repeat business for the restaurant and increased tips for the server.

The server needs to be prepared to serve all types of guests, particularly those who may need special attention, such as the following: The *procrastinator* needs suggestions to help with a decision; the *skeptic* needs reassurance; the *"sender backer"* knows what he or she wants and the server must understand those needs; the *handicapped guest* needs assistance; the *older guest* may need some special consideration and help; the *child* may need patience and understanding and a parent's approval for menu selection; the *wise guy* needs to be handled with tact, but very firmly; the *talker* needs to be given short answers and quick service; the *silent type* appreciates understanding; the *dieter* wants knowledgeable answers regarding ingredients and cooking methods; the *blind guest* will appreciate being accommodated with courtesy; the *coffee drinker* should be handled according to house policy; the *budgeter* will need to know the less expensive items on the menu; and the *bad tipper* should be treated with the same attention and service as everyone else.

A professional server will always anticipate the needs of guests by keeping an alert eye on guests and promptly attending to their needs. The server should also be aware of nonverbal cues and prompts from the guests, such as menu and napkin positioning, body language displays, and physical expressions.

Suggestive selling needs to be done with tact. It requires the server to have self-confidence and a positive attitude. It takes complete knowledge of the menu and of the combinations that go well with the item selected by the guest. Suggestions should be made with enthusiasm and by using the menu descriptions to create an appetizing image. The server who successfully uses suggestive selling will increase guest check averages and tips. The larger the guest check, the larger the tip. Also, suggestive selling provides a definite service to the guest with the opportunity to have a better meal and a better value. The different types of suggestive selling include: selling the guest "up," suggesting "related" menu items, suggesting new menu items or the "chef's specialties," suggesting items for special occasions, and suggesting "take home" items. Also, showmanship in the dining room with specially served food items can effectively enhance sales to other guests.

The proper procedure for taking the guest's order needs to follow a system, and most restaurants will have a designated system for servers to follow. Finally, all emergency situations should be handled according to the policy set forth by the restaurant.

DISCUSSION QUESTIONS AND EXERCISES

1. What is involved when a server makes a personal connection with a guest?

2. Give three examples of a server introductory greeting to guests.

3. How can a server measure the effects of his or her service enthusiasm?

4. What is the first step in developing server enthusiasm?

5. List and describe the characteristics of 10 different types of guests.

6. How should a server react if a rude guest looks at the server and loudly says, "Hey shorty, I need more bread?"

7. When anticipating guest needs, what does "reading the guest" mean?

8. Give five examples of when a server can be proactive in anticipating guest needs.

9. List and describe two nonverbal cues and prompts from guests that can assist the server in anticipating guests' needs.

10. What is suggestive selling?

11. Explain the five different types of suggestive selling.

12. Which offers a greater opportunity for suggestive selling, a dinner or an à la carte menu? Explain your answer.

13. Why should the server always include menu descriptions when describing menu items to guests?

14. What is the effect of suggestive selling?

15. When practicing suggestive selling, how many choices within each food and beverage category should the server suggest to the guest?

16. List the three basic guidelines to follow for suggestive selling.

17. Give an example of when dining room showmanship suggestively sells.

18. Describe the procedure to follow when taking a guest's order.

19. Since timing can be critical during rush periods, identify three procedures that could help a server conserve steps.

20. What should a server do in an emergency situation when a guest becomes ill?

The Technology
of Service

Learning Objectives

After reading this chapter and completing the discussion questions and exercises, you should be able to

1. Define the terms that are most commonly used when discussing the operation of a POS system.

2. Understand and explain the areas of improved guest service when technology is properly implemented.

3. Describe how a table service management system functions.

4. Explain the advantages of a guest paging system.

5. Discuss the advantages of product management software.

6. Know when the use of hand-held touch-screen terminals would have the best application.

7. Explain how a server paging system functions.

8. Describe the purpose of a kitchen display system and explain how it works.

9. Know how two-way radios would be used in a restaurant operation.

10. Understand the purpose of an Electronic Comment Card™ survey system.

11. Understand and describe the functions of various POS system software applications and their benefits.

12. Understand the benefits of using restaurant websites and restaurant customer e-mail and fax communications.

13. Know the methods of training available through the advances in technology.

Since 1970, annual restaurant sales have increased from $42.8 to $376.2 billion in the year 2000. That is a 779 percent increase in thirty years! Over 11 million employees serve almost half the U.S. adult population daily in restaurants across this country. Without technology this would not be possible. The advance and accessibility of technology in the industry benefits both restaurants and consumers worldwide.

Every restaurant operation relies on technology in one form or another and in varying degrees, from the small deli that uses a limited function point-of-sale (POS) terminal to the massive computer system with over 400 terminals and thousands of employees for food, beverage, and merchandise sales operations at Stadium Australia for the 2000 Summer Olympics in Sydney. The employees, managers, and owners of restaurants must become technologically literate in order to succeed and remain competitive. This chapter will discuss current applications of technology as it pertains primarily to the server and restaurants in general.

Basic Point-of-Sale (POS) Terms

The following is a list of terms that are most commonly used when discussing the operation of a POS system.

- *Back Office.* Interface between POS and "back office" generating management reports that can include accounting, inventory, and payroll.

- *Banked Server.* A server who handles transactions directly for the guest without going through a cashier. The server will typically start with a personal bank of $20.00 (his or her own money) in change, consisting of a five-dollar bill, 10 or 12 one-dollar bills and the balance in coins. It is the responsibility of the server to have the change amounts before the shift starts. The server settles with the house at the end of the shift.

- *Electronic Draft Capture.* A cashier or server swipes the guest's credit card at the POS terminal. Then, automatic processing of credit card authorization through a processing network takes place, followed by consolidation of daily transactions for single batch transmission to the bank for fund settlement.

- *Frequent Diner Program.* Discounts and incentives offered to guests and tracked via the POS. Can also be used to profile buying habits for target marketing and promotions.

- *Menu Engineering.* Using the information gathered from POS and inventory management to compose a mix of menu items for maximum variety, price, and profit.

- *Modifiers.* Instructions for food preparation (e.g., on the side, medium or rare, etc.).

- *Outlet.* A specific area of the restaurant, such as an outdoor patio or bar, in which sales are generated independently from the restaurant and represent a separate revenue center.

- *Pre-Check/Post-Check.* Pre-check is initiated by the server and generates service from the kitchen or bar. This step starts the guest check immediately and ensures that every item ordered is charged to the server's sales. Post-check totals items when the server is ready to produce a check for the guest.

- *Requisition Printer.* The device that prints out the entire order once it has been entered into the POS system.

- *Remote Printer.* A printer that is located in a different area of the restaurant, such as in the bar or kitchen. For example, the server rings up a drink order and a ticket is printed in the bar, instructing the bartender to start preparing the drinks.

- *Terminal.* Refers to the device the server uses to enter sales. It could be at a fixed location or a hand-held remote mobile device.

- *Touch-Screen.* A terminal whose entries are made by touching points on a screen. The screen is similar to a computer monitor. There may be several displays available on a touch-screen, such as one for beverages, one for appetizers, etc.

- *Up-Selling Prompts.* Prompts that are installed into a POS system that serve to encourage the server to suggest additional items, such as appetizers, desserts, and beverages. For example, beverage prompts: When a menu item is ordered it immediately goes to a beverage screen that is designed to increase beverage sales. This is a forced screen, which means that the server is forced to respond to this screen by suggesting a beverage.

Technology Applications

When technology is properly implemented the results are reflected in improved guest service. This can begin with efficiently taking reservations, reducing wait times for seating, and increasing the speed of service. A point-of-sale (POS) system is fast and easy to use, as shown in Figure 8-1, and is designed to accomplish the following:

- Seat guests more quickly.

- Increase the speed of guest service by reducing order turnaround time.

- Increase the accuracy of food and beverage preparation and pricing.

FIGURE **8-1**
Point-of-Sale Terminal *Courtesy of Micros Systems, Inc.*

- Allow for ease in splitting guest checks.
- Eliminate math computation errors.
- Provide prompt, accurate guest check presentation.
- Reduce cash handling problems and/or errors.
- Provide fast and efficient credit card authorization.

TABLE SERVICE MANAGEMENT

The graphical table screen, touch-screen, flow management system, as shown in Figure 8-2, maximizes a restaurant's guest service efficiency. This system reduces guest wait times by shortening the time a table remains empty between departing and arriving guests. The manager, host/hostess, or maître d' assigns guest seating and touches the screen at the appropriate table assignment. The table lights up on the screen to indicate the table is in use. Time colored alerts on screen help show the activity status at each table. This can alert the host or manager when tables turn different colors due to lack of activity with their guest checks. When the guests have left and the table has been quickly cleared and set, the host is informed and the light goes off, indicating that the table is available for seating.

GUEST PAGING SYSTEM

The guest anxiety associated with having to wait for an available table has been tremendously reduced with the use of a guest paging system as shown in Figure 8-3. The number of "no-shows" and walkouts is minimized with the guest-friendly system. The guests can be alerted that their table is ready with the touch of a button, rather than over a noisy public address system. The guest paging system developed by JTECH Communications, Inc. shown in Figure 8-3, GuestAlert™, vibrates and flashes, and plays an audio message informing the guest that the table is ready. It also alerts guests when they have gone too far from the restaurant.

If the restaurant has a lounge, the guest may prefer to have a drink while waiting for a table. The flashing light and audio message is most effective in alerting the guest. If a restaurant is located in or near a shopping mall, the guest may enjoy visiting the stores. The vibrating function of the pager

FIGURE 8-2
Table Service Management *Courtesy of Micros Systems, Inc.*

FIGURE 8-3
GuestAlert™ *Courtesy of JTECH Communications, Inc.*

would be ideal if the pager were in the guest's pocket. The guest pager serves to establish a commitment between the restaurant and the guest by promptly alerting the guest when the table is ready. It further reduces the chaos that sometimes occurs at the host stand during busy times, seats more people, and contributes to a smoother running operation.

PRODUCT MANAGEMENT SOFTWARE

When product management software is implemented into a POS system that is designed to handle it, guest service is brought to a higher level by having important information available for servers. At the touch of a button, the server can view a menu item picture, list of recipe ingredients, nutritional information, serving instructions, preparation instructions or even a video clip on how to serve or prepare the item, as shown in Figure 8-4. The information can even be printed on the POS printer for the server or the guest. This greatly aids in helping a guest avoid any possibility of an allergic reaction to a certain food item or recipe ingredient. Along with menu item descriptions, appropriate wine suggestions may also be included.

HAND–HELD TOUCH–SCREEN TERMINAL

The hand-held terminal, shown in Figure 8-5, speeds service and allows the server to take orders directly at the table. This provides flexibility and portability in remote locations like patios. It is also ideal for stadiums, casinos, and resorts where the server must go some distance to serve guests. If a menu item is out of stock, the terminal informs the server before he or she leaves the guest.

SERVER PAGING SYSTEM

The server paging system, shown in Figure 8-6, clips to the server's belt or pocket and quietly vibrates when activated from the kitchen. This informs the server when food items are ready to be picked up and served to guests. The

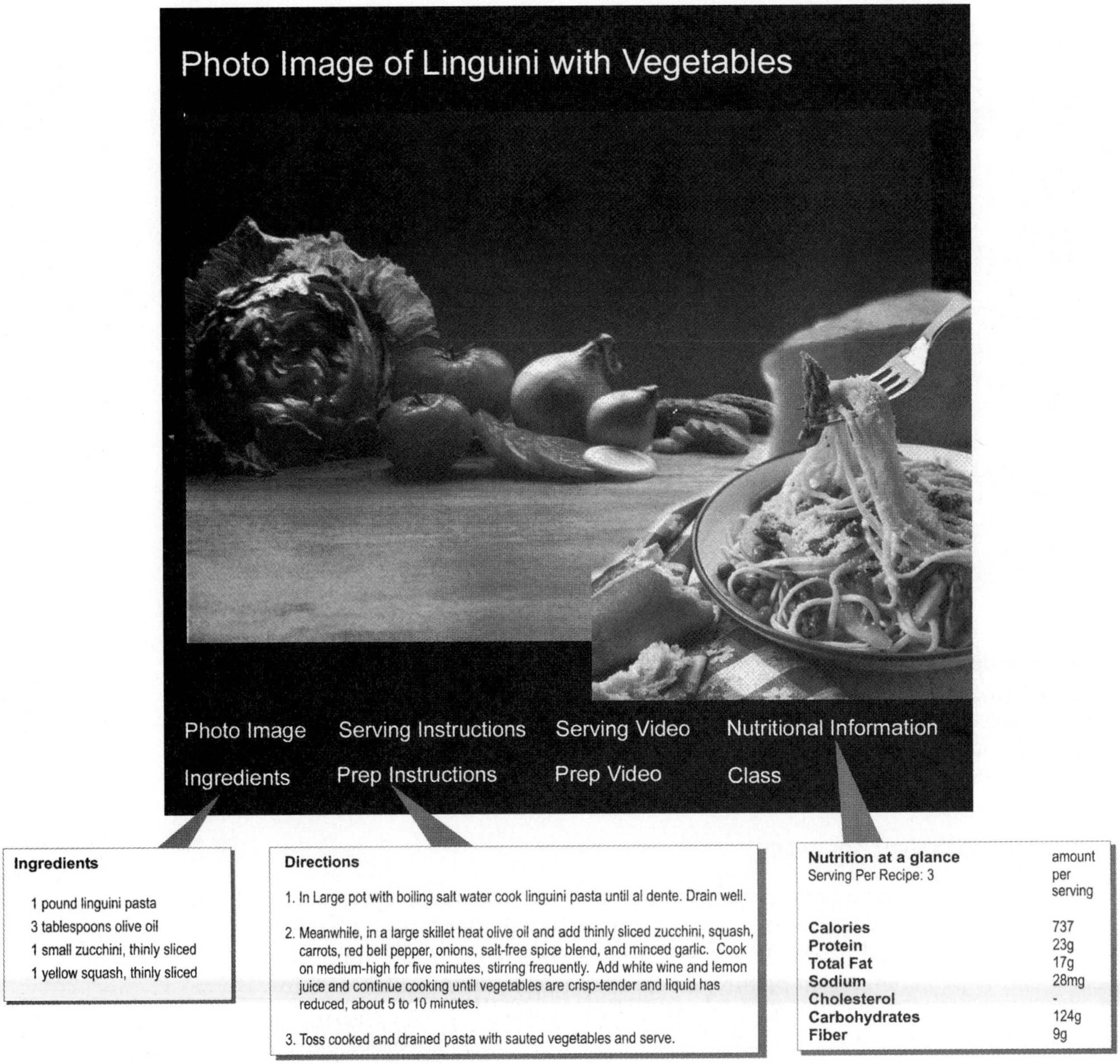

Photo Image of Linguini with Vegetables

Photo Image   Serving Instructions   Serving Video   Nutritional Information

Ingredients   Prep Instructions   Prep Video   Class

Ingredients

1 pound linguini pasta
3 tablespoons olive oil
1 small zucchini, thinly sliced
1 yellow squash, thinly sliced

Directions

1. In Large pot with boiling salt water cook linguini pasta until al dente. Drain well.

2. Meanwhile, in a large skillet heat olive oil and add thinly sliced zucchini, squash, carrots, red bell pepper, onions, salt-free spice blend, and minced garlic. Cook on medium-high for five minutes, stirring frequently. Add white wine and lemon juice and continue cooking until vegetables are crisp-tender and liquid has reduced, about 5 to 10 minutes.

3. Toss cooked and drained pasta with sauted vegetables and serve.

Nutrition at a glance	amount
Serving Per Recipe: 3	per serving
Calories	737
Protein	23g
Total Fat	17g
Sodium	28mg
Cholesterol	-
Carbohydrates	124g
Fiber	9g

FIGURE 8-4
Product Management Software *Courtesy of Micros Systems, Inc.*

system allows servers to be more efficient in promptly bringing guest orders from the kitchen.

Kitchen Display System The kitchen display system, shown in Figure 8-7, is a graphical software application designed to increase efficiency and improve guest service through better kitchen coordination. The system displays the dining room tables in one color. As guests are seated, the table designation on the screen changes color as controlled by the host staff. When the first order is entered, the color changes. After a certain time that color will change again, indicating the ticket time for the order working, thereby allowing the tracking of the production time. It can further identify the status of each table, and captures service times for each guest check and table. Each order is displayed, and the time is monitored for preparation. During order preparation, the system is programmed with highlight alert orders in different colors, such

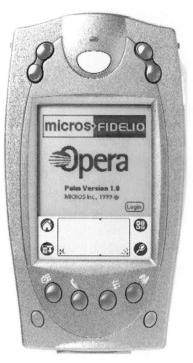

FIGURE 8-5
Hand-Held Touch-Screen Terminal *Courtesy of Micros Systems, Inc.*

as yellow or red, to indicate that an order has exceeded expected preparation time. Icons display a rush or VIP order and also display features to indicate when an order is done or recalled. The speed of service display views the status of each table in the restaurant at a glance. Table buttons change color to indicate: table vacant, guest seated, kitchen working on order, entrée served, or order late.

Two-Way Radio A restaurant can improve coordination between management, host/hostess, servers, and the kitchen in identifying open tables, notifying when food is ready to be served, and responding to any customer

FIGURE 8-6
ServAlert™ *Courtesy of JTECH Communications, Inc.*

FIGURE 8-7
Kitchen Display System *Courtesy of Micros Systems, Inc.*

request. Figure 8-8 shows a two-way radio that provides instant communication with the push of a button. Guests can be seated faster and servers can anticipate and react to guests' needs more quickly.

Electronic Comment Response The Electronic Comment Card™ survey system, shown in Figure 8-9, can be placed on the table along with the guest check. It allows the guest to immediately register his or her quality evaluation of the food and service. The card can be customized to meet a restaurant's needs, from the questions it asks, to the types of reports and summary information it requires. It can even notify the manager on the spot if a guest is dissatisfied, so immediate action can be taken.

FIGURE 8-8
TableAlert™ Motorola Spirit GT™ *Courtesy of JTECH Communications, Inc. and Motorola*

FIGURE 8-9
Electronic Comment Card™
Survey System *Courtesy of JTECH Communications, Inc.*

Software Applications POS systems typically have the capacity to add software that can strengthen every level of service in a restaurant operation, with the emphasis toward maximizing guest service and optimizing server productivity and selling time. Some of the more popular software applications are as follows:

- Credit card authorization to eliminate manual charge reconciliations to automate the settlement of funds.

- Speed tendering for a server, cashier, or bartender when taking various denominations of dollar bills; with one step the system can tender and compute exact change due back to the guest.

- Frequent diner programs that capture guest information and allow it to be accessed by name, telephone number, or other defined fields. Additional functionality can include creating, issuing, and redeeming gift certificates and rewards for frequent dining. Mailing labels can be generated in addition to a variety of database marketing and trend information, based on the data and sales history of a restaurant's guests.

- Multiple price levels that allow the restaurant to offer any happy hour or early bird menu pricing that may be needed. Prices can change by time of day and day of the week automatically.

- Separate or split guest check by item, person, group of seats or persons. This feature gives guests any format of guest check presentation they request.

- Gratuities automatically added to group guest checks. Large groups typically expect to pay a gratuity and it becomes easy to add it to the guest check.

- A "send" order allows the server to give appetizers or drinks from the bar a head start during the order process. The send order allows all the items entered at any given point to print immediately at their appropriate requisition printers or display monitors, such as in the kitchen (salad prep area) and in the bar.

■ A training mode (tutorial) for new servers, bartenders, cashiers, etc. that can be turned on or off and will not affect daily reports or print at remote requisition printers, but will walk the new employee through the ordering process.

■ Menu item modifiers that prompt the server in the exact way he or she wants to inform the kitchen, salad prep, or bar in specific preparation choices of the guest. If the modifier has not been programmed into the POS, a server can type what he or she wants to type and it will be relayed to the appropriate station. This can eliminate confusion over illegible handwriting and differences in abbreviations or terminology, and it reduces the server's trips to kitchen and/or bar.

■ Management reports that include the following functions:

   a. Labor management with labor scheduling
   b. Product management with inventory control, ordering, receiving, and supplier bids
   c. Financial management
   d. Employee time and attendance reporting
   e. Transaction analysis of sales activities, employee activities, etc.

B enefits of Technology

A POS system can provide a platform for a complete restaurant management system. The POS system can give the restaurant operator a solid foundation for all of the restaurant's information requirements and application needs. It begins with eliminating errors between servers and the kitchen, and it tracks everything being served and charged to the guest. Guest checks are fully accounted for according to each server. Guest orders instantaneously go directly to the kitchen's printer, with no chance of misplacement, which speeds up production and service, allowing the server to spend more time with guests for personalized service and merchandising. Printers print clean and clear type, reducing errors caused by poor handwriting.

Pre-check features allow the server to look up menu recipes to correctly advise guests with special requests about ingredients (no salt, diabetics, etc). It can also highlight features and promotions or alert the server of items no longer available. The post-check ensures a clean, clear check presentation for the guest. Additionally, some features enhance the speed and accuracy of producing separate checks, transfers between departments (bar tab transferred to the dining room), discounts, coupons, promotions, and adjustments to the bill.

Credit card transactions can be done on multiple terminals, reducing waiting time. Tips are automatically calculated and tallied, providing tip records for each server and the restaurant owner for tax reporting.

Server productivity, sales analysis, menu tracking (appetizers, wine, desserts, etc.) and labor can be tracked. This is useful for projecting service and menu focus, performance reviews, scheduling, contests, and seasonal adjustments. Promotions can be printed on guest checks (e.g., happy hour, holiday dinner special, etc). Some features include the ability for the server to create a personal message on the guest check, such as "Happy 25th Anniversary, Mr. & Mrs. Jones" or any other message with a total of 32 letters.

Hand-held terminals and two-way radios allow the server to provide enhanced tableside service. These are ideal for large properties such as resorts, hotels, convention centers, casinos, stadiums, theme parks, cruise ships, or caterers with multiple remote outlets. The speed of service is increased and the number of server trips is reduced. Guest pagers, which alert the customer when a table is ready, as well as server paging systems, are additional examples of technology that enhances a restaurant's efficiency.

A system can automatically track time and attendance information that can be downloaded to the back office or a payroll service (if used). Some systems have training mode applications that allow new hires to become productive on the POS in a short time. There are applications for direct automated purchasing, receiving, and inventory to control waste, theft, and stock levels. These can be programmed for simultaneous access to multiple products and suppliers.

Technology can manage and control all aspects of a restaurant operation if properly used. A POS system can be designed to simplify the difficult task of maintaining tight financial control, eliminate costly errors, save time, and be the vehicle that allows the servers to provide the best in customer service by being able to spend more time with guests.

R estaurant Websites

The use of the Internet for promotion is ever increasing. There are restaurant websites that include photos of the restaurant building, dinning and banquet rooms, the menu, wine lists, and actual plate presentations. In addition, they can include hours of operation, house specialties, newspaper and magazine reviews, upcoming promotions, online reservations, contact information, specialty items for sale, and a map with directions to the restaurant. The history of the restaurant along with professional profiles of the owner, chef, manager, and musical entertainers can further support the restaurant's reputation. Some restaurant sites even list key local events along with website links to the local chamber of commerce and convention and visitors bureau. This can motivate the diner to visit the restaurant's community. There is virtually no limit to what can be included on a website. An example of a very complete website is that of New Orleans famous Arnaud's Restaurant, www.arnauds.com. This site also includes a section for customer comments and an employment application for potential employees.

E -mail or Fax

E-mail and fax are used to promote daily or weekly menus, to announce a special meal or price incentives, and to inform patrons of upcoming entertainment or other activities that may be scheduled to take place in the restaurant. A restaurant can start a mailing list by offering the service to existing and potential customers. This allows the restaurant to connect with customers on a regular basis and on special occasions, such as birthdays, anniversaries, and holidays. It can also allow the restaurant to experiment with promoting party menus and take-out orders, as well as soliciting customer likes, dislikes, and preferences.

Training with Technology

Training at all levels of the restaurant and hospitality industry includes video, online training services, and use of CD-ROMs. Industry professionals, associations, and manufacturers have typically developed the material. It offers the advantage of flexibility, as the user decides when to view a training session.

Overview

Restaurant technology continues to grow and expand in fulfilling the requirements and application needs of the rapidly growing restaurant and hospitality industry. Employees, managers, and owners of restaurants must become technology literate in order to succeed and remain competitive.

Some of the most commonly used terms when discussing the operation of a point-of-sale (POS) system include the following: Back office, banked server, electronic draft capture, frequent diner program, menu engineering, modifiers, outlet, pre-check/post-check, requisition printer, terminal, touch-screen, and up-selling prompts. A POS system is fast and easy to use, and designed to accomplish the following:

- Seat guests more quickly.
- Increase the speed of guest service by reducing order turnaround time.
- Increase the accuracy of food and beverage preparation and pricing.
- Allow for ease in splitting guest checks.
- Eliminate math computation errors.
- Provide prompt, accurate guest check presentation.
- Reduce cash handling problems and/or errors.
- Provide fast and efficient credit card authorization.

Additional technology applications include table service management, guest paging, product management software, hand-held touch-screen terminals, server paging, kitchen display system, two-way radio usage, electronic customer comment response card, and various software applications. Technology can manage and control all aspects of a restaurant operation if properly used. A POS can be designed to simplify the difficult task of maintaining tight financial control, eliminate costly errors, save time, and be the vehicle that allows servers to provide the best customer service.

Restaurant websites have the capability of promoting a restaurant's business. E-mail communication between a restaurant and its customers can further serve to build customer loyalty and repeat business.

DISCUSSION QUESTIONS AND EXERCISES

1. Define the following list of terms that are commonly used when discussing the operation of a POS system:
   - Back Office
   - Banked Server
   - Electronic Draft Capture

- Frequent Diner Program
- Menu Engineering
- Modifiers
- Outlet
- Pre-Check/Post-Check
- Requisition Printer
- Terminal
- Touch-Screen
- Up-selling Prompts

2. Identify eight areas of improved guest service that result when technology is properly implemented.

3. Explain how a graphical table screen, touch-screen, flow management system functions.

4. Describe how the GuestAlert™ paging system works and how a restaurant benefits from its use.

5. What are the advantages of product management software?

6. Where would hand-held touch-screen terminals ideally be used?

7. Explain how a server paging system functions.

8. Describe the purpose of a kitchen display system and explain how it works.

9. List three examples of when a two-way radio might be used.

10. What is the purpose of the Electronic Comment Card™ survey system?

11. Identify and describe the functions of six different POS system software applications.

12. Visit a restaurant website and report your findings in a one-page written report.

13. Search out restaurants in your community that are using e-mail to communicate with their customers. Pick one such restaurant and describe your reaction to their e-mail messages.

14. View a training session (you pick the restaurant industry topic) either on a video, through an online training service, or on a CD-ROM and discuss your judgment of the competence and professionalism of the training presentation.

15. Schedule an appointment with the owner or manager of a restaurant in your community that may be using some or all of the technology presented in this chapter. Inquire how his or her information requirements and application needs are being met. Then write a one-page report describing your findings.

9

The Host/Hostess

Learning Objectives

After reading this chapter and completing the discussion questions and exercises, you should be able to

1. Understand the duties, functions, and responsibilities of a host/hostess.

2. Handle table delays when guests may have to wait 15 minutes or more for the next available table.

3. Understand how guests should be seated.

4. Explain how a table service management system functions.

5. Describe the correct way to present menus to guests.

6. List the many other duties that a host/hostess will be expected to perform when a restaurant is extremely busy.

7. Understand why the host/hostess-cashier would process a guest check payment before seating arriving guests.

8. Understand how the host/hostess should handle guest complaints.

9. Describe the procedure that the host/hostess should follow when taking a guest's reservations.

10. Describe the procedure that the host/hostess should follow when taking a "to go" order.

11. Explain the supervision functions that a host/hostess may have to perform.

12. Identify the items that would be discussed at a menu meeting.

The position of host/hostess can function in many different ways, according to the type and size of the restaurant and its organizational structure. A large fine dining restaurant may have a dining room manager who hires, trains, and schedules servers along with managing all the functions of the operation. The dining room manager may also organize food and/or wine tastings for servers in addition to ongoing training to review operational procedures and new menu items. The host/hostess may simply greet and seat guests. A maître d' or head waiter/waitress may assign server stations and supervise the service staff, as well as provide input to the manager for server performance evaluations.

A small family restaurant operation may have a manager who works the dining room floor in addition to managing all of these functions. Another type of operation may involve the host/hostess as a supervisor in the absence of the manager or owner, and he or she may be responsible for all or some part of these functions. Therefore, the responsibilities for the host/hostess position will vary and be set forth by the needs of each individual restaurant operation.

Greeting Guests

"The taste of the roast is often determined by the welcome of the host."

—Ben Franklin

This quote by Ben Franklin rings true. It is the host/hostess who creates the valuable first impression for guests. A warm, congenial atmosphere begins with a sincere smile and welcome greeting; guests will tend to feel wanted and appreciated immediately.

The host/hostess position in most restaurants is one of an official greeter, as this is the person who in some cases actually opens the door and welcomes guests into the restaurant. Therefore, the personality of the host/hostess requires the ability to take pressures such as handling a mealtime rush, accommodating various sizes of parties, effectively taking care of guests in a hurry, and assisting families with unruly children. The effective host/hostess will never allow this type of pressure to affect his or her performance with guests.

Whenever possible, guests should be greeted as soon as they enter the restaurant. The first thing that should happen is eye-to-eye contact with an accompanying smile and greeting, such as, "Good evening, how are you folks tonight?"

Guests expect the host/hostess to speak first, and then they will reply. The host/hostess who projects sincerity, maintains eye contact, and conveys a genuine interest in guests, will inspire a positive answer to the greeting, "Good evening, how are you folks tonight?"

As the guests respond to the question, listen attentively. The guest response will determine the next line of conversation. A host/hostess can develop impressive conversational abilities as he or she interrelates with guests. If a reservation is expected, ask if they have a reservation; if not, fine. If there are doubts about how many are in the party, ask. Then select an appropriate table according to party size. If an individual is dining alone, simply say: "Table for one, Sir/Ma'am?" Never refer to the person as a party of one or ask if he or she is eating alone. Whether one or a large party of guests, all guests should be made to feel important and treated as individuals. Also, the host/hostess should ask the guest's preference for either the smoking or non-smoking section of the restaurant.

When a guest's name is known by a reservation or remembered from a previous visit, the guest's name should always be used. "Mr. And Mrs. Jones, welcome to (the name of the restaurant)!" "Mr. & Mrs. Jones, it is always good to see you again!" As the theme song from the popular television show *Cheers* stated, "A place where everybody knows your name," is a place that people enjoy returning to time and again. Therefore, every effort should be made to remember guest's names to add value to their visit. Guests without reservations may be asked their name so the host/hostess could then record it properly on a waiting list. Additional marketing information could be gathered; for example—if this is a first time visit, how they found out about the restaurant, or if they are celebrating any special occasion, such as a birthday or anniversary.

During certain peak periods, guests may have to wait 15 minutes or more for the next available table. When this occurs, along with asking the guest's name for a waiting list, the host/hostess should say, "We are a bit busy tonight, but tables should be available shortly, only about a 15 minute wait." If the exact waiting time is uncertain, it is better to slightly overestimate the expected waiting time and be able to seat the guests sooner, rather than underestimating the time and having disappointed guests. If the restaurant has a lounge, offer to immediately seat the guests in the lounge where they can order drinks and appetizers. Further offering, "As soon as your table is available, I will come and get you." If the guests have not finished their drinks or appetizers, the host/hostess can help carry them to their table. Some restaurants use a guest paging system, as discussed in Chapter 8, where the guest is handed a small message device that is activated with the touch of a button, and alerts the guest by vibrating, flashing, or announcing when his or her table is ready.

Table Selection

Table selection begins by selecting tables that will provide the maximum comfort for guests. Therefore, guests should never be tightly seated at a table, and a large person should never be seated at a small table. In some situations two tables need to be put together. Guests should always have plenty of "elbow room" in order to be able to enjoy their meal. Since guest needs are not the same, the host/hostess should always personalize table selection. If regular guests request the same table, make a point of remembering it, and tell them that "their special table" is ready. These are the personal touches that can distinguish a restaurant's service.

To facilitate the speed of table selection, some restaurants use table service management systems, as discussed in Chapter 8. These systems provide a graphical table display on the POS screen that show available tables for immediate guest seating, as well as tables already in use. Controlling the seating flow is essential to maintaining a smooth tempo for the entire restaurant, as guests are alternately seated in servers' stations, allowing for a smooth flow of service and not overloading any one station.

At the beginning of a meal period or in the afternoon when the dining room may be empty, guests should be seated in the center of the room where they can be seen from the door, giving the impression that the dining room is somewhat busy. Large parties may tend to be noisy; if possible, they should be seated near the back of the restaurant so they will not disturb other guests. A handicapped guest should be seated in a convenient location away from traffic flow.

Professional Courtesies

The host/hostess should be prepared and ready to help remove guest coats, if appropriate, and if the guest acknowledges wanting the help. When this occurs, the procedure is to stand behind the guest and lift the shoulder of the coat while carefully slipping the coat off the arms. If the restaurant has a coat checkroom this should take place there; otherwise it should take place at the table. Coats then should be taken to a coat rack unless the guest wants to keep it and hang it on the chair. If that is the case, be careful that the coat does not drag on the floor where it could be soiled or tripped over.

When showing guests to a table, the host/hostess should always walk a step or two ahead of them at a comfortable pace, perhaps sharing a conversation that will allow them to feel comfortable and at ease. As you arrive at the table, pull out the chairs for guests to be seated. If a woman is being seated, you may want to lightly push the chair back as she sits down, unless her escort advances to do that for her. A high chair for infants or booster seat for small children may need to be furnished. Offer to help seat the child if the guests desire the service.

Open and present a menu directly in front of each guest, suggesting a specific appetizer, chef's specialty, or menu items that have made the restaurant famous. Make sure the guests are comfortable and tell them that their server will be right over. If you know their names, personalize it by saying, "Mr. and Mrs. Jones, Paul will be your server this evening." If it is extremely busy and Paul cannot immediately bring the water to the table, the host/ hostess should do so, while assuring the guests that any delay in service is only temporary. Also, the host/hostess should inform the server of guests' special occasions, such as a birthday, anniversary, school graduation, etc. Guests will often mention this to the host/hostess while making a reservation or while being seated at their table.

The host/hostess is usually expected to help in any way possible when needed. When it is extremely busy, he or she may be required to bus tables, pour coffee, fill waters, and help with orders. This means that the host/ hostess has to be flexible by nature as well as having the capacity to perform multiple tasks in order to help make the operation run smoothly. Therefore, a host/hostess should be able to set an effective and efficient pace for the service staff to follow. Then teamwork allows the guest to receive the best possible service.

The host/hostess, when also acting as the cashier, should always promptly process guest checks, even before seating arriving guests. Guests who have finished dining, and wish to leave, should not be inconvenienced by having to wait to pay for their meal. Also, many guests do not put down a tip until after they have paid and acquired change. Therefore, the process should be made quick and easy for the guest.

As guests are leaving the restaurant, the host/hostess may have the opportunity to open the door for the guests and bid them good-bye, along with an appreciative thanks and sincere invitation to return again soon.

Handling Complaints

The host/hostess-cashier will tend to get the bulk of any guest complaints. Guests who have a complaint about their visit to a restaurant sometimes wait until they have paid their check before they complain. The way the host/hostess-cashier handles a complaint could mean saving or losing this guest's future business. If the complaint is a serious one, the manager should be called immediately to discuss the problem with the guest. It might be a valid complaint that requires the manager's immediate attention. At any rate, the presence of the manager indicates to the guest that management is concerned and wants to correct problems that cause guest dissatisfaction. If the problem does not seem serious enough to call the manager and the guest does not request the manager, the host/hostess-cashier should write the complaint down on a notepad, in the presence of the guest, and assure him or her that it will receive the manager's attention. Further, ask the guest if he or she would like to leave a name and telephone number for the manager to call. Then thank the guest, sincerely apologize for the problem, and extend a warm invitation to return again soon. The note should be given to the manager with any further explanation, if necessary, at the close of the shift.

Taking Telephone Reservations and "To Go" Orders

The telephone should always be answered according to restaurant policy; for example, "Good evening, (name of the restaurant), may I help you please?"

When recording the reservation, repeat and spell the guest's name: "That is Mr. Wilkinson" (spell the name). Repeat the number in the party: "A party of four;" and the time, "6:00 P.M." Specify the day and date (Friday, month and day); also note any special occasion, such as a birthday or anniversary. Some restaurants request the guest's telephone number and/or e-mail address along with a credit card number to guarantee the reservation. This is particularly the case during peak times, such as Valentine's Day, Mother's Day, or New Year's Eve. If the guest does not keep the reservation, the restaurant may have a minimum service charge for holding the table that will be charged to the guest's credit card. If this is the policy of the restaurant, guests are informed when the reservation is made, and told what the charge would be.

When making the reservation, take the opportunity to pre-sell, such as, "We could have a fresh baked six-inch round double layer birthday cake ready and inscribed, should we order it for you?" "Since it is your anniversary, should we reserve a bottle of champagne?" "Our fresh stuffed mushrooms are mushroom caps with bay shrimp, baked with sherry and cheese, topped with fresh scallions, would you like to reserve an order?" When reservations are requested for larger than normal parties, they should be referred to the manager, according to the policy of the restaurant.

The host/hostess may also be responsible for "to go" orders. The specifics of those orders should be just as detailed as when taking a reservation. The host/hostess should know the restaurant menu well and up-sell using the appropriate suggestions. Repeat and spell the guest's name; repeat the guest's telephone number, menu order, and the time that the guest will be picking up the order. Then state the cost of the order.

Occasionally, people may call to request directions for getting to the restaurant. This is particularly the case for out-of-town visitors who may be staying in town for a few days or just traveling through. The host/hostess should be familiar enough with the community to be able to accurately give directions. Then ask the person to repeat the directions back so that he or she clearly understands them, and say, "We look forward to welcoming you to (name of the restaurant); shall we make a reservation for you?" Often, when paying their guest check, guests will ask for directions to a certain theater, museum, shopping mall, or other place of interest. The host/hostess should always be able to provide accurate directions.

People may also call the restaurant to inquire about the menu. The host/hostess should use the server skills of suggestive selling by first saying, "We have terrific beef, chicken, seafood, and pasta, which do you prefer?" When narrowing the person's interests, the host/hostess can then make the appropriate suggestions from the menu along with stating the menu prices. The key is to ask the right questions and attentively listen to the answers in order to be in a position to intelligently inform the person about the menu offerings. Then follow up by asking, "Can I make a reservation for you?"

Server Supervision

When the host/hostess is in charge of the service staff it is essential that he or she have total awareness and control of the front of the restaurant. This begins with proper planning that could include the following:

- Arrive at work at least 15 to 30 minutes before the service staff arrives in order to go through the normal checklists.

- Check the work schedules for servers and bus attendants to ensure proper staffing. Also inquire if anyone on the schedule has called in sick or unable to come to work for any other reason.

- Check the reservation book and compare the number of reservations with the normal amount of open business to verify that there is an adequate number of servers and bus attendants. If not, the manager should immediately be consulted.

- Assign servers to their stations. Also, assign reservations to stations, if needed. For example, to accommodate a party of 12, three tables may need to be moved together and set.

- Check restrooms to ensure that they are sparkling clean and adequately supplied.

- Check foyer (entrance area) for cleanliness.

- If appropriate, check lighting and music.

- When business is slow and it is evident that too many servers have been scheduled, it may become necessary to cut back on the number of servers, by either asking the first server who came in to check out or by tactfully asking if any of the servers would like to leave early. The host/hostess or the manager may have this responsibility, depending upon the policy of the restaurant.

The host/hostess may be responsible for many other front-of-the-restaurant details as assigned by the restaurant manager.

Menu Meetings

The host/hostess may schedule menu meetings for once a week or daily just before the shift begins, depending upon the needs of the restaurant operation. The meetings should be short and focused, with specific information to help the service staff be better informed, to generate enthusiasm, to develop teamwork, and to build morale. Items that could be discussed during these meetings include the following:

- New menu items or daily specials. The ingredients could be explained along with the cooking methods and serving procedures. The servers could also be allowed to taste a sample, preparing them to discuss these items when suggesting to guests.
- Recognition and performance praise for accomplishments and good work.
- Be open to feedback from servers and staff.
- Announce upcoming special events or other items pertaining to the restaurant.
- A quick review of restaurant policies, if needed.
- Share valid guest complaints and listen to any service staff complaints.
- Side-work schedules.
- Inspection of personal appearance and uniforms.

Overview

The host/hostess position can function in many different ways according to the type and size of restaurant along with the restaurant's organizational structure. The responsibilities of the position vary from simply greeting and seating guests to dining room and service staff supervision. The host/hostess must be able to take pressures such as handling a mealtime rush, accommodating various party sizes, effectively taking care of guests in a hurry, and assisting families with unruly children; he or she must never allow those pressures to affect his or her performance with the guests.

The host/hostess should be competent in tactfully handling table delays by offering to seat guests in the lounge, when possible, where they can order drinks and appetizers until their table is ready. It is important to keep communication going by giving realistic waiting times and keeping guests informed of the situation. The selection of tables that will provide maximum comfort for guests to fully enjoy their meal is also important. The host/hostess has the responsibility to control the seating flow in order to maintain a smooth tempo for the entire restaurant, as guests are alternately seated in servers' stations allowing for a smooth flow of service.

Among the many professional courtesies that the host/hostess should perform are helping guests with their coats, pulling out chairs for guests to be seated, and opening and presenting a menu in front of each guest. Also, he or she should be flexible during the busy times and assist with bussing tables, pouring coffee, filling waters, and helping with orders. The host/hostess, when also acting as the cashier, should be attentive in handling any guest complaints, and be sincere when inquiring about the guest's dining experience. When possible, ask about the guest's specific menu item, such as, "How was your New York steak?"

When taking telephone reservations and/or "to go" orders, a specific procedure should be followed to ensure accuracy at all times. The host/ hostess should also be familiar with the community in order to provide guests with directions and points of interest within the community.

The host/hostess will often have supervision responsibilities and therefore must be able to control the front-of-the-restaurant operations, including proper planning and assignments. They should schedule menu meetings to inform and motivate the service staff.

DISCUSSION QUESTIONS AND EXERCISES

1. What will determine the duties and responsibilities of a host/hostess?
2. When a guest's name is known, why should it always be used?
3. What should the host/hostess tell guests when they will have to wait 15 minutes or more for a table?
4. How should guests be seated?
5. Explain a table management system.
6. When should guests be seated in the center of the dining room and why?
7. How should guests' coats be handled?
8. How should menus be presented to guests?
9. When the restaurant is extremely busy, what other duties are the host/hostess often expected to perform?
10. Why would the host/hostess-cashier process the payment of a guest check before seating arriving guests?
11. How should the host/hostess, when acting as cashier, handle any guest complaints?
12. What procedure should the host/hostess follow when taking a guest's reservations?
13. What procedure should the host/hostess follow when taking a "to go" order?
14. Describe five supervision functions that a host/hostess may have to perform.
15. List five items that could be discussed at a menu meeting.

10
Waiter-Waitress Profiles

L earning Objectives

After reading this chapter and completing the discussion questions and exercises, you should be able to

1. Identify the successful characteristics of a waiter-waitress (server).
2. Relate to the individual server profiles.
3. Understand the functions and benefits of AIMHIRE® application software.
4. Complete a personal profile overview.

This chapter is designed to put a human face to the professional waiter-waitress (server). Brenda Carlos, Publisher of the Hospitality News Group, which publishes regional foodservice industry newspapers and an international education guide, conducted interviews with 10 successful servers from across the United States. Their employment experience ranges from fine dining to family and theme type restaurant operations. Some of the individuals interviewed have made serving their lifelong careers; others have used the position to meet their needs during certain times in their lives. All were recommended as top performers who epitomized the "best of the best."

Among those interviewed is the first place winner of the Sweet 'N Low® Great Waiter™ Awards Contest for 2000 and the winner of the California Restaurant Association's Front of the House Employee of the Year in 2000. The servers were working in the following cities: Kalamazoo, Salt Lake City, Honolulu, New Orleans, Salem, New York, Modesto, St. Louis, Portland, and San Francisco.

The AIMHIRE® Tutor software program that can be accessed via the Internet will introduce the reader/user to a personality assessment software that has been specifically developed for the foodservice industry. It will further allow the reader/user to experience a personal profile overview. The program is to be viewed as a tool to help identify personality characteristics that will allow an individual to be successful as a server, recognizing that success is a combination of personality characteristics, personal goals, experiences, desires, motivation, and determination.

Profiles

Chris Pabreza, Kalamazoo, MI

Brent Hendrickson, Salt Lake City, UT

Vilma Ang, Honolulu, HI

Reginald Broussard, New Orleans, LA

Shirley Mills, Salem, OR

Michel Meliarenne, New York, NY

Vicki Schultz, Modesto, CA

Jean Hawkins, St. Louis, MO

Joel Whitt, Portland, OR

George Vrakes, San Francisco, CA

Commentary by Brenda Carlos

From Sweet'n Low® comes the Great Waiter™ Awards Contest, a national program designed to recognize and reward quality service at all levels of the foodservice industry. In 2000 the award went to Chris Pabreza, a waitress from Kalamazoo, MI, with more than twenty years experience.

Chris Pabreza
Sinapore Aire's London Grill
Kalamazoo, MI

It all began when Pabreza's former boss nominated her by submitting an essay on why Pabreza should be recognized. Then Sweet'n Low® sent in "spies" to observe her in action. Judges were looking for the essential qualities of good service, including attention to customers' needs, a caring and committed attitude, and skills appropriate to the foodservice operation.

Pabreza had always planned on being a high school English teacher. In fact she went to college and obtained her degree. When high school teaching positions were scarce she enrolled in graduate school to learn computer programming. "It didn't take long for me to come to the conclusion that computer programming just wasn't for me. I'm a people lover and need to be around people," says Pabreza.

She had roots in the hospitality industry. At age 15 she started as a car hop at the local A&W restaurant. "I soon graduated from car hopping to table waiting and continued working at that A&W through college. It was fun work and I always enjoyed it," says Pabreza. So when the new college graduate left school she naturally turned to a profession that she loved.

Pabreza, who is single, has been able to purchase her own home and set money aside for her retirement. She admits that the money is decent but enjoying her work is worth more to her than a big paycheck. One drawback to the industry has always been the lack of benefits. But things are changing. For the first time in over 30 years Chris now works for a company that provides full health benefits.

Pabreza has a little advice to others entering the profession, "Learn to understand body language. By being observant a server should be able to know when a customer wants to talk or needs something. Be sure that you write things down unless you can memorize the order without ever faltering."

Pabreza says she can't imagine ever doing anything else except for possibly combining her love of the hospitality industry with her English skills. Some day she just might write a murder mystery that takes place, you guessed it, in a restaurant.

■ ■ ■ ■ ■

The Terrace Restaurant at the Salt Lake City airport is located on the upper deck and overlooks the flight deck. It is a casual, fine dining restaurant. Customers include travelers from all over the world and regular airline employees needing a good meal before a flight.

Brent Hendrickson
The Terrace Restaurant
SLC Airport
Salt Lake City, UT

Serving guests at a busy upscale airport restaurant is a unique experience. It is never predictable—a crowd can grow from just a few guests to several hundred in a matter of minutes. For Brent Hendrickson, who works at Salt Lake City Airport Terrace Restaurant operated by HMS Host, that's part of the intrigue and charm of being a server.

Hendrickson thinks his sense of humor is what gets him through the stressful times. "It's important to remember that many of my customers have been traveling all day. They are hungry and tired. Many have experienced flight delays or cancellations. A little touch of humor can often turn around their attitudes. I really try to have fun with the people that I serve," says Hendrickson, who began his career at age 15 working for a local Salt Lake City amusement park cafeteria.

When asked whether he is interested in restaurant management opportunities, Hendrickson replied, "I have worked in and out of this industry for over 20 years now and I have discovered that if your name isn't on the door then you'd better be on the floor. While management is a good path, there are a lot of dues to pay."

Being in an airport restaurant means that Hendrickson has the opportunity to serve customers over and over as they fly in and out of Salt Lake City. "Having a good memory has served me well. I seem to have a knack for remembering people and what they like to eat and drink. My customers are impressed that I care enough to remember," adds Hendrickson.

Much of his success can be traced back to one of his earliest jobs at the famed Hotel Utah where he worked in room service. "My boss taught me how to present the foods with careful attention to detail. She was a task master but I learned the art of serving well from her. To this day I anticipate the needs of my customers. I call it silent service. When a guest orders buffalo wings I anticipate that he or she will probably need a second napkin. Attention to detail is a must. That's why my customers ask for me. They appreciate that kind of service," concludes Hendrickson.

■ ■ ■ ■ ■

Vilma Ang
Roy's
6600 Kalanianaole Hwy.
Honolulu, HI

Roy's in Honolulu is the flagship restaurant of the ever-growing chain known for its upscale Euro-Asian cuisine.

It all began in her grandmother's kitchen in the Philippines. Vilma Ang practically grew up in that kitchen under the tutelage of her grandmother who loved to cook and loved to serve others. So years later, after her family immigrated to the US and Ang needed a job, it wasn't surprising that she turned to foodservice.

"After graduating from high school in Oregon I left home and moved to San Francisco. I found a job as a waitress in one of the Alioto's restaurants. Soon after, I moved on to the Hard Rock Café in San Francisco," notes Ang. The work was fun and easy and she excelled.

In 2000 Ang relocated to Oahu where her fiancé was transferred. There she found a new restaurant family to join—Roy's Restaurant.

"We are delighted to have Vilma Ang on our staff. When we interview individuals to work as servers at Roy's we look for individuals with 'heart.' We can teach them the techniques to become a great server but we can't give them 'heart.' Vilma has 'heart,' in other words, she has a passion to serve others and gives her customers over 100 percent of her time and energies," according to Roy's general manager, Rainer Kumbroch.

"I love to go to work. It's so much fun. My goal is to make my customers happy. There's an old Chinese proverb that states, 'Smiles open all doors.' I believe that—and always use my smile. Being a professional server has given me a very comfortable life. I generally work 25 hours a week and I earn a very comfortable living. In fact I know I earn more than I could if I was working in an office or teaching school. Plus my work doesn't interfere with my life. I have many outside interests and love to take classes during the day. This is a great lifestyle!" adds Ang.

Being able to upsell has certainly added to Ang's ability to make good tips. She continues "It's important to listen to what my customers are looking for—if they mention fish then I focus on fish and describe each entrée in detail making my words 'melt in their mouths.' I use facial expressions to help sell the food to my customers. It's really easy when you work at a restau, ant like Roy's that prepares such lovely food. But my greatest reward is seeing smiles come back to me from happy, satisfied guests."

■ ■ ■ ■ ■

Located in the heart of Bourbon Street in New Orleans is the Rue Bourbon Restaurant, known for its innovative culinary masterpieces and romantic Old World atmosphere.

Reginald Broussard
Rue Bourbon
241 Rue Bourbon
New Orleans, LA

The waitstaff constits of hospitality professionals who have dedicated their careers to fine dining. Attentive, courteous, and committed to providing the restaruant's guests with the best in fine dining service, Reginald Broussard, a Rue Bourbon waiter, epitomizes the restaurants's philosophy. Broussard has the hospitality business in his blood. A number of his uncles and several brothers work in the industry.

"I started as a dishwasher back when I was 17. Working my way up to busboy and eventually waiter, I have found being a waiter to be quite fulfilling," shares Broussard. After a hiatus working in the Louisiana oil fields, Broussard was happy to return to the industry 14 years ago and has been a waiter ever since. He claims that being a waiter has provided him with a rewarding career and given him the financial stability he has needed as a father of three growing children.

Broussard continues, "My job is to make people happy and to keep things flowing. As a waiter you must leave your problems at home. I have to be 100 percent attentive to my customers' needs from the minute I walk in the door to the minute I walk out. Over the years I've developed a knack of looking around my section and knowing immediately which table setting is missing a fork, a salt shaker, or who needs a napkin. You must become extremely observant."

Being a waiter in an historic Bourbon Street restaurant has given Broussard the opportunity of serving many famous guests including musicians, football players, and television and movie stars. "I try to serve every guest the same, it doesn't matter if they are famous or not, I am there to give them the best experience imaginable. I really like to make people happy. There aren't many other professions where you have the opportunity to do that over and over each day," says Broussard.

When asked if he would ever consider restaurant management positions Broussard quickly states, "No way, that would remove me from the people that I love to serve."

■ ■ ■ ■ ■

The Original Pancake House was started by Ferd and Gen Hueneke and their son Tom in 1958. Upon his parent's retirement, Tom took over the ownership and management of the restaurant. The Original Pancake House is known throughout the region as a high-quality breakfast house. Famous for its German and Apple Pancakes, freshly squeezed orange juice, and traditional breakfast fare, the restaurant has built a sterling reputation and loyal following.

Shirley Mills
The Original Pancake House
4685 Portland Road NE
Salem, OR

As a single 22-year-old, Shirley Mills relocated from Nebraska to Salem in 1957. Having worked as a waitress back home, Mills looked in the paper for a similar job opening. An announcement ran in the local paper about a new restaurant opening, The Original Pancake House. It sounded like a nice place to work and Mills applied for the job. She was hired and two weeks after the restaurant opened, Mills began her job—that was January, 1958.

Today, Mills has become an institution at the popular breakfast spot. For the first 20 years, she worked six days a week. She gradually lessened her schedule and now, over 40 years later, she works two days a week. "It's my life, I'm not ready to quit. My customers are my family," says Mills. During her tenure Mills has become a wife, (she married a man with the same last name as her maiden name, so she remained Shirley Mills) mother, and a grandmother. Her daughter now works at a second location of The Original Pancake House across town.

Mills believes that in order to be a successful server you must make three people happy. First and foremost you must make your boss happy. Going above and beyond what her boss expects has always been a trademark of Mills.

Second, Mills believes that you must make your customers happy. "Treat people with respect. Greet them and let them know you care." Mills adds that over the years she has become very close to many of her customers. It is not uncommon for Mills to receive invitations to weddings, and she has attended the funerals of many of her dear customers.

The third and final person that you must make happy is the one in the middle between the boss and the customer, and that's yourself. "I have to be happy in order to be able to fulfill my job responsibilities," adds Mills. "I'm really lucky. I love my work. I love my customers. I work for fantastic people who believe in offering top quality food. I am proud of everything on our menu and that makes serving it a real pleasure," ends Mills.

■ ■ ■ ■ ■

Michel Meliarenne
Payard Patisserie &
Bistro
1032 Lexington Ave.
New York, NY

Payard Patisserie & Bistro, established in August of 1997 by third-generation patissier Francois Payard, has provided New Yorkers with not only their favorite European sweet and savory delights, but also an intimate and elegant dining room.

Michel Meliarenne is currently training for his ninth New York City marathon. As a marathon runner he trains for one to two hours every day. Being physically fit has given him the stamina not only to achieve his marathon goals but also to serve between 30 and 40 guests on a busy night as a waiter for Payards.

An immigrant from France, Meliarenne began his restaurant career in 1964 when he was 24 years old. "I worked as a busboy for one year then was promoted as a waiter."

Meliarenne believes that a lot of what it takes to become a successful waiter comes from within. "A good waiter is really a psychologist. When guests come in I can sense if they want to talk, if not I give them some space. Many come in unhappy. My job is to make every guest happy before they leave," says Meliarenne.

Building a rapport with customers has been a "way of doing business" for Meliarenne. He has a faithful following of past customers who will wait a considerable amount of time to be served by him. He insists that good waiters are people who like people.

"The life of a waiter is a good one. It has provided a good life for my daughter and my son. In addition, it has afforded me the opportunity to rub shoulders with many famous people as I have waited on Jackie Onassis, numerous Kennedy family members, Michael J. Fox as well as numerous authors and artists from around the world."

Being fastidious and careful is another trait that Meliarenne believes good waiters share. "I have never spilled anything on any of my customers nor have I ever broken a dish." Some newcomers find the work to be stressful. "It helps to be positive during those times," he advises.

During his tenure Meliarenne has seen that there's upward mobility for professional waiters. From waiters to captains to maître d's and managers, there are many opportunities for ambitious employees. During his career he has worked in a variety of positions. However, nothing is as exciting or as rewarding to Michel Meliarenne as serving people.

■ ■ ■ ■ ■

Tony Roma's, in Modesto is part of a national chain restaurant famous for ribs. The casual family atmosphere and delicious barbecues, onion rings, and fresh salads appeal to families and business workers, which is why it is usually packed for lunch and dinner.

Vicki Schultz
Tony Roma's
2100 Standiford,
Suite E-9
Modesto, CA

Vicki Schultz is quick to admit that her first job is that of being a mother to two very busy teenagers. Those "mothering instincts" have helped her to find success as a professional server. "Being a server is not a job to me, I love people and love to nurture and take care of them," says Schultz.

Vicki's boss, Chris Hodges, manager of Tony Roma's in Modesto was quick to nominate her for the California Restaurant Association's Front of the House Employee of the Year in 2000. He wasn't a bit surprised when they proclaimed Vicki as the winner. "She is an incredible server. Vicki has been with us for over six years. It is not unusual for customers to line up and wait for a considerable length of time just to sit in her section," shares Hodges.

Vicki, who is now happily married, spent much of her adult life as a single mother. "Working as a server gave me the flexibility I needed to be a good mother. I worked nights and weekends. That meant that I was always home in the mornings to get my chldren off to school. Whenever we needed more money I would work more hours. There was always the opportunity to add more shifts. If my children were sick or had school events, that was my priority and I found others to cover for me," shares Schultz.

On the downside, the job requires physical stamina, and at 5 feet and only a little over 100 pounds, Schultz claims that she has developed muscles where others don't even think of having muscles. Wearing good shoes and a back brace when doing catering jobs is just part of Schultz's routine to keep herself healthy and ready for the job. "I really think that I can do this for many more years—until I retire," says Schultz.

■ ■ ■ ■ ■

At 53 years of age, Jean Hawkins has been working in the same restaurant as a waitress for half of her life. She began serving guests at the JW restaurant in St. Louis Airport Marriott Hotel in 1972, when the hotel opened. That was 28 years ago.

Jean Hawkins
JW Restaurant
Airport Marriott Hotel
St. Louis, MO

"Why would I leave? They treat me great. Marriott offers benefits when you work 30 hours a week. Since JW is a specialty restaurant primarily catering to business travelers, it is closed on all holidays. The tips are very good and I am able to meet wonderful people from all over the world. In addition, once you've worked for Marriott over 25 years you get all kinds of perks," says Hawkins.

Over the years Hawkins has developed her own formula for success that she often shares with new servers. "Know how to read the table and anticipate what they need when they need it. Second, know your menu. Know everything about the menu and the wine. How are the foods prepared? How many ounces is each portion, etc. Third, be courteous—no matter what. Always be nice and friendly. Also, know the proper way to serve. And never take anything for granted. I always ask questions such as, 'Do you want your appetizer with your soup or before?' " adds Hawkins.

"Marriott has a number of great programs that have helped me develop my skills as a server. When I started so many years ago, I was timid and shy and very unsure of myself. Over the years I have taken advantage of the many training opportunities that Marriott makes available for its employees," she continues.

Programs such as "At Your Service" suggest that every memeber of the Marriott family will bend over backwards to assist guests with whatever they need. "If I overhear that someone has lost luggage, I will let management know so that help can be rendered. If I see a mother open a bottle for a baby, I check to see if we can heat it. When a family comes in with small children I will make sure that the children have crackers to keep them happy until the dinner is served. It's the philosophy of Marriott, we will do anything it takes to make things right for our guests," states Hawkins.

■　■　■　■　■

Joel Whitt
Dental Student
Portland, OR
Red Robin Restaurant
Beaverton, OR

With 150 restaurants in 17 states, Red Robin Restaurants are known as a place to eat where guests can expect great meals and service from energetic Team Members (the Red Robin corporate term for employees) and fun!

Married, with one child and another on the way, Joel Whitt had his heart set on going to dental school. Armed with a recently earned business management degree, Joel decided to work for a year while waiting to get into dental school. Worried that many companies wouldn't give him the time of day once they heard of his plans for dental school, and needing more income than most temporary jobs could provide, Whitt turned to Red Robin Restaurants.

Beyond the good income potential, Whitt appreciated the flexibility of the job. If he needed more money he would pick up additional shifts. If he needed a day off it was easy to trade shifts. "There's not a lot of jobs with that kind of flexibility, which makes it a perfect job for a college student."

Now in his third year of dental school, Whitt reflects back to his experience as a server with Red Robin, "I learned traits there that will help me with my dental practice. As a server I had many opportunities to talk to people I didn't know. I've always been a little reserved and this was a good experience for me. In addition, Red Robin really emphasizes customer service and that philosophy will help me build my practice." He adds, "I even learned how to understand people with their mouths full."

Whitt is quick to offer advice to other students looking to work as servers. "Since making the most amount of money in the least amount of time is important, it's important to pick a restaurant that is busy all the time. Go sit out in the parking lot, drive by at various times of the day. Make sure that the restaurant can give you the number of hours that you need on a consistent basis. Look at the menu prices. It may be tough or virtually impossible for a college student to land a job in an upscale fine-dining establishment. But there are lots of casual dining restaurants with menu prices in a medium range that will hire students. Remember that tips usually reflect the menu prices."

Dr. Joel Whitt will soon graduate from Oregon Health Science University Dental School. His family hopes to settle in Oregon or Washington or perhaps Arizona or Nevada. Wherever he ends up he'll always remember the fun he had and the things he learned as a server for Red Robin.

■　■　■　■　■

Alioto's is a San Francisco landmark located on Fisherman's Wharf. The third-generation family-owned fine dining restaurant opened in 1925. The menu showcases the family's rich Sicilian heritage and features the abundant seafood harvest available from the waters below.

George Vrakes
Alioto's Restaurant
2285 Jackson St.
San Francisco, CA

An immigrant from Cyprus, Greece, found himself serving in the U.S. army after the Korean War. Trying to intimidate him into re-enlisting, the army suggested that jobs in the outside world were scarce. Young George Vrakes took his chances and was discharged at Ft. Lewis, WA. That was on May 28, 1958. By May 30, Vrakes had traveled to San Francisco and landed a job with the famed Alioto's restaurant. He started as a busboy. "One day the boss brought me a red jacket. Alioto's waiters wore red jackets in those days. That was my boss's way of telling me that I was ready to move on up," remembers Vrakes.

Today at age 70 and 42 years later, Vrakes continues to love his job at Alioto's. Working three to four days a week, Vrakes claims he will continue to work until an ambulance comes and takes him away from Alioto's.

Vrakes believes that in order to succeed as a professional waiter you must have a genuine love for the people you serve. "It doesn't matter if they drive up in a luxury car or walk in with soiled clothing. I give every customer respect and the best service possible," says Vrakes.

Smiling and getting to know your customers also tops his list of important traits for servers. Vrakes personally knows many of his clients. Some are grand-parents and he served their children, grandchildren, and now even great-grandchildren.

"A good server keeps an eye on people. Guests should never have to flag down their waiter. Making my customers feel comfortable is always my top priority," adds Vrakes.

Vrakes has successfully raised a family of three children on his wages as a waiter. He coninues, "My kids and my wife have had everything they need. I have always made more than most college educated people. I work now because I love it, not because I can't afford to retire. And I go home every night with a big smile on my face, because I love my job so much—not a lot of other people can say that."

■ ■ ■ ■ ■

Becoming a successful server, what inherent talents does it take? What personality traits are found amongst the best servers? The challenge was given—to conduct a nationwide search looking for successful servers with varied backgrounds and experience and determine the "characteristics" of a successful server. It took over six months to identify and interview ten successful servers, all with unique goals and personality traits. Serveral were on the horizons of great careers with top-notch restaurants. A few were beginning their life's work and found that being a server was perfect for this moment in their lives. We looked at male and female servers as well as young and mature servers. While each story is unique, I was amazed at the similarities. As I visited with server after server dejá vu set in, for I heard many of the same things over and over.

Whether reserved or outgoing, all servers mentioned having a love of people. Almost every server interviewed approached his or her job as a true professional by taking advantage of training provided by management and knowing the menu inside and out.

One common thread was, "I have fun with those I serve." Each server interviewed admitted that they enjoyed their work and had a genuine desire to make their guests happy. Most mentioned having the ability to be able to anticipate the needs of their guests and believe that giving attention to detail was very important.

**Commentary by
Brenda R. Carlos
Publisher,
Hospitality News Group**

A good memory, not only to remember the order but to remember the guests' likes and dislikes for their next visit, was a priority with these selected servers. Being a good listener was also mentioned time and again.

Treating all guests with utmost respect and with courteous service also seemed to be a common characteristic of our servers. While several mentioned that one frustration of the industry was the lack of benefits, most stated that they were able to earn a comfortable living and in some cases above average as a server. The flexibility of the working hours and the fact that the job was never boring also were repeated throughout our interviews.

In conclusion, I found that the successful servers I interviewed were all positive, upbeat individuals who love people and have the desire to please people. They are attentive to the needs of their guests and derive great joy and personal satisfaction out of making others happy.

About AIMHIRE® Software

AIMHIRE® is application software designed for the foodservice industry. Specifically, it is designed for use in restaurants to assist owners and managers in the selection, placement, and/or promotion of employees. Profit-Power Systems® developed the AIMHIRE® program, which has been designed to be fast and easy to use. Profit-Power Systems® is a software developer that has consistently provided the foodservice industry with functional software backed by technical support and training for over 20 years.

The AIMHIRE® employee selection program enables the owner/manager in a restaurant setting to successfully establish job models by creating profiles of top employees in each position within the restaurant, such as chef, cook, server, host/hostess, and supervisor, and rank them according to their ability to perform successfully. After the owner/manager has determined which employees are best suited to their positions and which of them continually perform well, he or she then can carefully examine their personal profiles and determine which of their characteristics help them succeed. From this data, the owner/manager can compile a profile of top performers in each job position. This information allows the owner/manager to be better able to hire applicants who best match the successful profile of the top employee. This allows "duplicating" successful employees by comparing each applicant's personal profile to the personal profiles of the restaurant's top employees and the position profile created.

When each applicant's personal profile is compared to the personal profile of top employees within the restaurant, the owner/manager can better determine the particular strengths an applicant will need to help increase productivity and create a highly effective team. The program's approach works because the individuals who perform well in a given position usually have common characteristics. These characteristics are generally not found in poorly performing employees.

This systematic approach to hiring and promotion is based on the premise that even when two candidates have identical skills, one can outperform the other. The difference in performance results from each individual's desires and competencies, as well as personal experience and characteristics. The program will enable the owner/manager to determine within minutes the employee characteristics needed to fill a new opening. The program further allows the owner/manager to determine the strengths and limitations of applicants and current employees. The personal profile overview, as shown in Figure 10–1, consists of 12 clearly presented questions, requiring an

Name: __________ Date: __________

Rank the following terms 1-4 according to how well each behavior describes you. If the behavior or attitude is **"most"** like you, rank it a **"4."** If the behavior is **"least"** like you, rank it a **"1."** Do not use the same ranking more than once for each section.

Example: 1. _4_ A. Enjoys eating Chocolate
_3_ B. Enjoys eating Fruit
_2_ C. Enjoys eating Meat
_1_ D. Enjoys eating Vegetables

In this example, the person most enjoys Chocolate (4), then Fruit (3), and then Meat (2). The person's least favorite is Vegtables (1).

1. ___ A. A Risk Taker ___ B. Accurate ___ C. Patient ___ D. Sociable	2. ___ A. Inventive ___ B. Casual ___ C. Factual ___ D. A Workaholic	3. ___ A. Aggressive ___ B. Calm ___ C. Logical ___ D. Trusting
4. ___ A. Serious ___ B. Sensitive ___ C. Involved ___ D. Generous	5. ___ A. Restless ___ B. Outgoing ___ C. Particular ___ D. Creative	6. ___ A. Authoritive ___ B. Loyal ___ C. Adventerous ___ D. Stable
7. ___ A. Blunt ___ B. Systematic ___ C. Relaxed ___ D. Flexible	8. ___ A. A Listener ___ B. Precise ___ C. Enthusiastic ___ D. Persistent	9. ___ A. Empathetic ___ B. Organized ___ C. Talkative ___ D. Industrious
10. ___ A. Cautious ___ B. Determined ___ C. A Delegator ___ D. Supportive	11. ___ A. Takes Charge ___ B. Impulsive ___ C. Conservative ___ D. Quiet	12. ___ A. Spontaneous ___ B. Forceful ___ C. A Perfectionist ___ D. Modest

FIGURE 10–1
Personal Profile Overview *Courtesy of AIMHIRE®*

applicant to prioritize responses. The program independently weighs the response given to each word in the questionnaire and assigns each response varying degrees of strength. Subsequently, each response is carefully weighed against every other response and is assigned an independent value. The program then merges each value into a composite profile of the applicant who responded to the questionnaire. The results will reflect the applicant's characteristics and strengths, and can be matched to the characteristics and strengths needed for the position profile. The profile is oriented towards the characteristics useful to the position. It does not deal with intelligence, job performance, aptitudes, skills, abilities, knowledge, motivation, or an individual's personal desire and determination to succeed. Furthermore, it is nondiscriminatory and will not provide information about sex, age, national origin, race, or physical challenge.

Personal profile characteristics are shown in Figure 10–2. A person whose characteristics are strong in one area will generally perform at his or her best if placed in a position requiring the same characteristics. Therefore, an applicant with only red characteristics who is applying for a position requiring mostly blue characteristics may be mismatched and not ideally suited for the position. The AIMHIRE® program can assist in matching the

EXTROVERT

<table>
<tr>
<td rowspan="2">T
A
S
K
S</td>
<td>

**RED Characteristics
(Director)**

- Wants tangible results
- Takes Charge
- Enjoys Tasks
- Forceful

</td>
<td>

**YELLOW Characteristics
(Socializer)**

- Extroverted
- Influential
- Likes People
- Coordinating

</td>
<td rowspan="2">P
E
O
P
L
E</td>
</tr>
<tr>
<td>

**GREEN Characteristics
(Thinker)**

- Orderly
- Structured
- Detailed
- Analytical

</td>
<td>

**BLUE Characteristics
(Relator)**

- Creative
- A Problem Solver
- Patient
- Loyal

</td>
</tr>
</table>

INTROVERT

FIGURE 10–2
Personal Profile Characteristics *Courtesy of AIMHIRE®*

applicants with the position by comparing their characteristics with the characteristics needed for the position.

SAVES TIME IN HIRING

The AIMHIRE® personal profile program helps the owner/manager to know beforehand if an applicant's personal characteristics (behavior patterns) will enable him or her to potentially work well in the position and be compatible with co-workers and supervisor. Matching the right applicant to the right position with compatible co-workers and supervisor, results in effective team building.

REDUCES EMPLOYEE TURNOVER

The program can help to reduce employee turnover by matching the characteristics of the applicant with the characteristics of the position. Furthermore, it can help to increase productivity and improve employee job satisfaction.

IMPROVES TRAINING METHODS

The program can help the owner/manager to determine the most effective training methods for new employees by understanding their needs and determining what motivates them. It will also enable the owner/manager to identify how a person learns, and therefore be able to apply the best strategy for training. This could decrease the tension in the training environment and increase trust and confidence.

The example that follows is a server position profile report. The profile provides a comprehensive description of the needs and requirements of the position. The example is based on the answers to the AIMHIRE® position evaluation questionnaire. The AIMHIRE® Tutor software, which can be visited through Internet access, has been programmed to include a completed server position evaluation questionnaire. The questionnaire was completed with the generally accepted characteristics for a server position in a family or theme restaurant operation. These characteristics have been presented in the Job Qualifications section of Chapter 2, The Professional Waiter-Waitress.

SERVER POSITION PROFILE REPORT

The results of the server position evaluation questionnaire (typically completed by the owner/manager) for a family or theme restaurant indicate that a successful server in that type of restaurant operation should have yellow and blue as the dominating characteristics. The AIMHIRE® program generates the requirements and expectations for the position, and are set forth as follows:

- An effective server has a pleasant manner and truly enjoys people. The server is able to sustain a friendly demeanor with poise and self-confidence while under pressure.

- An effective server is organized and systematically follows up. The server is always on time for work, provides prompt service to guests, completes all tasks including opening, shift change, closing cleanup, and restocking service areas.

- An effective server has a positive "professional attitude" that generates positive results. The server enjoys pleasing people and contributes to an atmosphere of trust and unity with co-workers and guests.

- An effective server takes charge of his or her station and recognizes when and what kind of service guests need, and responds with a sense of urgency. The server enjoys working at a fast pace.

- An effective server has a good cultural awareness of the lifestyle, ethnic and nationality mixes of co-workers and guests. The server enjoys and desires to work with many people of diverse backgrounds.

- An effective server has the ability to be flexible, diplomatic, patient, understanding, and cooperative. The server cooperatively works with co-workers in the fast-paced work environment that supports a common goal of providing the highest quality of guest service.

- An effective server is sensitive and is able to anticipate guest needs. The server has the ability to be a good and active listener, allowing guests to feel at ease. The server is able to quickly discern and understand guests' needs, and is concerned with accuracy and quality.

- An effective server demonstrates loyalty and commitment to the restaurant operation and co-workers. The server has a strong sense of honesty when handling guest payment transactions, when sharing tips, and when equally sharing work responsibilities.

- An effective server has the ability to adjust timing and service according to the expectations and needs of multiple guest situations. The server will continually develop and refine his or her service skills based upon personal experience.

- An effective server understands food and beverage menu descriptions and is able to comfortably guide guests through meal selections. The server constantly takes the initiative to keep informed about new food and beverage items.

- An effective server demonstrates politeness, courtesy, and respect at all times, allowing co-workers and guests to feel comfortable. The server works to support an environment that is relaxed and free from discord.

- An effective server has endurance and a high energy level and enjoys working at a quick, steady, and methodical pace. The server is enthusiastic, and has the ability to step back and find a sense of humor in order to minimize the stress and tension of the job.

The position profile chart is compared to the profile overview of two applicants, as shown in Figure 10–3. By comparing the profile overview of the two applicants, it is apparent that applicant A's profile overview is similar to the position profile chart. Therefore, Applicant A is probably a good candidate for the position. If the applicant's profile overview is different from the position profile, management should carefully examine whether the applicant will be able to perform the job successfully. It is important to recognize that although an applicant may not have all of the personal characteristics required for a given position, he or she may still perform well, and can acquire through experience the specific characteristics necessary to successfully perform the job. These characteristics are often referred to as "learned" behaviors.

A IMHIRE® Tutorial Program

The AIMHIRE® Tutor program can be accessed by going to www.hiresuperstars.com and following the instructional prompts to complete your personal profile overview. The program allows the reader/user to identify the

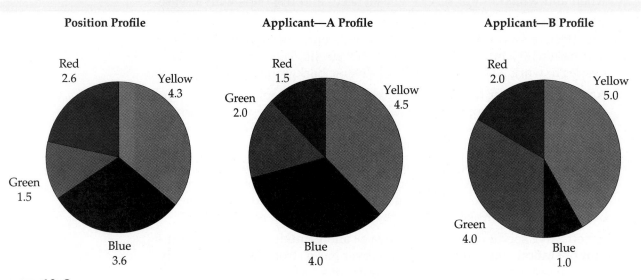

FIGURE 10–3
Position Profile Chart Compared with Two Applicants *Courtesy of AIMHIRE®*

characteristics of a successful server in a family or theme style of restaurant environment, which represents the broadest segment of server positions. For additional information on the full AIMHIRE® program, call Profit-Power Systems® in Orem, Utah, at 877 AIMHIRE (877.246.4473) or visit their complete website at www.hiresuperstars.com.

Overview

The professional servers who were interviewed from across the United States all possess similar characteristics, as reviewed in the commentary by Brenda Carlos, publisher of the Hospitality News Group. Their employment ranged from fine dining to family and theme type restaurant operations.

The AIMHIRE® personality assessment software is specifically designed for the foodservice industry. The software is a tool that can be used by owners and managers in identifying the individual characteristics of successful employees. The complete AIMHIRE® program can allow the owner/manager to successfully build job models by creating profiles of employees in each position within the restaurant, such as chef, cook, server, host/hostess, or supervisor, and rank them according to their ability to perform successfully. From this data, the owner/manager can compile a profile of top performers in each job position. This information allows the owner/manager to be able to hire applicants who best match the successful profile. Comparing each applicant's personal profile to the personal profiles of the restaurant's top employees allows "duplication" of successful employees. The proper use of the program can result in saving time when hiring, reduce employee turnover, and improve training methods.

The AIMHIRE® Tutor software program can be accessed by going to www.hiresuperstars.com, and will allow the user to identify his or her own personal characteristics and compare them to the characteristics of a successful server in a family or theme type restaurant operation.

DISCUSSION QUESTIONS AND EXERCISES

1. List 12 characteristics of a successful server.

2. After reading the server profiles, discuss the ones that you may have found to be of particular interest and state the reasons.

3. Explain how the AIMHIRE® software program functions.

4. What are the benefits of the AIMHIRE® program?

5. Identify your characteristic strengths by completing a personal profile overview with the AIMHIRE® Tutor Program.

6. Visit a family or theme type restaurant within your community and observe the characteristics of the servers, taking note of those who demonstrate the characteristics presented in this chapter.

7. Interview a server and write a one-page report similar to the profiles at the beginning of the chapter.

A
Common Menu Terms

À la (ah-la): After the style or fashion

À la broche (ah-lah-brosh): Cooked on a skewer

À la carte (ah-lah-cart): A separate price for each item on the menu

À la king (ah-lah-king): Served in a cream sauce with mushrooms, green peppers, and pimentos

À la mode (ah-lah-mode): Usually a dessert (pie) served with ice cream

Al dente (ahl-den-ta): Cooked firm to the bite—pasta

Amandine (ah-mahn-deen): Almonds added

Ambrosia (am-broh-zha): Fruit mixture of oranges, grapefruit, bananas, cherries, and shredded coconut

Antipasto (ahn-tee-pahs-toh): An appetizer that can have a variety of Italian meats, cheeses, olives, and vegetables

Aspic (ass-pik): A clear jelly made from meat, fish, poultry, or vegetables

Au gratin (oh-grah-tin): Foods with bread crumbs, cheese, or sauce topping usually made by browning top

Au jus (oh-ju): Meat served in natural juices

Basted: Cooking juices (drippings) spooned over meat while cooking

Battered: Covered with flour or other starch mixture

Béarnaise (bear-naz): A sauce usually containing butter, egg yolks, tarragon, shallots, and white wine or vinegar

Béchamel (bay-shah-mehl): A white sauce usually containing butter, flour, milk, and seasonings

Bill of fare: List of foods on the menu

Bisque (bisk): Cream soup usually made with seafood (shellfish)

Blanquette (blang-ket): White stew usually made with veal or poultry

Bombe glacé (bongh-glaz-ay): Frozen dessert usually made with cake, ice cream, or a combination of several dessert items, and molded in a round ball

Bon appetit (bone-ah-pet-tee): "A good appetite to you," "May you enjoy your meal"

Bordelaise (bohr-dih-layz): A brown sauce usually made with meat stock, beef marrow, butter, carrots, onions, red wine, bay leaf, and a variety of seasonings

Borscht (borsht): A beet soup, may also include cabbage

Bouillabaisse (boo-yah-bays): A fish stew usually made with several types of fish and vegetables

Breaded: Rolled in bread crumbs (plain or seasoned), cracker crumbs, cornmeal, or other dry meal, generally used prior to pan- or deep-frying

Brioche (bre-ohsh): A sweetened soft bread with eggs and butter

Brochette (bro-shet): Meat chunks broiled, grilled, or baked on a skewer, often with onion, green or red pepper, and tomato

Cacciatore (kah-che-ah-toh-reh): An Italian sauce usually made with tomatoes, garlic, onions, peppers, sausage, and spices

Calamari (kah-lah-mah-re): Squid

Canapé (kah-nah-pay): Small bread, toast, or cracker spread (topped) with tasty food mixtures and served as an appetizer

Cannelloni (kan-a-lo-ne): A pasta stuffed with cheese and/or spicy meat and served with Italian tomato or meat sauce

Capers: Small flower buds from the caper plant that have been pickled

Carbonara (car-boh-nah-rah): A sauce usually made with cream, butter, onion, peas, bacon, Parmesan cheese, and various seasonings

Carte du jour (kahrt-du-joor): Menu of the day

Chanterelle (shahn-the-rehl): A funnel-shaped mushroom mild in taste

Chantilly cream (shahn-tee-lee): Vanilla whipped cream

Chantilly sauce (shahn-tee-yee): A mixture of thick sauce supreme and whipped cream

Chatêaubriand (shah-toh-bree-ahn): A roasted tenderloin of beef, center cut

Chiffonade (sher-fon-ad): Shredded vegetables used as a topping for salads or soups, or as a garnish or bedding

Chive (ch-eye-vuh): Slender, green, dried onion tops

Chorizo (choh-re-soh): A mild or spicy Mexican pork sausage

Chowchow: A spicy hot relish usually made with pickles and pickled vegetables

Chutney (chuht-ne): A sweet and sour condiment that is usually made of fruits or vegetables

Cobbler: A deep-dish fruit dessert

Compote (kahm-pote): A stewed fruit mixture

Consomme (kon-so-may): A clear broth

Couscous (koos-koos): Crushed wheat grain often cooked by steaming and served as an alternative to potatoes or rice

Crème brûlée (krehm broo-lay): Cream custard with a caramelized sugar glaze top

Creole (kree-ol): Style of cooking common in Louisiana, prepared with tomatoes, peppers, onion, and unique seasoning blends

Crêpe (krehp): A thin pancake

Crêpes suzette (krehp-soo-zeht): Crêpes cooked in a sweet orange sauce consisting of sugar, lemon juice, butter and oil from the skins of Mandarin oranges

Croquettes (crow-kets): A mixture of chopped cooked foods, shaped into small balls, rolled in egg and bread crumbs, and deep-fried

Croutons (crew-tahns): Bread cubes sautéed and seasoned

Currants: Small red or black dried fruit from a shrub related to gooseberries

Drawn butter: Melted butter

Duchesses potatoes: Mashed potatoes usually made with egg yolks, butter, milk, salt, ground white pepper, and nutmeg

Duxelles (ducks-elz): Finely chopped mushrooms, shallots, and garlic sautéed in butter and then simmered in a stock and made into a coarse paste

En casserole (ahn-kahs-eroll): Baked or served in an individual dish

Endive (ahn-dev): A leafy salad vegetable with a bitter taste

Escargot (es-kar-go): Snails served as an appetizer

Escarole (ehs-kah-rohl): A curly leaf salad vegetable similar in taste to endive

Feta (feh-tah): A Greek white cheese that has been pickled

Filet (fih-lay): A boneless loin of meat or a boneless strip of fish

Filet mignon (fih-lay-meen-yoon): Tenderloin of beef

Flambé (flahm-bay): Flamed

Flan (flahn): A caramel custard

Florentine (floor-ahn-teen): Prepared and/or served with spinach

Foie Gras (fwah-grah): Goose or duck liver, of a pâté

Fondue (fon-du): Melted or blended for dipping bread, meat, etc.; most common is cheese fondue; dessert fondues often feature chocolate or caramel for dipping fruits

Frappé (frap-pay): A frozen drink served over crushed ice

Fricassée (frick-ah-see): Stewed meat or chicken served with thickened white sauce

Gazpacho (gahs-pah-choh): A cold tomato and vegetable soup

Glacé (glaz-ay): A glazed coating made by reducing fish, meat, or poultry stock

Gnocchi (nyoh-ke): A small Italian dumpling usually made from potato

Gouda (goo-dah): A smooth mild Dutch cheese

Granita (grah-ne-tah): A flavored frozen beverage

Gratinée (grah-tan-ay): A food that is sprinkled with bread crumbs and/or cheese and baked until browned

Gruyère (grue-yair): A sharp dry cheese with a nutlike flavor

Guava (gwah-vah): A tropical fruit with a sweet flavor

Gumbo: A soup usually made with seafood or chicken, tomatoes, peppers, and various ingredients and spices

Hollandaise (haw-lawn-dez): A sauce made with egg yolk, butter, and lemon juice

Hors d'oeuvres (ohr-durv): Savory foods served before meal as appetizers, to stimulate the appetite

Hush puppies: A popular southern dish of deep-fried cornmeal

Indian pudding: A baked pudding made with cornmeal, milk, eggs, brown sugar, and raisins

Jardinière (jar-duhn-air): A mixture of vegetables

Jarlsberg (yahrls-berg): A Norwegian cheese with large holes, like Swiss cheese, and a smooth nut-like flavor

Julienne (julie-en): Thin strips of food about 2 or 3 inches long

Kabob (keh-bahb): Cubes of meat and other foods, such as peppers, onion, and tomato, grilled or broiled on a skewer

Kimchi (kihm-che): A Korean relish usually made from spicy, pickled vegetables

Kipper (kih-per): A cold, smoked herring

Kiwi (ke-we): A fruit with brown skin, green flesh, and tart taste

Knockwurst: A large smoked German sausage

Kosher: A method of cooking that strictly follows Jewish dietary laws

Kumquat (kuhm-kwaht): A mildly bittersweet citrus fruit

Langostino (lang-goh-ste-noh): A large prawn that has the appearance and taste of a small lobster tail

Leek: A very sweet type of onion

Lox: Smoked salmon

Mango: A fruit with a juicy light orange flesh and a pineapple and peach taste

Marengo: A chicken or veal sautéed in olive oil with tomatoes, mushrooms, and olives

Marinara (mah-re-nah-rah): An Italian tomato sauce with various spices

Medallions: Small round cuts of food, often round cuts of meat

Meringue (mar-rang): Baked dessert of beaten egg whites and sugar

Meunière (moon-yair): A lightly floured piece of fish, sautéed in butter, seasonings, parsley, and lemon juice

Milanaise (me-lan-ayz): A food item that is breaded, sautéed, and topped with Parmesan cheese

Mornay (mor-nay): A white cheese sauce

Mortadella (mohr-tah-dehl-lah): An spicy Italian pork and beef sausage

Mousse (moos): A chilled, light, whipped dessert made with cream, egg white, gelatin, and flavoring; or a cold molded purée of meat, fish, or poultry

Mozzarella (moth-sah-rehl-lah): A soft white mild Italian cheese

Münster (moon-ster): A semi-soft German cheese with a light pungent flavor and aroma

Napoleon: A layered pastry with custard or cream filling

Neapolitan: (ne-oh-pah-le-than): A layered ice cream and cake dessert, layered in different colors of ice cream and cake

Newberg: A creamed seafood dish made with egg yolks, sherry, and various spices

Panettone (pa-neh-toh-neh): A bread with candied fruit

Parboiled: Boiled until partially cooked

Parfait (par-fay): A chilled dessert of layered ice cream, fruit, whipped cream, and/or other confections served in a parfait glass

Parisienne potatoes: Small round potatoes that can be cooked by boiling, steaming, or baking

Parmesan (pahr-meh-jzahn): A hard sharp Italian cheese that is served grated and used as toppings for salads and soups

Pastrami (pa-stra-mi): Beef that has been slowly cured with spices

Pâté (pah-tay): A meat or fish mixture often baked in a small pastry shell

Pâté de foie gras (pah-tay-de-fwah-grah): A goose or duck-liver pâté

Pesto (pehs-toh): An Italian sauce made of olive oil, garlic, basil, and cheese

Petite marmite (puh-teet-mahr-meet): A consommé made with beef, chicken or turkey, and vegetables, such as carrots, peas, and celery

Petits fours (puh-tee-foor): Small layered and frosted cakes or cookies, or small fruits glazed with sugar

Pilaf (pee-lof): Rice that has been cooked slowly with onions and stock

Piquant (pee-kahnt): Heavily seasoned

Polenta: Boiled cornmeal

Prâline: Almonds or pecans caramelized in boiling sugar

Primavera (pre-mah-veh-rah): Fresh spring vegetables served as part of a main dish

Prosciutto (proh-she-oo-toh): Dry-cured smoked ham

Provençale (pro-vahn-sahl): An item usually cooked with tomatoes, garlic, and spices

Provolone (proh-voh-loh-neh): A hard, sweet-tasting Italian white cheese

Purée (pu-ray): Fruits or vegetables that have been sieved or blended into a thick liquid, also a thick soup

Quiche: A mixture of cream, eggs, Swiss cheese, and various other ingredients baked in a pie shell

Radicchio (rah-de-ke-oh): A small red leaf lettuce

Ragoût (rah-goo): A stew of highly seasoned meat and vegetables

Ramekin (ram-kin): A small oven-proof baking dish used for individual food portions

Ricotta (re-kah-tah): A soft bland Italian cheese

Risotto (re-soh-toh): Sautéed grains or rice that is boiled in stock and seasoned with cheese

Rissole (ree-soh-lay): Browned

Romano (roh-mah-noh): A hard Italian cheese with a strong flavor and aroma

Roquefort (roke-furt): A French white cheese made only in Roquefort, France

Roulade (rue-lad): Thin meat that can be braised or sautéed and rolled around stuffing

Scalappine (skah-loh-pe-na): Small pieces of veal

Scampi: Shrimp in butter sauce

Shallot: An onion variety

Shiitake (she-e-tah-keh): A Japanese mushroom

Sorbet (sore-bay) (or sherbet): A frozen mixture made with fruit juice or fruit purée

Soufflé (soo-flay): A baked, fluffy, light egg mixture combined with ingredients such as cheese, spinach, or chocolate

Spumoni (spoo-moh-ne): An Italian ice cream made with chocolate, vanilla, and cherry flavors along with candied fruit

Stir-fry: To cook vegetables alone or with meat or poultry in oil over high heat in a wok, frequently stirring to retain the crispness of the vegetables

Sweetbreads: The thymus glands of young animals such as calves and lambs

Tortoni (tore-toh-ne): An Italian vanilla ice cream topped with crushed almonds or macaroons

Tournedos (toor-nuh-doe): Small size tenderloin steaks

Trifle: A decorative dessert made with several layers of sponge cake, fresh fruit, soaked with brandy or rum, and topped with custard or whipped cream

Truffles: A fungi-like tuber similar to a mushroom but with a strong aroma; or can be ganache-filled rich chocolate candies

Velouté (vel-oot-eh): A thick cream sauce made from fish, veal, or chicken stock

Vichyssoise (vee-shee-swaz): Potato and leek soup served cold

Vinaigrette (vee-neh-gret): A dressing made with oil, vinegar, salt, and pepper

Watercress: Green type of small crisp salad leaves used on sandwiches, in salads, and as garnishes

Wiener schnitzel (vee-ner-schnit-zl): Breaded veal sautéed and served with lemon wedge

Wonton: Noodle stuffed with ground pork or chicken served in Oriental soup

B

Wine Terminology
General, Sight, Smell, and Taste

GENERAL

Acetic: Vinegar smell and taste. Spoiled wine.

Aeration: Letting a wine "breathe" before drinking it, preferably in the glass, in order to soften the tannins and improve the overall quality. Red wines benefit most from aeration.

Alcoholic: Used to describe a wine that has too much alcohol for its body and weight, making it unbalanced. A wine with too much alcohol will taste uncharacteristically heavy or hot as a result. This quality is noticeable in aroma and aftertaste.

Awkward: Poor structure, clumsy or out of balance.

Backbone: Full-bodied, well structured and balanced by a desirable level of acidity.

Backward: Used to describe a young wine that is less developed than others of its type and class from the same vintage.

Balance: A wine has balance when its elements are harmonious and no single element dominates.

Character: Describes distinct attributes of a wine.

Clean: Wine without disagreeable aromas or taste.

Closed: Wines that are concentrated and have character yet are shy in aroma or flavor.

Complexity: Displays subtle, layered aromas, flavors, and texture.

Cooked: Wine that has been exposed to excessively high temperature; spoiled.

Delicate: Light, soft, fresh—usually describes a white wine.

Dense: Describes a wine that has concentrated aromas on the nose and palate. A good sign in young wines.

Dumb: Describes a phase young wine undergoes when the flavors and aromas are undeveloped. The same as "closed."

Earthy: Used to describe both positive and negative attributes in wine. At its best, a pleasant, clean quality that adds complexity to aroma and flavors. The flip side is a funky, barnyard character that borders on or crosses into dirtiness.

Elegance: Well balanced and full wine with a pleasant distinct character.

Fading: Describes a wine that is losing color, fruit or flavor, usually as a result of age.

Flawed: Wine that is poorly made and shows mistakes.

Flinty: Extremely dry white wines such as Sauvignon Blanc. More often an aroma than flavor. Smell of flint struck against steel; a mineral tone.

Floral: Tasting and smelling of flowers. Mostly associated with white wines.

Fresh: Having a lively, clean, and fruity character. An essential for young wines.

Fruity: Having obvious aroma and taste of fruit(s).

Graceful: Describes a wine that is harmonious and pleasing in a subtle way.

Grapey: Characterized by simple flavors and aromas associated with fresh table grapes; distinct from the more complex fruit flavors (currant, black cherry, fig, or apricot) found in fine wines.

Grassy: Aromas and flavors of fresh cut grass or herbs. A signature descriptor for Sauvignon Blanc.

Harmonious: Well balanced, with no component obtrusive or lacking.

Hearty: Used to describe the full, warm, sometimes-rustic qualities found in red wines with high alcohol.

Heady: High in alcohol.

Herbaceous: Herbal or vegetal in flavor and aroma.

Length: The time the sensations of taste and aroma persist after swallowing. The longer the better.

Light: Soft, delicate wine; pleasant but light in aroma, flavor, and texture.

Madeirized: The brownish color and slightly sweet, somewhat caramelized and often nutty character found in mature dessert wines.

Mature: Ready to drink.

Meaty: Describes red wines that show plenty of concentration and a chewy quality; they may even have an aroma of cooked meat.

Medium-Bodied: Good weight and texture but softer than "full-bodied."

Nouveau: A light fruity red wine bottled and sold as soon as possible. Applies mostly to Beaujolais.

Oaky: Describes the aroma or taste quality imparted to a wine by the oak barrels or casks in which it was aged. Can be either positive or negative. The terms toasty, vanilla, dill, cedary, and smoky indicate the desirable qualities of oak. Charred, burnt, green cedar, lumber, and plywood describe its unpleasant side.

Peak: The time when a wine tastes it's best—very subjective.

Potent: Intense and powerful.

Raw: Young and undeveloped. A good descriptor of barrel samples of red wine. Raw wines are often tannic and high in alcohol or acidity.

Robust: Means full-bodied, intense and vigorous, perhaps a little too much so.

Rustic: Describes wines made by old-fashioned methods or tasting like wines made in an earlier era. Can be a positive quality in distinctive wines that require aging. Can also be a negative quality when used to describe a young, earthy wine that should be fresh and fruity.

Simple: Light wine with limited aromas, flavors, and texture, similar to thin.

Stale: Wines that have lost their fresh, youthful qualities are called stale. Opposite of fresh.

Stalky: Smells and tastes of grape stems or has leaf- or hay-like aromas.

Stemmy: Wines fermented too long with the grape stems may develop an unpleasant and often dominant stemmy aroma and green astringency.

Vegetal: When wines taste or smell like plants or vegetables.

Vinous: Literally means "wine-like" and is usually applied to dull wines lacking in distinct varietal character.

Yeasty: Fresh dough, biscuit-like aroma and or flavor.

SIGHT

Appearance: Refers to a wine's clarity, not color.

Brilliant: Absolutely clear appearance of a wine.

Browning: Describes a wine's color, and is a sign that a wine is mature and may be faded. A bad sign in young red (or white) wines, but less significant in older wines. Wines 20 to 30 years old may have a brownish edge yet still be enjoyable.

Cloudiness: Lack of clarity to the eye. Fine for old wines with sediment, but it can be a warning signal of protein instability, yeast spoilage or re-fermentation in the bottle in younger wines.

Hazy: Used to describe a wine that has small amounts of visible matter. A good quality if a wine is unrefined and unfiltered.

Legs: The drops of wine that slide down the sides of the glass when it is swirled.

Murky: More than deeply colored, lacking brightness, turbid and sometimes a bit swampy, mainly a fault of red wines.

SMELL

Acetic: Vinegar smell. Spoiled wine.

Acrid: Describes a harsh or pungent smell that is due to excess sulfur.

Aroma: Traditionally defined as the smell that wine acquires from the grapes and from fermentation. Now it more commonly means the wine's total smell, including changes that resulted from oak aging or that occurred in the bottle—good or bad. "Bouquet" has a similar meaning.

Bouquet: Wine's aroma from aging.

Cigar Box: Another descriptor for a cedary aroma.

Cedary: Denotes the smell of cedar wood associated with mature Cabernet Sauvignon and Cabernet blends aged in French or American oak.

Dirty: Covers any and all foul, rank, off-putting smells that can occur in a wine, including those caused by bad barrels or corks. A sign of poor winemaking.

Esters: The aromatic compounds of wine.

Mercaptains: An unpleasant sulfur smell found in some very old white wines.

Musty: Having a moldy or mildew smell. The result of a wine being made from moldy grapes, stored in improperly cleaned tanks and barrels, or contaminated by a poor cork.

Nose: The smell, aroma, or bouquet of wine.

Nutty: Aroma found in sherry, Madeira, port, and "cooked" wine.

Perfumed: Describes the strong, usually sweet and floral aromas of some white wines.

Pungent: Having a powerful, assertive smell linked to a high level of volatile acidity.

Smoky: Aromas caused by low acid, tannin or both. Imparted from the oak barrel.

Toasty: Wine aroma derived from the fire bending of the oak barrels staves.

TASTE

Acidic: Used to describe wines whose total acid is so high that they taste tart or sour and have a sharp edge on the palate.

Acrid: Describes a harsh or bitter taste that is due to excess sulfur.

Aeration: Letting a wine "breathe" before drinking it, preferably in the glass, in order to soften the tannins and improve the overall quality. Red wines benefit most from aeration.

Aftertaste: The taste or flavors that linger in the mouth after the wine is tasted, spit or swallowed. The aftertaste or "finish" is the most important factor in judging a wine's character and quality. Great wines have rich, long, complex aftertastes.

Aggressive: Unpleasantly harsh in taste or texture, usually due to a high level of tannin or acid.

Astringent: Extremely dry acidity, bitter; gives a dehydrated sensation in the mouth.

Austere: Used to describe relatively hard, high-acid wines that lack depth and roundness. Usually said of young wines that need time to soften, or wines that lack richness and body.

Bite: A noticeable level of tannin or acidity. Desirable in rich full-bodied wines.

Bitter: Along with salty, sweet and sour, this is one of the four basic tastes. Not a desirable trait in wine, it often signifies too much tannin.

Blunt: Strong in flavor and high in alcohol.

Body: Tactile impression of weight or fullness on the palate. Commonly expressed as full-bodied, medium-bodied or medium-weight, or light-bodied.

Brawny: Used to describe wines that are hard, intense, and tannic and that have raw, woody flavors. The opposite of elegant.

Briary: Describes young wines with an earthy or stemmy wild-berry character.

Bright: Used for fresh, ripe, zesty, lively young wines with vivid, focused flavors.

Brut: A general term used to designate a relatively dry-finished Champagne or sparkling wine, often the driest wine made by the producer.

Burnt: Describes wines that have an overdone, smoky, toasty, or singed edge. Also used to describe overripe grapes.

Buttery: Rich, creamy aroma and flavor associated with barrel fermentation, often referring to Chardonnay.

Chewy: Deep, heavy, tannic wines that are full-bodied with mouth filling texture.

Cloying: Describes ultra-sweet or sugary wines that lack the balance provided by acid, alcohol, bitterness, or intense flavor.

Coarse: Usually refers to excessive tannin or oak. Also used to describe harsh bubbles in sparkling wines. The opposite of smooth.

Corked: A wine that has been tainted with moldy smell from a bad cork.

Depth: Describes the complexity and concentration of flavors in a wine. The opposite of shallow.

Dry: No sugar or sweetness remaining. A fruity wine can be dry.

Empty: Similar to hollow or devoid of flavor and interest.

Extra-Dry: A common Champagne term not to be taken literally. Most Champagne so labeled is sweet.

Extract: Richness and depth of concentration of fruit in a wine. Usually a positive quality, although high extract wine can also be highly tannic.

Fat: Full-bodied, high alcohol wines low in acidity give a "fat" impression on the palate.

Finesse: Delicate and refined texture and structure.

Finish: The lasting impression, or aftertaste, of a wine on the palate. Can be long or short.

Firm: High in acidity or tannins, usually describes young reds.

Flabby: Soft, feeble, lacking acidity and mouth feel.

Flat: Having low acidity; the next stage after flabby. Can also refer to a sparkling wine that has lost its bubbles.

Fleshy: Soft and smooth in texture with deep flavor.

Full-Bodied: Rich, mouth-filling texture and weight on the palate; opposite of thin.

Green: Tasting of unripe fruit, tart, and sometimes-harsh flavors and texture.

Grip: A welcome firmness of texture, usually from tannin, which helps give definition to wines such as Cabernet and Port.

Hard: High in acidity or tannins that do not allow flavor perception.

Harsh: Astringent or burns the palate. Wines that are tannic or high in alcohol.

Hollow: Lacking in flavor.

Hot: High alcohol content that tends to burn. Acceptable in Port wines.

Jammy: Sweet concentrated fruit character.

Leafy: Describes the slightly herbaceous, vegetal quality reminiscent of leaves. Can be a positive or a negative, depending on whether it adds to or detracts from a wine's flavor.

Lean: Lacking in fruit.

Lingering: Used to describe the flavor and persistence of flavor in a wine after tasting. When the aftertaste remains on the palate for several seconds, it is said to be lingering.

Lively: Young wines that are fresh and fruity with bright vivacious flavors.

Lush: Wines that are high in residual sugar.

Malic: The green apple-like flavor found in young grapes that diminish as they mature.

Off Dry: A slightly sweet wine.

Pruny: Having the flavor of overripe, dried-out grapes. Can add complexity in the right dose.

Puckery: Describes highly tannic and very dry wines.

Raisiny: Having the taste of raisins from ultra-ripe or overripe grapes. Can be pleasant in small doses in some wines.

Rich: Intense, generous, full flavors and texture.

Round: Smooth flavors and texture; well balanced, not coarse or tannic.

Soft: Describes wines low in acid or tannin (sometimes both), making for easy drinking. Opposite of hard.

Spicy: Spice flavors such as anise, cinnamon, cloves, mint, nutmeg, or pepper.

Structure: A wine's texture and mouth feel—a result of a particular combination of acid, tannin, alcohol, and body.

Subtle: Describes delicate wines with finesse, or flavors that are understated rather than full-blown and overt, a positive characteristic.

Supple: Describes a smooth soft texture, mostly with reds.

Tanky: Describes dull, dank qualities that show up in wines aged too long in tanks.

Tannin: The mouth-puckering substance, mostly in red wines, that is derived primarily from grape skins, seeds and stems, but also from oak barrels. Tannin acts as a natural preservative that helps wine age and develop.

Tart: Sharp-tasting because of acidity. Occasionally used as a synonym for acidic.

Thin: Lacking body and depth, unpleasantly watery.

Tight: Describes a wine's structure, concentration and body, as in a "tightly wound" wine. Closed or compact are similar terms.

Tinny: Metallic tasting.

Tired: Limp, feeble, or lackluster.

Velvety: Having rich flavor and smooth texture.

Volatile (or Volatile Acidity): Describes an excessive and undesirable amount of acidity, which gives a wine a slightly sour, vinegary edge. At very low levels (0.1 percent), it is largely undetectable; at higher levels it is considered a major defect.

C

Spirit Brands and Related Cocktails

AMERICAN BOURBON WHISKEY

STRAIGHT BOURBON

Ancient Age	Jim Beam	Old Grand Dad
Beams Choice	Jim Beam Black	Makers Mark
Ezra Brooks 90	Knob Creek	Bookers
Evan Williams	Mattingly & More (M&M)	Wild Turkey
Gentleman Jack	Old Crow	Wild Turkey 101
Jack Daniels	Old Forrester	

BLENDED BOURBON

Beams Blend 8 Star	McCormick	Brokers Reserve
Kessler	Seagrams 7 Crown	Monarch

STRAIGHT RYE WHISKEY

Old Overholt	Wild Turkey Rye

CANADIAN WHISKEY

BOTTLED IN CANADA

Black Velvet Sipping	Crown Royal Sp. Resv.	Seagrams V.O.
Canadian Club	MacNaughton	V.O. Bold
Canadian Mist 1885	Northern Light	
Canadian R&R	Seagrams Crown Royal	

BOTTLED IN U.S.

Black Velvet	Lord Calvert	Monarch Canadian
Canadian Mist	MacNaughton Lt. Wt.	Potters Crown Canadian

COMMON BOURBON WHISKEY COCKTAILS:

CC - 7	Old Fashioned
Manhattan	7&7
Mint Julep	Whiskey Sour

IRISH WHISKEY

Black Bush Irish	Jameson	Tullamore Dew
Bushmills Irish	Jameson 1780	
Bushmills Single Malt	Tyrconnel	

SCOTCH WHISKEY

BLENDED SCOTCH

Ballantine	Grants	Pinch
Black & White Grant's	J&B	Scoresby
Chivas Regal	Johnnie Walker Blue	Sheep Dip
Clan MacGregor	Johnnie Walker Red	Teachers
Cutty Sark	Old Smuggler	
Dewars (White Horse)	Passport	

BLENDED SCOTCH – 12 YEAR

Buchanan's Deluxe	Chivas Regal	Johnnie Walker Black

BLENDED SCOTCH – 15 YEAR

Haig & Haig Pinch	Glenfiddich Solera

SINGLE MALT SCOTCH

Balvenie	Glenlivet	Lagavulin
Cardhu Highland Malt	Glenmorangie 10 Year	Laphroaig
Cragganmore	Glenmorangie 18 Year	Macallan 12 Year
Dalmore	Glenmorey 12 Year	Macallan 18 Year
Dalwhinnie	Glenmoray Tin	Oban
Glenfarclas 12 Year	Glendronach	Talisker
Glenfiddich Ancient	Highland Park	Tambowie
Glenkinchie	Knockando	Tamnavulin

COMMON SCOTCH COCKTAILS:

Rob Roy	Rusty Nail	Scotch Mist

COGNAC AND BRANDY

TERMS

V.S. - Very Superior

V.S.O.P. - Very Superior Old Pale

X.O. Extra Reserve - Usually denote the oldest cognac from a particular producer.

Brandy

AMERICAN BRANDY

Christian Brothers	Korbel	Paul Masson
Clear Creek	Lejon	Potters
Domain Charbay	Martel	
E&J	Monarch	

IMPORTED BRANDY

Asbach Uralt	Funador	Presidente
Boulard Calvados	Maraska Sliovitz	St. Remy VSOP
Don Pedro	Mextaxa	Viejo Vergel

Cognac

Courvoisier VS	Hennessey VSOP	Remy Martin Louis XIII
Courvoisier VSOP	Hennessey XO	Remy Martin VSOP
Hennessey VS	Martel VS	Remy Martin XO

GRAPPA

Acqua Di Amore	Clear Creek	Peak

LIQUEURS

(Liqueurs listed with identifiable flavors)

LIQUEURS – FLAVORS

Amaretto Di Saronno - almond	Goldschlager - cinnamon (100 proof)
Bailey's Irish Cream - chocolate	Grand Marnier - cognac/orange
Benedictine - herb spice	Irish Mist - honey
B & B - cognac	Kahlua - coffee
Carolans Irish Cream - chocolate	Kamora - coffee
Chambord - cognac/raspberry	Midori - honeydew
Cointreau - orange	Ouzo - licorice
Crème de Bananas - bananas	Peppermint Schnapps - mint
Crème de Cocoa - chocolate/ vanilla	Sambuca - licorice
Crème de Cassis - currants	Sloe Gin - plum
Crème de Menthe - mint	Southern Comfort - bourbon/peach
Crème de Noyaux - almond	Tia Maria - Jamaican coffee
Curacao - orange	Triple Sec - orange
Drambuie - scotch/honey	Tuaca - cocoa
Frangelico - hazelnut	Yukon Jack - Lt whiskey
Godiva - chocolate	
Galliano - anise-vanilla/licorice	

GIN

AMERICAN GIN

Gilbey's	McCormick	Seagrams Extra Dry
Boords	Monarch	Seagrams Lime Twisted
Gordon's	Potters	

IMPORTED GIN

Beefeater	Bombay
Boodles	Tanqueray

COMMON GIN COCKTAILS

Gibson	Gimlet	Tom Collins
Gin Tonic	Martini	

RUM

JAMAICAN

Bacardi Anejo   Bacardi Solera

PUERTO RICO

Bacardi 8	Bacardi 151 (proof)	Lemon Hart
Bacardi Dark	Captain Morgan	Malibu
Bacardi Light	Captain Morgan Spiced	Mt. Gay
Bacardi Limon	Castillo	Ronrico

VIRGIN ISLANDS

Cruzan Clipper	Montego	Redrum
Monarch	Potters	

COMMON RUM COCKTAILS

Cuba Libra
Piña Colada
Mai Tai
Daiquiri

TEQUILA

Aguila Blue Agave	Monarch	Sauza Commerativo
Arandas Oro	Monte Alban	Sauza Hornitos
Baja	Montezuma	Tarantula Azul
Cuervo 1800	Pancho Villa	Torada
Cuervo Anejo	Patron Anejo	Tres Generationes
Don Julio	Patron Reposado	Two Fingers
Giro	Patron Silver	Rio Grande
Herradura	Pepe Lopez	Sauza
Hussongs	Potters	Matador
Jose Cuervo Gold	Puerto Vallarta 100%	
Jose Cuervo White	Agave	

COMMON TEQUILA COCKTAILS

Bloody Maria	Tequila Shot
Margarita	Tequila Sunrise

VODKA

Absolut - Sweden	Gordon's - US	Smirnoff - U.S.
Absolut Citron - Sweden	Kamchatka - US	Stolichnaya -
Belvedere - Poland	Lukweska - Poland	Russia
Finlandia - Finland	Popov - US	Tanqueray
Gibley's - US	Skyy - US	Sterling - U.K.

COMMON VODKA COCKTAILS

Bloody Mary	Kamikazi	Vodka Collins
Chi Chi	Lemon Drop	Vodka Martini
Cosmopolitan	Martini	Vodka Rocks
Gibson	Salty Dog	Vodka Tonic
Gimlet	Sea Breeze	
Greyhound	Screwdriver	

B-52
Black Russian
Champagne Cocktail
Collins
Colorado Bull Dog
Creamsicle
Dr. Pepper
Eggnog
Fuzzy Navel
Godfather

Boiler Maker
Brave Bull
Godmother
Golden Cadillac
Grasshopper
Harvey Wallbanger
Long Island Iced Tea
Melon Ball
Midori Sour
Mimosa

Café Royal
Cape Codder
Mud Slide
Pink Lady
Pink Squirrel
Presbyterian
Whiskey Sour
White Russian

ALCOHOLIC COFFEE/TEA DRINKS

Coffee Jitz
Irish Coffee
B-52
BFK

Blueberry Tea
Hot Apple Toddy
Hot Toddy
Jamaican Coffee

Kioke Coffee
Nudge
Spanish Coffee

D

Ales, Lagers, and Non-Alcoholic Beers

TYPES OF ALES

Altbier: "Alt" in German means "old". This style of top fermenting light ale is cold conditioned making them more in taste like lagers than ales.

Barleywines: A high alcohol ale (7.5%–14%) with a dark brown hue, usually bittersweet, it is matured for a long time in casks.

Bitters: Style of English ale that is dry and usually served draft. Should not be served too cold.

Brown Ale: A strong, dark colored ale that is somewhat sweet, from the stewing of barley. Brown ale is stronger than pale ale and lightly carbonated.

Cream Ale: Mild and sweet ale made in the US.

Golden Ale: Light to medium body with some hop aroma and clean finish.

India Pale Ale: Fruity, super-premium ale that has a strong flavor of hops. India Pale Ale sometimes has a touch of oak.

Lambic: A spontaneously fermented style of wheat beer unique to Belgium. Usually full bodied with an acidic, yeasty palate.

Pale Ale: Dry, delicate flavored, English-style ale.

Porter: Deep brown ale, lighter in body than a stout, originating in London in 1722.

Scotch Ale: Strong, malt style ale, which is often served as a nightcap. Can be served in winter with hearty food.

Stout: Descended from Porter, stout is a thick, sweet, and relatively low alcohol content.

Trappist: There are six breweries operated by monks of the Trappist order, typically producing strong, fruity, sedimented ale, bottle conditioned, undergoing secondary or even third fermentations in the bottle.

Weisse: German word meaning "wheat". Top fermented, most are light and tart in taste with bread or yeast aroma.

COMMON ALE BRANDS

Alaska Amber - U.S.	Rolling Rock - U.S.
Bridgeport Blue Heron - U.S.	Thomas Kemper - U.S.
Full Sail - U.S.	Widmere Hefeweizen - U.S.
McTarnahan's - U.S.	Widmere Hop Jack - U.S.
Napa Ale Works – U.S.	Widmere Wildberry - U.S.

Anderson Valley - U.S.   Napa Ale Works - U.S.
Guinness - Ireland   Red Hook - U.S.
McAuslan - Canada   Youngs & Co. - U.K.
Murphy's Irish Stout - Ireland

TYPES OF LAGERS

American Lager: Largest selling beer in the USA with broad categories. Derived from European Pilsners, clean and crisp with more carbonation and less hop character.

Bock: A strong lager that is served very cold, usually bottom fermented. It is full bodied, sweet, and sometimes syrupy.

Dortmunder: From the German city with the same name. Their export style of beer is pale and medium dry, with more body and alcohol content than pale lagers from Munich to Pilsen.

Dry: Styled in Germany with thorough fermentation creating high-alcohol content. Popularized by Japanese brewers. The American version has no "beery" aftertaste with conventional alcohol content.

Ice: Developed by Labatt of Canada.

Marzen: Originally brewed in the month of March for consumption in the summer months. Eventually became a malty, medium-strong version of the Vienna-style beer.

Munchener: Dark brown lager with a sweet malt and slight hop flavor that is more creamy and aromatic than light lagers. The dark color and malty flavor come from roasted barley.

Pilsner: A very dry, pale lager. Lots of hop aroma. A true Pilsner can only come from the town of Pilsen, Czechoslovakia. Most light lagers are styled after Pilsner beer but have less body and character.

Vienna: Amber-red kilned malt producing style beer. Originally produced in Vienna.

COMMON LAGER BRANDS

Amstel Light - Holland   Moosehead - Canada
Asahi - Japan   Samuel Adams - U.S.
Budweiser - U.S.   Sapporo - Japan
Bud Light - U.S.   Saxer Lemon - U.S.
Coors - U.S.   St. Pauli Girl - Germany
Corona - Mexico   Steinlager - New Zealand
Dos Equis XX - Mexico   Thomas Kemper - U.S.
Fosters - Australia   Tsing Tao - China
Grolsch - Holland
Harps - Ireland
Heineken - Holland
Henry Weinhard - U.S.
Henry Weinhard Dark - U.S.
Lowenbrau - Germany
Michelob - U.S.
Miller Genuine Draft - U.S.
Miller Lite - U.S.

COMMON NON-ALCOHOLIC BEERS

Bavaria Malt Bier - Germany
Bitburger Drive - Germany
Buckler - Holland
Dortmunder Union - Germany
Gerstel Brau - Germany

Grolsch - Special Malt, Holland
Haake Beck - Germany
Kaliber - England
O'Douls - U.S.
Sharps - U.S.

Index